"Noël and I listened to most of this book driving in the car! Wise words. Authentic experience. Provocative application. Turned a long trip into a fruitful two-person marriage seminar."

John Piper, Chancellor of Bethlehem College and Seminary, Minneapolis, Minnesota

"When Paul Tripp teaches, preaches, or writes he does so through the lens of the gospel. In *What Did You Expect?,* Paul faithfully and brilliantly lets the gospel bear its weight on the messiness and beauty of marriage. I, personally, found the book to be helpful, and we use it extensively at The Village."

Matt Chandler, Lead Pastor of Teaching, The Village Church, Dallas, Texas

"The reason *What Did You Expect?* is so powerful is not because Paul Tripp is a marriage expert with tips and tricks to fix your problems, it's because his teaching is drenched in the gospel and the Word of God. This honest book will help you see yourself and your spouse in a new light as it shows you who Jesus is and how to connect his redeeming grace to the daily realities of your marriage. Singles and engaged couples will benefit from it, too."

Joshua Harris, Former Senior Pastor, Covenant Life Church, Gaithersburg, Maryland

"At once deeply theological and practically relevant, this is one of the top books on marriage I have ever read. Paul Tripp allows readers to examine marriage through a biblical lens so that we understand how God can graciously heal our hurting homes. As a pastor, I will implore our people to read this book as soon as it is available."

Chris Brauns, author, *Unpacking Forgiveness*; Pastor, The Red Brick Church, Stillman Valley, Illinois

"What I've come to expect from Paul Tripp is consistently deep, transparent, biblical, wise, practical, gospel-driven counsel. Rather than muddying the water with self-focused strategies designed to meet our ever-multiplying needs, Paul, as the seasoned soul-physician he is, correctly diagnoses our problems and provides the cure—humble faith in Jesus Christ. I wasn't disappointed. You won't be either."

Elyse M. Fitzpatrick, counselor; speaker; author, *Give Them Grace*

"Paul Tripp brings many years of counseling, growth as a husband, and deepening discovery of the liberating power of grace to this realistic and challenging guide to God's engagement in redeeming marriages that are threatened by complacency, misunderstanding, and selfishness. The Bible's message of the humbling and healing power of Christ's mercy and the powerful presence of his Spirit in our homes comes through loud and clear. The daily practicality of gospel doctrine is made crystal clear by Tripp's transparency about his personal missteps in becoming a Christ-reflecting husband and the many examples of couples who have discovered that they are sinners married to sinners. But that the third, divine Party in marriage gives hope and change when unrealistic expectations are shattered and when we confront our sin. But be warned: Tripp's diagnostic questions are downright uncomfortable. Even those with strong marriages by God's grace will find their deep tendencies toward self-coronation challenged!"

Dennis E. Johnson, Professor of Practical Theology, Westminster Seminary, California

"Paul Tripp issues a challenge for couples to roll up their sleeves, get to work, and do what it takes to build a God-honoring relationship. He presents six commitments for couples to make, and contained within each is insightful, practical, and effective advice on how to construct a loving, growing, grace-soaked marriage."

Mary A. Kassian, Professor of Women's Studies, The Southern Baptist Theological Seminary; author, *Girls Gone Wise in a World Gone Wild*

What did you Expect?

Other Crossway books by Paul David Tripp:

Awe: Why It Matters for Everything We Think, Say, and Do (2015)

Come, Let Us Adore Him: A Daily Advent Devotional (2017)

Dangerous Calling: Confronting the Unique Challenges of Pastoral Ministry (2012)

New Morning Mercies: A Daily Gospel Devotional (2014)

Parenting: 14 Gospel Principles That Can Radically Change Your Family (2016)

Redeeming Money: How God Reveals and Reorients Our Hearts (2018)

Sex in a Broken World: How Christ Redeems What Sin Distorts (2018)

A Shelter in the Time of Storm: Meditations on God and Trouble (2009)

Suffering: Gospel Hope When Life Doesn't Make Sense (2018)

Whiter Than Snow: Meditations on Sin and Mercy (2008)

What did you Expect?

Redeeming the Realities of Marriage

PAUL DAVID TRIPP

CROSSWAY®

WHEATON, ILLINOIS

First printing 2010

Reprinted with new cover 2012, 2015

Printed in the United States of America

Unless otherwise indicated, Scripture quotations are from the ESV® Bible (The Holy Bible, English Standard Version®), copyright © 2001 by Crossway, a publishing ministry of Good News Publishers. Used by permission. All rights reserved.

Scripture quotations marked ASV are from the American Standard Version of the Bible.

Scripture quotations marked NASB are from *The New American Standard Bible®*. Copyright © The Lockman Foundation 1960, 1962, 1963, 1968, 1971, 1972, 1973, 1975, 1977, 1995. Used by permission.

Scripture references marked NIV are from The Holy Bible: New International Version®, NIV®. Copyright © 1973, 1978, 1984 by Biblica, Inc.™ Used by permission. All rights reserved worldwide.

All emphases in Scripture quotations have been added by the author.

ISBN-13: 978-1-4335-4945-8
ISBN-10: 1-4335-4945-X
ePub ISBN: 978-1-4335-4948-9
PDF ISBN: 978-1-4335-4946-5
Mobipocket ISBN: 978-1-4335-4947-2

Library of Congress Cataloging-in-Publication Data

Tripp, Paul David, 1950–
   What did you expect? : redeeming the realities of marriage / Paul David Tripp.
      p. cm.
   ISBN: 978-1-4335-1176-9 (hc)
   1. Marriage—Religious aspects—Christianity. I. Title.
BV835.T75   2010
248.8'44—dc22   2009040500

Crossway is a publishing ministry of Good News Publishers.

LB		28	27	26	25	24	23	22	21	20	19	18
17	16	15	14	13	12	11	10	9	8	7	6	5

There aren't many couples who are graced
by having such fine examples go
before them.
Thanks, Tedd and Margy,
for giving us a living example
of how to live in marriage
God's way.

Contents

Preface   11

1 What Did You Expect?   15

2 Reason to Continue   29

3 Whose Kingdom?   43

4 Day by Day   55

COMMITMENT 1: *We will give ourselves to a regular lifestyle of confession and forgiveness.*

5 Coming Clean: Confession   71

6 Canceling Debts   85

COMMITMENT 2: *We will make growth and change our daily agenda.*

7 Pulling Weeds   101

8 Planting Seeds   115

COMMITMENT 3: *We will work together to build a sturdy bond of trust.*

9 Sticking Out Your Neck   133

10 Someone to Be Trusted   151

COMMITMENT 4: *We will commit to building a relationship of love.*

11 All You Need Is Love   167

12 Ready, Willing, and Waiting   185

COMMITMENT 5: *We will deal with our differences with appreciation and grace.*

13 Amazing Grace   205

14 Before Dark   219

COMMITMENT 6: *We will work to protect our marriage.*

15 Eyes Wide Open   233

16 On Your Knees   249

17 Worship, Work, and Grace   267

Preface

For some reason I seem to be drawn to write about things I'm not very good at. Marriage is a prime example. I got married at twenty and was all too sure of myself. I was convinced of my character and maturity, and I thought marriage would be easy for me. It wasn't! It didn't take long for the true selfishness and impatience of my heart to be revealed. But I worked to deny what God was clearly revealing. I fought to convince myself that I was not the problem. I got good at persuading myself and worked hard at persuading Luella, my wife, that I was right and she was wrong. But God, in his gorgeous grace, was unrelenting in his pursuit of me, and Luella was committed to being honest with me.

I was heading for disaster and I didn't even know it. Now, don't misunderstand; I wasn't a constant monster, and I really did want my marriage to Luella to work. The problem was that there were things inside me that made the kind of marriage this book is about utterly impossible. I analyzed, rationalized, criticized, and generally pointed the finger. But there was no escaping it—I was the problem. I had been surrounded by grace, grace that would not rest until I had been delivered from the one thing I could not escape by myself—me. I went down kicking and screaming, but God was gracious and Luella was patient until I began to face the one thing I had fought so hard to admit: I desperately needed to change.

Luella and I just celebrated another anniversary. When we look back, we are amazed at all that has happened, all that God has done. We love one another dearly, and we are very grateful for our years together. They have been rich and exciting. We have not experienced too many boring days. We love being with one another, and we love celebrating shared life. But there is something that we love even more. We love Jesus and his transforming grace. We love his Word and the stunning wisdom that it contains. We know our story isn't a story of marital success. No, our story is the story of two people who have been rescued by grace and wisdom again and again. Over and over we have been forgiven and empowered by God's grace. Over and over we have been convicted, convinced, transformed, and directed by his Word.

If you could watch a video of our life together, you would soon realize that we have not "arrived." We are still being rescued by that same wisdom and grace. God is still working to reveal and win our hearts. We wish we could say that the war of love is over in our marriage, but we can't. Love of self still gets in the way of love for God and for one another. And when it does, our marriage suffers. There are still times when we have a greater trust in our instincts than we do in God's wisdom, and when we do, our marriage suffers the results of our foolishness. So, we rest in God's wisdom and grace, but we do not rest in our marriage. As long as we are two sinners living in a fallen world, there will be work to do.

Sometimes that means being willing to serve when it's the last thing we want to do. Sometimes it means being willing to listen when our instinct is to argue. Sometimes it means being willing to love, even in those moments when the other doesn't seem deserving. Sometimes it means humbly asking for forgiveness when we are tempted to argue that we were right. Sometimes it means being willing to go through a moment of tension so that truth can get on the table. Sometimes it means being willing to overlook a minor offense. But there is one thing that we know for sure: as we rest in God's grace, we are called to give grace to one another. And as we celebrate God's wisdom, we must be willing to let that wisdom be our moment-by-moment guide as we relate and respond to each other.

I don't have any personal brilliance to give you. In a real way, this book is a testimony to my own rescue. I offer to you and your marriage two things: God's powerful, transforming grace and his life-rearranging wisdom. In these two things you will find hope and real change for your marriage, and as you do, you too will learn what it means to rest and work at the same time.

—Paul David Tripp
August 31, 2009

COMMITMENT 1:   We will give ourselves to a regular lifestyle of confession and forgiveness.

COMMITMENT 2:   We will make growth and change our daily agenda.

COMMITMENT 3:   We will work together to build a sturdy bond of trust.

COMMITMENT 4:   We will commit to building a relationship of love.

COMMITMENT 5:   We will deal with our differences with appreciation and grace.

COMMITMENT 6:   We will work to protect our marriage.

1

What Did You Expect?

"I just didn't think it would be like this," Mary said. She looked completely exhausted and defeated.

Sam just looked angry. He didn't want to be with me talking about his marriage to Mary. In fact, if the truth be told, he didn't want to be married to Mary. He'd had it! "Fifteen years—fifteen years!—and this is what I get?"

Mary refused to answer; she just sat there and sobbed.

"Look what my hard work gave you. No one you know lives in a house like yours. No one you know has the things I've provided for you. No one has had the wonderful experiences around the world that I've given you. But, no, it's never enough. Mary, I'm tired of your constant complaining. I'm tired of daily criticism. I just don't want to do this anymore, and I don't think you do either," Sam said, as his voice trailed off.

I looked at Sam and Mary, and I knew it had not always been like this. I've sat with many couples while they were in the process of considering marriage, which has often been a bit of a frustrating experience for me. No, I haven't been frustrated because they were "madly" in love; I think it's wonderful when a man and woman adore one another. I think it's wonderful when they decide to spend their lives with one another. I understand that in the throes of the romance of the moment, they find it hard to concentrate on the preparatory work that needs to get done. None of this has frustrated me. I think that deep mutual affection is a beautiful thing.

Here's what has frustrated me again and again: *unrealistic expecta-*

tions. There—I've said it. I am persuaded that it is more regular than irregular for couples to get married with unrealistic expectations. Again and again I have sat with couples who simply do not seem to be taking seriously the important things the Bible has to say about what every marriage will encounter in the here and now. Unrealistic expectations always lead to disappointment.

You know this is true if you have ever looked at a vacation Web site before traveling there. No vacation site will actually look as nice and function as well as it does on its promotional site on the Internet. You inevitably end up disappointed because you started out with unrealistic expectations.

We took our family on a vacation to Disney World. We looked at that beautiful Disney literature. But we weren't told that we would stand under a blazing sun for 90 minutes in 120-degree heat and 200-percent humidity to ride a ride that takes 33 seconds!

My son, who was at this time just a little guy, saw a ride that he wanted to go on. We walked for what seemed like forever and finally found the end of the line. We stood in line so long that my son and I had this conversation: "Dad," he said, "why are we standing here?" I said, "There is a ride at the end of this line." And he said, with a look of complete exhaustion, "And what ride is it?" We had been in the line so long that he had forgotten why we were standing there. Unrealistic expectations always lead to disappointment.

Using the Bible Biblically

Part of the problem is the way we use Scripture. We mistakenly treat the Bible as if it were arranged by topic—you know, the world's best compendium of human problems and divine solutions. So when we're thinking about marriage, we run to all the marriage passages. But the Bible isn't an encyclopedia; it is a story, the great origin-to-destiny story of redemption. In fact, it is more than a story. It is a theologically annotated story. It is a story with God's notes. This means that we cannot understand what the Bible has to say about marriage by looking only at the marriage passages, because there is a vast amount of biblical information about marriage not found in the marriage passages.

In fact, we could argue, to the degree that every portion of the

Bible tells us things about God, about ourselves, about life in this present world, and about the nature of the human struggle and the divine solution, to that degree every passage in the Bible is a marriage passage. Every passage imparts to us insight that is vital for a proper understanding of the passages that directly address marriage, and every passage tells us what we should expect as we deal with the comprehensive relationship of marriage.

One of our problems is that we have not used the Bible biblically, and this has set us up for surprises we shouldn't have had.

Please Don't Mess This Up

But the unrealistic expectations have another source. It's almost as though the potential husband and wife are motivated not to hear the truth about what they will inevitably face, because they don't want anything to mess up the unfettered affection that has left them in a virtual romantic delirium. Now again, I want to say that I think that deep and mutual affection is a beautiful thing, but we must not let it motivate us to deny reality.

That dynamic is like what happens to you while you are consuming a wonderful meal of deep-fried fish and chips, which will be followed by a dessert of rich chocolate cake and ice cream. You simply have no interest in considering what this meal is doing to your heart and waistline. You do not want to discuss calories and cholesterol. You are not very motivated to consider fat and sugar content. No, you want to savor every delectable morsel. You want to consume all the fish and fries you can while they are still warm and crunchy. And no matter how full you are, you are planning to consume a hearty piece of that four-layer, double-chocolate mousse cake.

You see, in the midst of the power of premarital romance, it is very hard to get yourself to want to take a hard and honest look at reality, that is, those things that every couple will face someday, somehow, someway. You are scared that under the heat of the light of truth, your affection may evaporate. You fear that something is going to mess up the delight of what you are experiencing at the moment. What you are experiencing is one of the most powerful things a human being can experience. Love is compelling. It is motivating. It is intoxicating. It can command your mind and control your emotions. You sit with the one you love, considering your marriage to come, and you want what you are now feeling and experiencing to last forever. And you're not about to do anything that will mess it up.

Here's how it tends to work: you're in love and convinced that the love you are now feeling will get you through anything you might face. You simply don't want to dig up potential difficulty. You don't want to consider what could be. You don't want to let the future get in the way of what you are experiencing in the moment. Your attention span is short. You are in love, and you like it, and you are not about to let anything get in the way. You look at one another with glazed eyes, and you are sure that the powerful love you are feeling will get you through anything. You don't feel that you have much to fear. You are sure that few people have felt the love that you feel for one another. You know that other couples have problems, but you are convinced you are not like them. You are sure they must not have felt what you are feeling. You are in love, and you are sure that everything will work out right. You are simply not interested in being realistic.

Between the Already and the Not Yet

There is a way that theologians think about life in the here and now that is very helpful and can impart to us realistic expectations. Everything we say and do, everything we commit ourselves to, and every situation, location, and relationship we experience is experienced between the *already* and the *not yet*. You will never understand the things you face every day until you understand that you live in the middle. Everything in your life is shaped by what the middle is like. Perhaps you're thinking, "Paul, I don't know what you're talking about." Permit me to explain.

Knowing that you are living between the already and the not yet tells you where you are located in God's story of redemption. Stay with me; this is intensely practical. Already God has given us his Word as our guide. Already he has sent his Son to live, die, and rise again for our salvation. Already he has given us his Spirit to live within us. But the world has not yet been restored. Sin has not yet been completely eradicated. We have not yet been formed in the perfect likeness of Jesus. Suffering, sadness, and death are not yet no more.

It is hard to live in the middle, but that is exactly where we live. We live in a world that is still sadly and terribly broken. Your marriage will not escape its brokenness. We live with flawed people. Your marriage will not be protected from those flaws. When you start unpacking what life is really like between the already and the not yet, you gain perspectives that are enormously helpful for understanding the things you need to face if you want a marriage that is wholesome and healthy in the eyes of God.

Prepared Spontaneity

You and I simply never know for sure what is coming next. Think about it: your life has not worked according to your plan. You could not have written yourself into your present situation twenty years ago. Last week didn't work according to your plan. Today won't work according to your plan. Your life is under the wise and sovereign plan of another (see Acts 17:26–27; Dan. 4:34b–35). This means that, every day, you deal with the unexpected, with things you didn't plan to have on your plate. This is surely true of your marriage. Problems come your way that have a huge impact on you and your spouse. Sickness and sin get in the way of what you thought you would be sharing together. Every marriage is required to face the unexpected. But dealing with the unexpected doesn't mean you have to be unprepared. This book is all about the principle of *prepared spontaneity*.

Now, I know it sounds like a contradiction, but it isn't. You actually can be prepared for things that you don't yet know you will face. You can be ready for things that you had no idea would come your way. In fact, I am persuaded that this is one of the main functions of Scripture. It enables us to be prepared to decide, think, desire, act, and speak well in a world in which we aren't sovereign. Here's how it works: if we have taken in what the Bible says about God, ourselves, life, sin, and the surrounding world, we are ready to deal spontaneously with things we didn't know we would be dealing with.

Again and again I have sat with couples who are surprised by what they are dealing with. Yet, when I give them an opportunity to tell their story, I am impressed to find, once again, that the things they are dealing with are the kinds of things the Bible predicts that flawed people in a fallen world will face. It is troubling when I sit with a wife who is shocked that her husband is a sinner or with a husband who was unprepared for the fact that his wife is tempted to be selfish.

More couples than I can number have been surprised that their marriage needs the regular rescue of grace. And because they did not take the Bible seriously, they were caught short in that moment, when the rubber meets the road in daily life, where grace was their only hope.

It's not just the prediction of *potential problems* that people haven't taken seriously, but the message of *promised provision* as well. Prepared spontaneity is not just about being aware of what you are going to face and therefore being ready to face it. It is also about knowing what you have been given so that you can face it with practical courage and hope.

This book will lay out for you a lifestyle of readiness that takes seriously the practical and life-giving wisdom perspectives of the Word of God. These wisdom insights will cause you to live prepared, even though your hand isn't on the joystick, and you don't really know what is around the next corner of your marriage.

You Can Expect the Expected

Jim got sick and had to forsake his climb up the corporate ladder. This brought stress into his marriage to Jen that he would never have anticipated. Brad and Savannah got busier and busier and quit communicating as they should, and their relationship paid the price. Brent struggled with a secret sin for years, and when Liz discovered it, it almost ended their marriage. India and Frank always seemed to be in a battle for control. It was an exhausting marriage to be a part of. Alfie and Sue never seemed to be in the same place spiritually. Jared and Sally had an infectious affection for one another, but their financial woes brought much stress to their marriage. Jung's mother pulled her into loyalty battles again and again. It caused lots of conflict between her and Kim.

There are two observations to make about all these marriages. First, none was a bad marriage. No one was about to walk out. No one had been unfaithful as yet. There had been no abuse or violence. But none was experiencing what God had in mind when he created their union in the first place. And all of them were surprised at what they had to face as a couple.

Second, everything that each couple faced is predicted by command, principle, proposition, or perspective in the Bible. These couples should have expected the expected. If they had approached the Bible as a wonderful window onto their marriage, they would have known what to expect and not been surprised at what came their way.

So what are the essential wisdom perspectives that Scripture gives us that enable us to have realistic expectations for our marriage?

1) You Are Conducting Your Marriage in a Fallen World

Sam can't believe he has been suddenly laid-off after all these years. Julie struggles with the thought of living with a man with a chronic disease. Jared never thought he would be dealing with the things he is facing with his son. Mary feels like a prisoner in the house she loves, which is located in a neighborhood now gone bad. Sherrie struggles with the responses she has received to her biracial marriage. John often wonders why life has to be so hard.

We all face the same thing. Our marriages live in the middle of a world that does not function as God intended. Somehow, someway, your marriage is touched every day by the brokenness of our world. Maybe it simply has to do with the necessity of living with the low-grade hassles of a broken world, or maybe you are facing major issues that have altered the course of your life and your marriage. But there is one thing for sure: you will not escape the environment in which God has chosen you to live. It is not an accident that you are conducting your marriage in this broken world. It is not an accident that you have to deal with the things you do. None of this is fate, chance, or luck. It is all a part of God's redemptive plan. Acts 17 says that he determines the exact place where you live and the exact length of your life. He knows where you live, and he is not surprised at what you are facing. Even though you face things that make no sense to you, there is meaning and purpose to everything you face. I am persuaded that understanding your fallen world and God's purpose for keeping you in it is foundational to building a marriage of unity, understanding, and love.

There is no better window on what we face in the here-and-now world in which we live than the descriptive words that the Bible uses: "grieved," "trials," and "tested" (1 Pet. 1:6–7). Now, these words should cause you to pause. Of all the descriptive words that Peter has at his disposal to describe what God is doing in us through the environment in which we live, it is very significant that he uses these three words. Each is instructive and interpretive. First, you will not escape the grief of life in the fallen world. That grief can be the momentary pain of a little disappointment or the long-term mourning of a significant moment of loss. The point is that, along the way, grief touches us all in little or significant ways. Second, we all face trials. We will deal with things we would never have planned for ourselves or inserted into our schedules. We will grieve because we will face difficulty that we neither anticipated nor planned. The final word brings the portrait of life in this fallen world together. The word *tested* does not mean tested like in an exam. No, it means "tempered" or "refined."

With this word, *tested*, God tells you one of the most significant things you will ever understand about your marriage in the here and now. God decided to leave you in this fallen world to live, love, and work, because he intended to use the difficulties you face to do something in you that couldn't be done any other way. You see, most of us have a *personal happiness paradigm*. Now, it is not wrong to want to be happy, and it is not wrong to work toward marital happiness. God has given you the capacity for enjoyment and placed wonderful things around you to enjoy. The problem is not that this is a wrong goal, but that it is way too small a goal. God is working on something deep, necessary, and eternal. If he was not working on this, he would not be faithful to his promises to you. God has a *personal holiness paradigm*. Don't be put off by the language here. The words mean that God is working through your daily circumstances to change you.

In his love, he knows that you are not all that you were created to be. Even though it may be hard to admit, there is still sin inside you, and that sin gets in the way of what you are meant to be and designed to do. And, by the way, that sin is the biggest obstacle of all to a marriage of unity, understanding, and love. God is using the difficulties of the here and now to transform you, that is, to rescue you from *you*. And because he loves you, he will willingly interrupt or compromise your momentary happiness in order to accomplish one more step in the process of rescue and transformation, which he is unshakably committed to.

When you begin to get on God's paradigm page, life not only makes sense (the things you face are not irrational troubles, but transforming tools) but immediately becomes more hopeful. There is hope for you and your marriage because God is in the middle of your circumstances, and he is using them to mold you into what he created you to be. As he does this, you not only respond to life better, but you become a better person to live with, which results in a better marriage.

This does not mean that you will stop being grieved. In fact, Jesus wept when he walked the roads of our world. But this grief is not a dark tunnel that fate has sent your way. It is a wise tool in the hands of a loving God who knows how deep your need is and wants to give you gifts of grace that will last forever.

So, somehow, someway, this fallen world and what it contains will enter your door, but you do not have to be afraid. God is with you, and he is working so that these grieving things will result in good things in and through you.

2) You Are a Sinner Married to a Sinner

I will say much more about this throughout the book, but you and I just don't get to be married to someone perfect. It seems true when you read it, but even though this seems obvious, many people get married with unrealistic expectations about who they are marrying. Here is the point: you both bring something into your marriage that is destructive to what a marriage needs and must do. That thing is called sin. Most of the troubles we face in marriage are not *intentional* or *personal*. In most marriage situations, you do not face difficulty because your spouse intentionally did something to make your life difficult. Yes, in moments of anger that may happen. But most often, what is really happening is that your life is being affected by the sin, weakness, and failure of the person you are living with. So, if your wife is having a bad day, that bad day will splash up on you in some way. If your husband is angry with his job, there is a good possibility that he will bring that anger home with him.

At some point you will be selfish. In some situation you will speak unkindly. There will be moments of jealousy, bitterness, and conflict. You will not avoid this, because you are a sinner and you are married to a sinner. If you minimize the heart struggle that both of you have carried into your marriage, here's what will happen: *you will tend to turn moments of ministry into moments of anger.* When your ears hear and your eyes see the sin, weakness, or failure of your husband or wife, it is never an accident; it is always grace. God loves your spouse, and he is committed to transforming him or her by his grace, and he has chosen you to be one of his regular tools of change. So, he will cause you to see, hear, and experience your spouse's need for change so that you can be an agent of his rescue.

Often, in these God-given moments of ministry, rather than serving God's purpose we get angry because somehow our spouse is in the way of what we want. This leads to the second thing that happens: the reason we turn moments of ministry into moments of anger is that *we tend to personalize what is not personal.* At the end of his bad day at work, your husband doesn't say to himself, "I know what I'll do. I'll take my bad day out on my wife so that her day gets as wrecked as mine." No, the trouble you are experiencing is not about you directly. Yes, it is your trouble, because this angry man is your husband. But what you are experiencing is not personal in terms of conscious intentionality. You are living with a sinner, so you will experience his sin.

Now, when you personalize what is not personal you *tend to be adversarial in your response.* When that happens, what motivates you is not the spiritual need in your spouse that God has revealed but your spouse's offense against you, your schedule, your peace, etc. So, your response is not a "for him" response but an "against him" response. Rather than wanting to minister to him, what you actually want to do is get him out of your way so you can go back to whatever was engaging you beforehand. Let's be honest—all of us have been there.

When we respond in an adversarial way, we actually escalate the trouble that the other person splashed up on us. This leads to one more thing: because we have turned a moment of ministry into a moment of anger by personalizing what is not personal, we are adversarial in our response, and because we are, we *settle for quick situational solutions that do not get to the heart of the matter.* Rather than searching for ways to help, we tell the other to get a grip, we attempt to threaten them into silence, or we get angry and turn a moment of weakness into a major confrontation.

This is one place where I think the Bible is so helpful. The world of the Bible is like your world—messy and broken. The people of the Bible are like you and your spouse—weak and failing. The situations of the Bible are like yours—complicated and unexpected. The Bible just isn't a cosmetic religious book. It will shock you with its honesty about what happens in the broken world in which we live. From the sibling homicide of Cain to the money-driven betrayal of Judas, the blood and guts of a broken world are strewn across every page. The honesty of God about the address where we all live is itself an act of love and grace. He sticks our head through the biblical peephole so we will be forced to see the world as it really is, not as we fantasize it to be. He does this so that we will be realistic in our expectations, then humbly reach out for the help that he alone is able to give us.

3) God Is Faithful, Powerful, and Willing

There is one more reality that you have to include as you are trying to look at your marriage as realistically as possible. Not only must you consider the fallenness of the world you live in and the fact that both of you are less than perfect, but you must also remember that you are not alone in your struggle. The Bible says that God is near, so near that in your moment of need you can reach out and touch him because he is not far from each one of us (Acts 17:27). Yes, you live in a bad neighborhood (fallen world), and the two of you are less than perfect (sin), but in all this you are not left to your own resources. The God who determined your address lives there with you and is committed to giving you everything you need.

I am writing this a few days after Easter, so my mind has been on the empty tomb. Consider for a moment what the empty tomb of the Lord Jesus Christ teaches us. First, it teaches us that God is *faithful*. Centuries earlier, after Adam and Eve had disobeyed God, God promised that he would crush wrong once and for all. So he sent his Son to defeat sin and death by his crucifixion and resurrection. For thousands of years God neither forgot nor turned from his promise. He did not grow weary, nor would he be distracted. He made a promise, and he controlled the events of history (large and small) so that at just the right moment Jesus Christ would come and fulfill what had been promised.

But the open tomb also reminds us that God is *powerful*. He is powerful in authority and powerful in strength. Think of the authority you would have to have to control all the situations, locations, and relationships in order to guarantee that Jesus would come at the precise moment and do what he was appointed to do! Also, could there be a more pointed demonstration of power than to have power over death? By God's awesome power, Jesus took off his grave clothes and walked out of that tomb. Those guys in power-lifter competitions may be able to pull a bus with their teeth, but they will all die, and there is nothing they can do about it.

The empty tomb points us to one more amazing thing. It teaches us that God is *willing*. Why would he go to such an extent to help us? Why would he care to notice us, let alone rescue us? Why would he ever sacrifice his own Son? Because he is willing. You and I need to recognize that his willingness was motivated not by what he saw in us but by what is inside of him. He is willing because he is the definition of mercy. He is willing because he is the source of love. He is willing because he is full of amazing grace. He is willing because he is good, gentle, patient, and kind. Even when we are unwilling, full of ourselves and wanting our own way, he is still willing. He delights in transforming us by his grace. He delights in rescuing us by his powerful love.

So, when you are sinned against or when the fallen world breaks your door down, don't lash out or run away. Stand in your weakness and confusion and say, "I am not alone. God is with me, and he is faithful, powerful, and willing." You can be realistic and hopeful at the very same time. Realistic expectations are not about hope without honesty, and they are not about honesty without hope. Realism is found at the intersection of unabashed honesty and uncompromising hope. God's Word and God's grace make both possible in your marriage.

Are your expectations for your marriage realistic?

COMMITMENT 1:   We will give ourselves to a regular
                lifestyle of confession and forgiveness.

COMMITMENT 2:   We will make growth and change our
                daily agenda.

COMMITMENT 3:   We will work together to build a sturdy
                bond of trust.

COMMITMENT 4:   We will commit to building a relationship
                of love.

COMMITMENT 5:   We will deal with our differences with
                appreciation and grace.

COMMITMENT 6:   We will work to protect our marriage.

2

Reason to Continue

Everyone searches for hope. Everybody looks for a reason to continue. Everyone hooks their daily functioning to some kind of dream. Everyone wants to know that what they give themselves to will prove to be worth it. Human beings don't live by instinct. Made in God's likeness, we are rational beings. The things we do and say are rooted in deeply ingrained thoughts and desires. There is a way in which it is accurate to say that we are all on one big, lifelong, treasure hunt. Your treasure may not be my treasure, but we're both treasure hunters nonetheless. If you didn't think the things you are doing would pay off in some way, you'd probably quit doing them.

Tom was struggling and ready to pack it in. No, it wasn't that he had been dealt some disaster that had left him devastated and alone. In fact, from a distance, it seemed that Tom had a pretty good life. He had a bright, beautiful, and intelligent wife. He had three beautiful children under the age of seven. His job was never boring or mundane. Yet Tom toyed with the desire to quit his own life. It simply wasn't enjoyable anymore. He and Dara seemed to function with low-grade irritation toward one another all the time. Their schedule was ridiculously demanding, and their children seemed to be in need of endless attention. Tom felt that there was seldom a day in which he didn't upset Dara in some way. He was tired of working hard and having little to show for it, and he couldn't find much reason to continue.

Cindy lay in bed awake. She was looking at Mac. It was hard for her to grasp that the man she was lying next to was the same man who had swept her off her feet. As a tear coursed down her cheek, she remembered Mac's infectious smile and his sense of humor. She thought about how Mac had the ability to make the most mundane things enjoyable. She remembered getting excited at the sound of his voice; but no more. Somewhere along the way Mac had quit being Mac. He seemed perennially distracted and frustrated. He spent his time watching sports or on the computer. Going to bed was particularly hard for Cindy. She longed for a little bit of tenderness before they both caved into exhaustion and slept, but there was no tenderness. Mac would crumble into bed, sullen once again, mumble good night, give her a perfunctory kiss, and roll over into sleep. Night after night Cindy would lie awake searching for a reason to continue.

From the beginning, Erin knew that Will was very close to his family, but she never thought it would be like this. Erin feels like an outsider in her own life. She is tired of spending every holiday and vacation with Will's family. She is tired of all the intertwining of marriage, extended family, work, and church. How many holidays has she spent watching Will and his brothers having the time of their lives, quite oblivious to the fact that she isn't? She had long ago faced where Will's loyalty lies, and she knows that there will never be a decision that Will won't discuss with his family. She has thought a lot about what the Bible says about "leaving and cleaving," and in her heart of hearts she knows that Will has never left his family. Erin is tired of being the outsider and is finding it hard to continue.

Nathan stood there with the crumpled note in his hand. He had found it several weeks ago on the floor of their walk-in closet. Things have been hard since then. Anita had made no denials. She had become emotionally infatuated with a coworker. No, this relationship had not been physical in any way. In fact, they had never been together outside work, but the note was devastating nonetheless. Anyone reading it would've called it a love letter. Nathan doesn't know why he keeps it. He doesn't know why he digs it out day after day and reads it again and again. He just does. Anita seems remorseful and is doing everything she can to make amends. Nathan is thankful that she quit her job, but he can't get beyond the note. It stands in the middle of his life like an Everest that he knows he needs to climb but never will. It is as though the note has taken away every reason he has to continue.

Sandy looks at the uncooked egg that her three-year-old has just dropped on the floor, and she wants to scream. She feels more like a custodian than a wife. It seems to Sandy that day after day she gets up to clean and straighten things until she goes to bed, and then she gets up and does it all over again. She lives in sweats and sneakers; those days of feeling attractive have almost faded from memory. Fred has gained some weight and doesn't look too great himself. She passes by the full-length mirror in the upstairs hallway and thinks, "What happened to us?" The morning when the first-years-of-marriage photo album had fallen off the closet shelf and onto the floor, she had hit the wall. It seemed that the pictures were of a different couple from a different time and place. The comparisons were devastating. She is tired of a domestic's existence, and she is not finding much encouragement to continue.

Brandon is simply tired of the hard work. It is difficult not to wish for the early days once again. Being with Jessie had been so much fun. He had loved the spontaneous freedom of their relationship and schedule. He had loved the fact that Jess seemed ready for anything at anytime. Back then he knew it wouldn't always be that way, but he never imagined that it would be like this. With his new job and the arrival of the twins, he and Jess do little but work hard. Busy and exhausting, life isn't very much fun, even in the rare moments when they have time to be together. When Brandon works late, Jess complains that he isn't home to help, and when he is home to help, she complains that he isn't making enough money. Brandon summarized it well to a coworker: "When you feel that you can't win, it's hard to continue trying."

Nora and Chris are both tired of arguing, but they don't know how to stop. They get up on different sides of the universe every morning and look at everything from opposing perspectives. They are both convinced they are right and are constantly frustrated that the other doesn't see things their way. It has gotten to the point where everything seems to matter. The crumpled towels in the bathroom or the dried-out cheese in the refrigerator have become much bigger issues than they ever should have been. They would both say that they love one another, and they apologize after the heat of another argument has waned, but they don't stop arguing. It is an unhappy existence, and they both feel it. Quietly they both wonder what it will take for things to be different and what in the world they will do if nothing changes.

Not the Way It Was Meant to Be

It happens to everyone. It is the unavoidable reality of marriage. Somehow, someway, every marriage becomes a struggle. Life after the honeymoon is radically different from the honeymoon that preceded it. The person you loved to play with, you are now living and working with. The person who was once your escape from responsibility has become your most significant responsibility. Spending time together is radically different from living together. Reasons for attraction now become sources of irritation. We are all confronted with the fact that in some way our marriage is not what it was meant to be. Why? Well, the reasons are found in what we looked at in the first chapter.

Somewhere along the way you realize that you, too, are a sinner, married to a sinner, and you are together living in a broken world. Sometimes this reality just makes mundane little moments more difficult than they should be, and sometimes it means facing devastating things you thought you would never face. But it happens to all. At some point you need something sturdier than romance. You need something deeper than shared interests and mutual attraction. You need something more than marital survival skills. You need something that gives you peace of heart and strength of resolve when you aren't feeling romantic and your problems are getting you down.

Everyone's marriage becomes something they didn't intend it to be. You are required to deal with things you didn't plan to face. In every marriage sin complicates what would otherwise be simple. In every marriage the brokenness of the world makes things more complicated and difficult. In every marriage either giddy romance wanes and is replaced with a sturdier and more mature love, or the selfishness of sin reduces the marriage to a state of relational détente.

So, what do you do when your marriage becomes what it was not intended to be? What do you do in those moments when you aren't so attracted to your spouse? Where do you look when you are irritated, hurt, or discouraged? Where do you reach? Where do you run?

Rooted in Worship

So, what does give you reason to continue when the little problems have gotten under your skin or the big problems have left you devastated? What does produce a marriage with sturdy love, unity, and understanding? I think the answer I am about to give will surprise many of you. Here it is: *a marriage of love, unity, and understanding is not rooted in romance; it is rooted in worship.* Now, you may be able to read all the words, but you still might not understand the depth of the insight of this principle.

What does it mean to say that a marriage is "rooted in worship?" The word *worship* is a tricky word. When the average person hears the word *worship* he thinks of a gathering, of hymns, an offering, and a sermon. But there is a biblical truth embedded in this word that is vital to understand if you are ever going to figure out why you struggle in your marriage and how those struggles will ever get solved. Worship is first your identity before it is ever your activity. You *are* a worshiper, so everything you think, desire, choose, do, or say is shaped by worship. There is simply no more profound insight into the reason people do the things they do than this, and once you get hold of it, it opens doors of understanding and change that were never before opened to you. Let me explain.

When the Bible teaches that we are worshipers (see Rom. 1:19–25), it is not first talking about a religious function that is separate from the other aspects of our more regular functioning. No, in naming us as worshipers, the Bible is providing for us a radical insight into fundamental human motivation. Because you are not an animal, which functions by ingrained instinct, the things you do and say are driven by some kind of purpose. In other words, whether or not your words and actions make sense on the surface, you have acted or spoken for a reason. The most general and fundamental reason for doing what you do is worship. Now, you are probably already sensing that this insight needs further explanation.

Think about this. Isn't it interesting that some of the things that upset you don't bother your spouse at all? Why is it that something that delights you is, at the very same time, a thing that your husband or wife could easily live without? Why are some things much more important to you than to others? And why is it that your list of what is important doesn't completely agree with your husband's? Why are there themes to your anger (certain times, places, situations, relationships, etc.) and certain themes to your discouragement? Well, all these things I have been describing are connected to worship.

When the Bible says that we are worshipers, it means that every human being lives for something. All of us are digging for treasure. All of us are in pursuit of some kind of dream. Behind everything we do is some kind of hope. Every one of us is in constant pursuit of life. Perhaps you're thinking, "Paul, I get all this, but I don't understand how it helps me understand my marriage." Let me take you further.

Being a worshiper means that you attach your identity, your meaning and purpose, and your inner sense of well-being to something. You either get these things vertically (from the Creator) or you look to get them horizontally (from the creation). This insight has everything to do with how a marriage becomes what it is. No marriage will be unaffected when the people in the marriage are seeking to get from the creation what they were only ever meant to get from the Creator.

Comfort had become Jeanie's functional god. No, she hadn't quit going to church. She loved Sunday worship services, and she loved her pastor's preaching, but comfort is what ruled her heart. Jeanie got her comfort from turning her home into a museum to her domestic dexterity. Jeanie owned a thousand decorating magazines. She was always redecorating or remodeling. She cleaned relentlessly and was obsessively neat. She would tell herself that she wanted to make her home a beautiful place for her family, but what drove her was not concern for her family. Jeanie had attached her identity, her inner sense of well-being, to the beauty of her home.

Jeanie was never really relaxed at home; neither were her husband and family. Jeanie didn't want her family to wear shoes in the house. She was upset at every hint of disorder and went after whoever she thought was the culprit. In a moment of anger, Jeanie's husband captured it very well: "Jean, we don't have a home to come home to anymore. This place is not our home; it's your museum, and we are feeling less and less welcome here!"

Tony had attached his identity to success. He had no idea that what he was supposed to be getting from the Creator, he was seeking to get from the creation, but that is exactly what was going on. The place where Tony looked for the success that made him want to get up in the morning was his job. Tony was good at what he did; the more he did it, the better he got, and the better he got, the more money and power he was given. It was all very exciting and intoxicating. It was as if he were living a dream. No, work wasn't perfect by any means, but it gave him a reason to get up in the morning.

But with every new promotion, the pressure got greater and the hours got longer. By the time Tony got home, long after his wife and children had eaten dinner, he had little energy left for his family. Yet something even deeper than this was going on. Because Tony got his value as a person from his job, when he drove away from his job and toward his house, he was driving away from what gave him value. His marriage actually existed outside his circle of value. So, while Tony would tell you that he loved his wife, he was not excited to arrive at home after work. He was easily irritated and often a non-participant in what was going on.

Abby hooked her meaning and purpose to Cameron. She didn't know it, but he had become her personal messiah. She would say that he was all she had ever wanted in a husband. You would think that would mean she was always happy and satisfied in her marriage, but the opposite was true. Abby was perennially dissatisfied. She got up every morning and rode the roller coaster of every action, reaction, or response that Cameron had toward her. She paid too much attention to his tone of voice, the look on his face, and his body posture. Even the littlest things had the potential to wreck her day. She was not only focused on how Cameron responded to her, but she also watched very closely how he responded to other women. For Cameron, it was marriage as a final exam, and he felt he was always being given a failing grade. It was all very exhausting and unappealing. Cameron needed a reason to continue.

I have become more and more persuaded that marriages are fixed vertically before they are ever fixed horizontally. We have to deal with what is driving us before we ever deal with how we are reacting to one another. Every relationship is victimized in some way when we seek to get from the surrounding creation what we were designed to get from God. When God is in his rightful place, then we are on the way to putting people in their rightful place. But there is more. I am convinced that *it is only in the worship of God in our marriages that we find reason to continue.*

What Does a Marriage Rooted in the Worship of God Look Like?

Paul said something startling in Galatians 5:14: "The entire law is summed up in a single command: 'Love your neighbor as yourself'" (NIV). Now, I've thought about this many times. If I had written those words, "The entire law is summed up in a single command," I think I would have followed with, "Love God above all else." But that is not what Paul wrote. How is it that love of neighbor summarizes all that God has called us to? The principle embedded in these words is incredibly practical and insightful once you see it. It is only when I love God above all else that I will ever love my neighbor as myself. At the foundational level, the difficulties in our marriages do not first come because we don't love one another enough. They happen because we don't love God enough; and because we don't love God enough we don't treat one another with the kind of love that makes marriages work.

Consider the Ten Commandments: it is only when we keep the first four commands (having to do with the worship of God) that we will keep the last six commands (having to do with love for our neighbor). *Sturdy horizontal love always begins vertically.* Lasting, persevering, other-centered living does not flow out of romantic attraction, personality coalescence, or lifestyle similarity. It is only when I live in a celebratory and restful worship of God that I am able not to take myself too seriously and I am free to serve and celebrate another.

I probably taxed your patience here, and you're thinking, "Come on, Paul, get to the point and help me understand what this looks like!" Worship that gives you sturdy marital love and a reason to continue will flow out of three ways that you must worship God.

1) *A marriage of love, unity, and understanding will flow out of a daily worship of God as creator.* It is only when you look at your spouse and see the glory of God's creative artistry that you will treat her with

the dignity and respect that a healthy marriage requires. God created every aspect of your personhood. He administrated every choice of your hardwiring. He determined how tall you would be, whether you would tend to gain weight, the color of your eyes, the texture of your hair, the shape of your nose, the size of your hands, the tone of your voice, your innate personality, your natural gifts, the tone of your skin, your natural degree of physicality or athleticism, and whether you are mechanical, analytical, or relational. You didn't choose any of these things. You didn't wake up at six months and say, "I think I'll grow up and be a mechanical guy," or "I'm going to work on developing a long, thin nose because that will benefit the symmetry of my face."

All these choices were made by the Divine Artist who has infinite creativity. But there are moments in our selfishness, when that other person is in the way of what we want, that we all wish we could rise to the throne of the Creator and re-create our husband or wife into our own image, or at least into someone who would be easier for us to live with. The relational wife wants to turn her mechanical husband into her clone. The analytical husband wants to re-create his more emotionally wired wife into a dispassionate thinker like himself. The husband allows himself to be irritated by the screechiness of his wife's voice, or the wife is impatient with how slowly her husband does everything.

In subtle and not so subtle ways we all question the Creator, and in so doing we dishonor and disrespect our husband or wife. We end up criticizing the other for choices he or she didn't make. We all end up asking the other to change in areas where change simply is not possible. I cannot think myself taller. I cannot alter my natural Creator-initiated range of gifts.

When we celebrate the Creator, we look at one another with wonder and joy. When you look at your spouse and see the Creator's glory, then you feel blessed by the ways he is different. You are amazed and respectful of the experiences and perspectives that he has brought into your life, which you never would have had without him. And you look for ways to communicate your honor for him and what the fingers of the Creator formed him to be.

2) *A marriage of love, unity, and understanding will flow out of a daily worship of God as sovereign.* You've probably noticed that your

life hasn't worked according to your plan! Last week didn't work the way you had planned it to work. Each of our stories is being written by Another. Think about this: fifteen years ago you couldn't have written yourself into whatever situation you are in as you are reading this book. In the same way, your marriage is an unfolding drama written by the wise control of a loving and sovereign God.

I was confronted with this in the very first moments of my relationship to Luella. I stood behind her in the very first lunch line of a new college year. The line was on a campus in South Carolina. Luella was raised in Cuba, and I was raised in Toledo, Ohio. There is no possible way that we could have controlled all the things that would have to be controlled to guarantee that we would be in that line together, not only on the same day, but at the precise same moment during that day.

God ruled the whole process. He controlled all the cultural influences that shaped us. He controlled all the family values that helped shape us. He controlled all the situations, locations, and experiences that helped shape the particular ways that we think about and respond to life.

In marriage, we bring all those cultural, familial, experiential influences with us. So, we come into marriage with a list of givens that aren't the givens of our spouse. We come with cultural expectations that aren't the expectations of the other. We come in with schedule, aesthetic, and relational expectations that the other person doesn't have. One expects dinner to be a quick moment of food consumption, while the other expects dinner to be a time of relaxed eating and conversation. One person doesn't really care if the house is messy, while the other was trained to expect and maintain a neat environment. In one family, the roles of husband and wife were very defined and evident; in the other family they were there, but blurred. One family thought of money as something to be spent; the other thought of it as something to be saved. We could multiply example after example.

It doesn't take long in marriage before you realize that your spouse doesn't share your instincts. At that point, either you worship God as sovereign and celebrate the different way of looking at the world that your spouse has blessed you with, or you dishonor him by trying to rewrite his story. For example, the house you live in shouldn't be a reflection of one of you. It should be a beautiful mix of the sovereignly produced sensibilities of both. Many husbands and wives carry with them the pain of dishonor and disrespect that results when their spouse has mocked or denigrated their way of doing things or rejected their family and their way of relating or doing things.

But when you begin to celebrate the sovereignty of God and how he formed you and brought you and your spouse together for his glory and your good, you quit being irritated by your differences and start celebrating how your life has been enhanced by them. As a result, you will not only give room to your spouse's sensibilities, but you will honor him or her in what you do and say in the moments when you are confronted with the differences in your approach to the very same things.

3) *A marriage of love, unity, and understanding will flow out of a daily worship of God as Savior.* There is no area that is more important than this. It doesn't take long to realize that you have married a sinner, and what you do when you make this discovery will determine the character and quality of your union. You will only respond in a way that is right, good, and helpful to your spouse's sin, weakness, and struggle when you are celebrating the transforming grace of an ever-present, always-faithful Redeemer.

You cannot let your responses to your spouse in these moments be driven by hurt or self-righteousness. They must be driven by worship. What does this mean? Well, first it means that when you celebrate God as Savior, you are confronted with the reality of how much you are in desperate need of his grace. This makes it impossible for you to look at your spouse as the only sinner in the room, or more of a sinner than you are. The fact is that no one gives grace better than someone who is convinced that he needs it, as well.

Worshiping God as Savior also means that you find joy in being part of the work of grace that God is unrelentingly committed to doing in your spouse's life. So, when your spouse blows it, you will not throw her sin in her face. You will not make her feel guilty for how hard her failure makes life for you. You will not use her sins against her. You will not keep a detailed history of her wrongs against you. Rather, you will look for ways of incarnating the transforming grace of the Savior. You will be ready to encourage her when she fails and restore her when she falls, and you will not treat her as less righteous than you.

Reason to Continue

Where will you find the reasons to continue working on your marriage in those disappointing moments when those reasons are most needed? Well, you won't find them in your spouse. He or she shares your condition; your spouse is still a flawed person in need of God's transforming grace. You won't find them in the ease of your circumstances. You still live in a world that is groaning and broken. You won't find them in surface strategies and techniques; your struggles are deeper than that. You will only find your reasons to continue by looking up.

When your heart rests in the amazing wisdom of the choices of a powerful Creator, you have given yourself reason to continue. When your heart celebrates the myriad of careful choices that were made to bring your stories together, you have given yourself reason to continue. When your heart is filled with gratitude for the amazing grace that you both have been and are being given, you have given yourself reason to continue. You are not alone. Your creating, ruling, transforming Lord is still with you. He has brought your stories together and placed them smack-dab in the middle of his redemptive story. As long as he is Creator, as long as he is sovereign, and as long as he is the Savior, you have reason to get up in the morning and love one another, even though you aren't yet what he created you to be.

COMMITMENT 1: We will give ourselves to a regular lifestyle of confession and forgiveness.

COMMITMENT 2: We will make growth and change our daily agenda.

COMMITMENT 3: We will work together to build a sturdy bond of trust.

COMMITMENT 4: We will commit to building a relationship of love.

COMMITMENT 5: We will deal with our differences with appreciation and grace.

COMMITMENT 6: We will work to protect our marriage.

3

Whose Kingdom?

Gwen had always carried her dream with her like a precious jewel in a velvet bag. At twelve years old she would leaf through her mother's home magazines and imagine her future home and family. By the time Gwen went to college, she knew what kind of home and family she wanted. She wasn't just hoping that she would be happy; she knew what would make her happy. Gwen wasn't aware of it but she didn't really date men in college; no, she shopped for a man. She was looking for that special man who would help her realize her dream. So, the more she got to know Barry, the more she was attracted to him. Gwen really did think she was falling in love with Barry, and he loved the fact that she was crazy about him.

It was a quick courtship. Neither Gwen nor Barry wanted anything to get in the way of their developing union. The wedding between their junior and senior years of college was exciting and beautiful. They really did seem like the perfect couple. Gwen was vibrant and relational, and Barry was administrative and analytical; they seemed to complement each other perfectly. Gwen couldn't believe it. She remembered the scrapbook she had made as a little girl. She was about to live what she had pasted on the pages!

Getting pregnant right away wasn't part of Gwen's dream, but so many other things had fallen into place so perfectly that she took it in stride. It bothered her that she wouldn't graduate with Barry, but she knew there would be a time in the future when she would finish her studies. Barry wasn't prepared for the pressure of a full-time job and full-time school, but he knew he had to make it work. They were both shocked to learn that Gwen was carrying twins. Gwen was overwhelmed at the thought of her instant family, but she couldn't tell Barry. There simply wasn't time in his busy schedule to listen to her worry and complaints. They both settled into separate daily routines, as Gwen tried to convince herself that she was still taking steps toward living her dream.

There were no pictures in Gwen's girlhood scrapbook of colicky twins, a small house, heavy school loans, or a poorly paying, entry-level job. Gwen tried not to be depressed, but she was. Their house had no yard whatsoever, and the interior was so small that it seemed to be cluttered all the time. Life seemed to be no more than get up in the morning, work all day, go to bed, get up in the morning, and do it all over again. But Gwen's disappointment was deeper than her physical surroundings and busy schedule. She was disappointed with Barry.

The way he looked at life had been so helpful during their courtship; now it tended to irritate Gwen more than interest her. It seemed that Barry was perennially dissatisfied with the disorganization of their life together. He constantly complained about how messy the house was, and he was always telling Gwen how she could be more efficient. To Gwen he seemed cold, distant, and constantly just a few steps from anger.

Barry was struggling as well. Gwen seemed more interested in talking for hours on the phone than she did in taking care of their daughters and the home. He was tired of seeing the woman he thought was as beautiful as they get now living in sweats and looking as though she had just gotten up. He knew it was unkind to think these things, but he did. It seemed that Gwen seldom had dinner ready when he got home and never seemed able to get the girls in bed in a timely manner.

Gwen silently wondered where the man who had attracted her so had gone. Barry could dress any way he wanted to at work, and he did. He had no time for working out and seemed often to eat on the fly, so he had put on some pounds. He surely wasn't as responsive or as solicitous as he had been in courtship. It became harder and harder for Gwen to convince herself that she was living any part of her dream. The facts were the facts, and Gwen couldn't escape them. Life was hard, and it was going to stay that way for awhile.

At first, Gwen and Barry hunkered down together and tried to make things work, but that didn't last very long. Gwen was very disappointed at what her life had become and hurt at how Barry treated her. Barry was frustrated that in all his attempts to help Gwen, she simply didn't want to change. The silent unhappiness both of them felt didn't remain silent for very long. It started with little comments meant to inflict guilt and little statements that were meant to register dissatisfaction. But before long, Gwen and Barry were in a pattern of regular arguments. They both had a lot to say, and neither one seemed willing to listen. The more they argued, the more their negative view of one another and their life together grew. Neither one will ever forget the night when Gwen said it. It had been a long time in coming, but it was hard to move beyond its actually being said.

She blurted the words out at the end of an evening when Barry had come home late, even though he knew the twins were sick and Gwen was exhausted. "I think I made a big mistake, Barry. Every day I find it harder not to regret that we ever got married." It cut Barry like a knife. She knew how hard he worked for her; she knew all the things he had given up for her, and this was the thanks she gave him!

The next day it was hard for Barry to come home from work. It was hard to face living with someone who didn't really want to be with him. It was hard for Gwen too; her dream had become a nightmare, and she didn't know what to do.

A Deeper Battle

Poor Gwen and Barry—so hurt, so confused, and so wanting to turn the clock back, but they didn't know what was going on, and that was the problem. It's hard to fix something you don't understand, and it's even harder to fix it when you think your problem is really the other person. As Barry drove to work the next day, he rehearsed to himself all the good things he had done for Gwen. The deck had made their small house a little more livable. The vacation, which they really couldn't afford, had brought some needed sanity to Gwen's frenetic life with the twins. His willingness to work from home all Fridays had complicated his work life, but he was willing to do it for Gwen. He couldn't believe the way she had been acting, and it was even harder to believe she had said those things!

Gwen was stung too. She spent most of the next day in a bit of an emotional daze. Yes, she did some laundry and took care of the twins' needs, but she really wasn't there. When she spilled her coffee, she began to cry and had trouble stopping. It wasn't supposed to be this way! Life with Barry was all she had ever wanted. She could accept the unplanned pregnancy. She could accept the small house. She could accept Barry's long hours. But his coldness and constant irritation were things she never thought she would be dealing with. She just couldn't make sense of it. Maybe he was regretting that he had married her. Maybe he was having an affair. Maybe he was wanting out and didn't know how to tell her. Her mind raced and her heart broke, but she didn't know what to do.

Sadly, many couples have arrived at that point. Yes, the details are different, but they've arrived there nonetheless. The sweetness has evaporated from their marriage. The friendship has faded away. The person they courted doesn't seem to be the person they are now living with. There is distance, coldness, impatience, and conflict that weren't there in the beginning. Sometimes a couple will settle for cold war, sometimes they will settle into marital détente, and sometimes they will nip at one another as if they are looking for any opportunity to express their dissatisfaction. Sometimes it becomes all-out war. Sometimes couples hide behind their busyness. Sadly, many couples just walk away, never fully understanding what happened to the relationship that once brought them so much joy.

There are few couples that understand the one thing they need to understand in order for lasting change to take place in their marriage. They think their battle is with the other, or they think the circumstances in which they find themselves are what need to change. But here is the reality: *all of the horizontal battles are the fruit of a deeper war*. The most important war, the one that needs to be won, is not the war they are having with each other, but a war that wages within them individually. Real change is all about winning this war.

Attraction or Love?

The way to begin to understand this deeper war is to look at the beginning of couples' courtship and marriage. Considering the beginning of the relationship between Gwen and Barry will help us here. Let me suggest something that will upset some of you, and then I will explain.

Perhaps, from the very beginning, what Gwen and Barry thought was love was not actually love. Now, to help you understand this possibility, I have to take you on a bit of a biblical tour.

I have written before about what 2 Corinthians 5:14–15 says about the fundamental nature of sin, but I think it is particularly helpful here. The passage reads, "For Christ's love compels us, because we are convinced that one died for all, and therefore all died. And he died for all, that those who live *should no longer live for themselves* but for him who died for them and was raised again" (NIV). The apostle Paul summarizes here what sin does to all of us. Sin turns us in on ourselves. Sin makes us shrink our lives to the narrow confines of our little self-defined world. Sin cause us to shrink our focus, motivation, and concern to the size of our own wants, needs, and feelings. Sin causes all of us to be way too self-aware and self-important. Sin causes us to be offended most by offenses against us and to be concerned most for what concerns us. Sin causes us to dream selfish dreams and to plan self-oriented plans. Because of sin, we really do love us, and we have a wonderful plan for our own lives!

What all this means is that *sin is essentially antisocial.* We don't really have time to love our spouse, in the purest sense of what that means, because we are too busy loving ourselves. What we actually want is for our spouse to love us as much as we love ourselves, and if our spouse is willing to do that, we will have a wonderful relationship. So we try to co-opt our spouse into a willing submission to the plans and purposes of our claustrophobic kingdom of one.

But there is more. Because sin is antisocial, it tends to dehumanize the people in our lives. No longer are they objects of our willing affection. No, they quit being the people we find joy in loving. Rather, they get reduced to one of two things. They are either *vehicles* to help us get what we want or *obstacles* in the way of what we want. When your wife is meeting the demands of your wants, needs, and feelings, you are quite excited about her, and you treat her with affection. But when she becomes an obstacle in the way of your wants, needs, and feelings, you have a hard time hiding your disappointment, impatience, and irritation.

This is where another eloquent biblical observation comes in. It is that we are kingdom-oriented people. We always live in the service of one of two kingdoms. We live in service of the small, personal happiness agenda of the kingdom of self, or we live in service of the huge, origin-to-destiny agenda of the kingdom of God. When we live for the kingdom of self, our decisions, thoughts, plans, actions, and words are directed by personal desire. We know what we want, where we want it, why we want it, how we want it, when we want it, and who we would prefer to deliver it. Our relationships are shaped by an infrastructure of subtle expectations and silent demands. We know what we want from people and how to get it from them. We seek to surround ourselves with people who will serve our kingdom purposes, and we evaluate them not from the perspective of the laws of God's kingdom but from the perspective of the laws of our kingdom.

Think about Gwen. She was not angry that Barry had broken the laws of God's kingdom. She was not grieved that he was in the way of what God wanted to accomplish in and through her marriage. No, Gwen was hurt and angry because Barry had broken the laws of her kingdom. This side of heaven, there is a constant war being fought in all our hearts between the kingdom of self and the kingdom of God. Every battle you have with other people is the result of that deeper war. When you are losing this war, you live for yourself, and invariably it ends in conflict with your husband or wife.

Perhaps these two perspectives tell us much more about the beginning of Gwen and Barry's relationship than we tend to think. Maybe what they thought was love was not love at all, but something very different, masquerading as love. Remember, Gwen had had specific marriage and family dreams for most of her life. Although she did not realize it, Gwen was searching for the one man who would be the missing piece to the puzzle that was her dream for her life. Barry seemed to be that piece, and she wouldn't even have to bend any of his tabs to make him fit. From day one she was powerfully attracted to Barry. She couldn't wait to see him the next time. She loved his quirky text messages. It made her happy to imagine him in the middle of her marital daydreams. She hung on every word as they began to talk about a future together. Gwen knew months before he asked that she would say yes to his proposal. She was convinced that she was deeply in love for the very first time.

Barry hadn't dated much, so it was hard not to like the attention Gwen gave him. The silly e-cards were not his style, but they were so Gwen. She listened to him. She respected his opinion. She enjoyed his company. What was not to like? The more Barry was around Gwen, the more he was attracted to her. He loved that she would pick him up at midnight from his after-class job. He would laugh at how specific her dreams about their future were, but he kind of liked it. It seemed logical that they should get married. He could marry Gwen and still be himself. He would get his dream and Gwen's too. The whole thing was very attractive.

On the surface it all seemed wonderful, but perhaps that was the problem. There was no doubt that Gwen and Barry were very attracted to one another and that this attraction had produced strong affection. That in itself was a wonderful thing. The question is, however, whether what they were experiencing was love. Could it be that Gwen was not attracted to Barry because she loved Barry, but because she loved Gwen? Could it be that her attraction was much more self-oriented than she knew? What felt like love may actually have been excitement that this man she had gotten to know seemed to fit nicely into the dream she had always had for her life.

I have counseled many soon-to-be-married couples just like Barry and Gwen. They were so excited to be together that it was hard for me to get enough of their attention to actually help prepare them for marriage. Together they were convinced that they would never have any problems. Together they were persuaded that nothing would ever get in the way of the feelings they had for one another. Together they were convinced that they were a perfect match. They would sit on my couch, holding hands and looking at one another with glazed eyes, while I tried my best to warn them that they were flawed people marrying a flawed person. But it was always hard for them to take me seriously.

The self-orientation of sin can produce a powerful attraction to another person, but that attraction should not be confused with love, because that attraction cannot do what love will do when the reasons for the attraction die. And the death of the dream happens to every couple. None of us gets our dream in the way that we dreamt it, because none of us is writing our own story. God, in his love, writes a better story than we could ever write for ourselves. He has a better dream than the one we conceive. He knows much better than we do what is best for us. He will take us places that we never intended to go because, in doing so, we become more of what he re-created us in Christ to be.

Could it be that as Gwen and Barry begin to face the harsh reality of the death of their individual and shared dreams, they are not struggling to love one another but are being given the opportunity to love one another more than ever before? It is when attraction wanes, flaws show, and the dream dies that real love has its best opportunity to germinate and grow. For Gwen and Barry, this sad and disillusioning moment is not the end of it all, but the beginning of something wonderful. We could argue that God now has them right where he wants them. They are no longer attracted to one another out of self-centered desire. They are no longer holding onto their dream, because it has melted away before their very eyes. They are hurt and frightened because what had fueled their relationship is gone, and they don't know what to do. But this is not a defeat; this is an opportunity to exit the small space of the kingdom of self and to begin to enjoy the beauty and benefits of the kingdom of God. What appears to be love may not be love, and when God reveals that, it is a very good thing. What happened to Gwen and Barry did not happen because God was absent from their marriage. No, it happened precisely because God was present and was rescuing them from themselves and giving them what they could not produce on their own.

Gwen and Barry's marriage did not die; the selfish dream did, and when it did, real, sturdy, satisfying, other-centered, God-honoring, perseverant love began to grow. Their life together doesn't look anything like the dream they once had, but they love one another more than ever, and they are very thankful that God wanted something better for them than they wanted for themselves.

The Cart before the Horse?

It would be tempting to think that perhaps God got it wrong. Perhaps he really did get the cart before the horse. Think about it: wouldn't it have saved so much heartache, conflict, hurt, and disappointment if God had done things another way? Why do we have to marry flawed people? Wouldn't it have been much easier if God had worked it out so that we would be fully sanctified, then married? Who wouldn't want to marry a perfected person? Wouldn't that make marriage fundamentally easier and more enjoyable? Maybe God did get the order mixed up.

Now, the reason we tend to think this way is precisely because we are so captivated by the kingdom of self. We are drawn to order, predictability, comfort, ease, pleasure, appreciation, fun, and personal happiness. These things are not wrong in and of themselves, but they must not control us. We struggle with God's plan because, at street level, we don't really want what God wants. We want what we want, and we want him to deliver it. But that is not the plan. You see, God didn't give us his grace to make our kingdoms work; he gave us his grace to invite us to a much, much better kingdom.

Think of the sturdiness of your allegiance to your own kingdom purposes. Let me help you see what I mean. Think about how little of your anger over the last month had anything whatsoever to do with the kingdom of God. Your anger seldom comes out of a zeal for the plans, purposes, values, and calling of the kingdom of God. When you are hurt, angry, or disappointed with your husband or wife, it is not because he or she has broken the laws of God's kingdom, and it really concerns you. No, you are most often angry because your spouse has broken the laws of your kingdom. Your spouse is in the way of what you want, and that makes you mad, and it mobilizes you to do or say something that will rein your spouse back into service of your wants, needs, and feelings.

But God's grace is intended to explode that. His grace purposes to expose and free you from your bondage to you. His grace is meant to bring you to the end of yourself so that you will finally begin to place your identity, your meaning and purpose, and your inner sense of well-being in him. So he places you in a comprehensive relationship with another flawed person, and he places that relationship right in the middle of a very broken world. To add to this, he designs circumstances for you that you would have never designed for yourself. All this is meant to bring you to the end of yourself, because that is where true righteousness begins. He wants you to give up. He wants you to abandon your dream.

He wants you to face the futility of trying to manipulate the other person into your service. He knows there is no life to be found in these things.

What does this practically mean? It means the trouble that you face in your marriage is not an evidence of the failure of grace. No, those troubles *are* grace. They are the tools God uses to pry us out of the stultifying confines of the kingdom of self so that we can be free to luxuriate in the big-sky glories of the kingdom of God. This means that you and I will never understand our marriages and never be satisfied with them until we understand that marriage is not an end to itself. No, the reality is that marriage has been designed by God to be a means to an end. When you make it the end, bad things happen. But when you begin to understand that it is a means to an end, then you begin to enjoy and see the value in things that you would not have been able to enjoy before.

When the war between the kingdom of God and the kingdom of self, which rages in all of our hearts, is not being won, then we enter marriage driven by little-kingdom purposes. The problem is that our spouse does the same thing. So, it will just be a matter of time before the carnage begins as our little kingdoms of one collide.

It is only when a husband and wife each live in a purposeful and joyful allegiance to the plans, purpose, and Lord of the kingdom of God that their marriage can really be a place of unity, understanding, and love. Now free from the debilitating anxieties of the wants, needs, and feelings-fulfillment agenda of the kingdom of self, they are free to rest in God's goodness, and because they are, they are also free to love and serve one another. *Marriage is a beautiful thing that only reaches what it was designed to be through the methodology of a painful process.*

Our problem is that we don't like difficulty of any kind. We hate pain and despise suffering. There are many of us who would rather have an easy life than a God-honoring one. So before we ever battle with one another, we are actually battling the Lord. We are fighting his plan. We are critiquing his will. We bring him into the court of our judgment and find him unloving and unwise. We begin to wonder if what we have believed is true and if following him is really worth it. At the very same time, as our hearts are pondering these things, God is near and loves us with transforming love. He is carefully bringing us to the end of ourselves, and he is making us into people who find joy in loving others with the same kind of costly love he has given us.

So, as you read, I would ask you these questions: Whose kingdom shapes your marriage? Whose kingdom defines your dream? What really makes you happy? What is it that you want so badly for your marriage to be? Could it perhaps be that what you thought was love was not really kingdom-of-God, other-centered, other-service love? Could it be that what you actually wanted was for that other person to love you as much as you do? Could it be that your anger reveals how zealously committed you are to the purposes of your own kingdom? Could it be that the troubles you face in your marriage, both big and small, are not so much hassles as they are opportunities? Could it be that just when you thought God had abandoned you and your marriage that he is really very near, giving you the best gift ever—transforming grace? This grace rescues you from the one thing that you cannot rescue yourself from—you.

Reconciling your marriage begins when you begin to reconcile with God. It begins when you begin to pray this radical prayer: "Your kingdom come, your will be done, right here, right now in this marriage as it is in heaven." Good things happen as the result of that prayer!

COMMITMENT 1: We will give ourselves to a regular lifestyle of confession and forgiveness.

COMMITMENT 2: We will make growth and change our daily agenda.

COMMITMENT 3: We will work together to build a sturdy bond of trust.

COMMITMENT 4: We will commit to building a relationship of love.

COMMITMENT 5: We will deal with our differences with appreciation and grace.

COMMITMENT 6: We will work to protect our marriage.

4

Day by Day

I'll never forget the moment. It was 1974, and Luella and I were on the first mezzanine level of the Forrest Theatre in Philadelphia. It was a packed house at the end of the play *Godspell*. It was no longer a theater audience. It was a celebration, a party. The reprise was being sung and played over and over. The air was filled with magic. The scene was electric. The doors were open, but no one was interested in leaving. The story of the gospel had, for a moment, transported us to another place. People grabbed the hands of people they didn't know and would probably never see again. We danced and hugged and laughed. We were all taken beyond our fears and our self-interest. We were celebrating a victory that many of us didn't really understand. We had seen Wisdom come to earth and transform fools into heroes.

In that once-in-a-lifetime moment we all sang the same song. We sang it over and over. No one in that room wanted that song to stop. The musicians smiled as they cranked it up even more. They knew they may not ever experience that again. It was as though they had a sense that they hadn't made this happen either. Perhaps for the first time they understood what the production they had been part of for many months was all about.

We thought we had the best seats in the house. We could look down and see exuberance like we hadn't seen before and probably wouldn't see again until eternity. As Luella and I glanced at one another, we knew we didn't need to say what we were thinking. We knew the other knew. Then, suddenly, my mind became freshly aware of the words we were singing, words that all humanity was meant to sing. Tears began to fill my eyes. "This is what we were made for, this is what the gospel is about, and this is what grace alone is able to do," I thought, as I mouthed the words with the crowd, which had become my for-the-moment family:

Day by day
Day by day
Oh Dear Lord
Three things I pray
To see thee more clearly
Love thee more dearly
Follow thee more nearly
Day by day.

I don't think it would be possible to have a more appropriate mission statement for a marriage. I am deeply convinced from Scripture, my own experience, and the stories of others that you fix a marriage vertically before you ever fix it horizontally. Before you can really gain significant ground in your relationship with your spouse, ground where real, lasting change takes place, you have to be willing to accept and deal with what God says about you, your spouse, your world, and God himself, his purpose, and his grace. These things aren't just the focus of super-spiritual people who want marriage plus a whole lot of spirituality. No, dealing with these things in a way that forms a day-by-day lifestyle is the foundation of a marriage that is what God designed it to be and does what God intended it to do. You cannot avoid dealing with these things any more than you can avoid removing trees from the wooded lot where your new home is going to be located.

What we so joyously sang that night was much more than a song, although most of the crowd didn't know it. It is rather a radical paradigm for a way of living that fills every day with honesty and hope. The things that the lyrics call you to are not one-time decisions; they are meant to be daily commitments that become regular ways of living. When the commitments and actions that follow are applied to marriage, something very simple but quite revolutionary happens, and once it does, you will never want to go back again!

Brick by Brick

I performed the marriage, so I got the call. It is almost always made by the wife, and she is calling because she has actually been forced to face what, somewhere in the recesses of her mind, she knew to be true—she and her husband are sinners. The call is usually made a few days or weeks after the honeymoon. On the honeymoon the self-orientation of sin is overshadowed by exotic cuisine and gorgeous sites, but when the couple returns to real, everyday life, minus these distractions, they are forced to face who they really are and what their marriage is actually about.

I have always thought of this moment of reality recognition as a very positive thing, although the caller rarely does. Usually the wife is in a panic; she thinks she has made a mistake, she thinks their love is over, and she imagines she is going to live a life of loveless torment. But at this moment I think she is about to experience the good stuff that only honest marriage can experience. She is about to be taken beyond herself, and in being taken beyond herself she will abandon her dream, and in abandoning her dream she will pick up a better dream, and in picking up a better dream she will commit herself to a set of daily habits that will not only heal her marriage but make it something better than she ever conceived of. The problem is that none of this is what she expected.

Sara called me at 6:30 AM the day after the ceremony. I picked up the phone to these two words: "It's over!" I knew it wasn't over. In fact, I was happy that she was making the call so soon. I thought Sara and Ben were the smart kids in the class. They had gotten to the end of themselves quickly and were doing something very wise—reaching out for help. I was delighted to help, and I knew that the journey we were about to take together would change them and their marriage.

Here is what I have told couples again and again. It is what I have endeavored to live in my own marriage as well. *The reconciliation of a marriage must be a lifestyle, not just the response you have when things go bad.* Consider why this must be the case. If you are a sinner married to a sinner—and you are—then it is very dangerous and potentially destructive to allow yourself to coast as a couple. You simply will not live a day together where no act of thoughtlessness, self-interest, anger, arrogance, self-righteousness, bitterness, or disloyalty will rear its ugly head. Often it will be benign and low-level, but it will still be there.

Now, I want to introduce you to a theme that will come up again and again in this book: *if you are going to have a marriage that lives in unity, understanding, and love, you must have a little-moment approach to your marriage.* All this does is recognize the nature of the life God has designed for us. In his wisdom, God has crafted a life for us that does not careen from huge, consequential moment to huge, consequential moment. In fact, if you examine your life, you will see that you have actually had few of those moments. You can probably name only two or three life-changing situations you have lived through. We are all the same; the character and quality of our life is forged in little moments. Every day we lay little bricks on the foundation of what our life will be. The bricks of words said, the bricks of actions taken, the bricks of little decisions, the bricks of little thoughts, and the bricks of small-moment desires all work together to form the functional edifice that is your marriage. So, you have to view yourself as a marital mason. You are daily on the job adding another layer of bricks that will determine the shape of your marriage for days, weeks, and years to come.

Perhaps this is precisely the problem. It is the problem of perception. We just don't tend to live life this way. We tend to fall into quasi-thoughtless routines and instinctive ways of doing things that are less self-conscious than they need to be. And we tend to back away from the significance of these little moments because they *are* little moments. You see, the opposite is true: little moments are significant because they are little moments. These are the moments that make up our lives. These are the moments that set up our future. These are the moments that shape our relationships. We must have a "day-by-day" approach to everything in our lives, and if we do, we will choose our bricks carefully and place them strategically.

Things don't go bad in a marriage in an instant. The character of a marriage is not formed in one grand moment. Things in a marriage go bad progressively. Things become sweet and beautiful progressively. The development and deepening of the love in a marriage happens by things that are done daily; this is also true with the sad deterioration of a marriage. The problem is that we simply don't pay attention, and because of this we allow ourselves to think, desire, say, and do things that we shouldn't.

Let me play out this life of little-moment inattention for you. You squeeze and crinkle the toothpaste tube even though you know it bothers your spouse. You complain about the dirty dishes instead of putting them in the dishwasher. You fight for your own way in little things, rather than seeing them as an opportunity to serve. You allow yourself to go to bed irritated after a little disagreement. Day after day you leave for work without a moment of tenderness between you. You fight for your view of beauty rather than making your home a visual expression of the tastes of both of you. You allow yourself to do little rude things you would never have done in courtship. You quit asking for forgiveness in the little moments of wrong. You complain about how the other does little things, when it really doesn't make any difference. You make little decisions without consultation.

You quit investing in the friendship intimacy of your marriage. You fight for your own way rather than for unity in little moments of disagreement. You complain about the other's foibles and weaknesses. You fail to seize those openings to encourage. You quit searching for little avenues for expressing love. You begin to keep a record of little wrongs. You allow yourself to be irritated by what you once appreciated. You quit making sure that every day is punctuated with tenderness before sleep takes you away. You quit regularly expressing appreciation and respect. You allow your physical eyes and the eyes of your heart to wander. You swallow little hurts that you would have once discussed. You begin to turn little requests into regular demands. You quit taking care of yourself. You become willing to live with more silence and distance than you would have when you were approaching marriage. You quit working in those little moments to make your marriage better, and you begin to succumb to what is.

Why do we quit paying attention? Because it is hard work to care, it is hard work to discipline ourselves to be careful, and it is hard work to always be thinking of the other person. Now, be prepared to have your feelings hurt: you and I tend to want the other to work hard because that will make our lives easier, but we don't really want to have to sign in for the hard work ourselves. Oh, I'm not done! I think there is an epidemic of marital laziness among us. We want to be able to coast and have things not only stay the same but get better. And I am absolutely persuaded that laziness is rooted in the self-centeredness of sin. We have already examined the antisocial danger of this thing inside us that the Bible calls sin. We have already considered that it turns us in on ourselves, but it does something else. It reduces us to marital passivity. We want the good things to come to us without the hard work of laying the daily bricks that will result in the good things. And we are often more focused on what the other is failing to do and more focused on waiting for him to get his act together than we are on our own commitment to doing whatever is daily necessary to make our marriages what God intended them to be.

You can have a good marriage, but you must understand that a good marriage is not a mysterious gift. No, it is, rather, a set of commitments that forges itself into a moment-by-moment lifestyle.

Reconciliation as a Lifestyle: What Does This Mean?

There is a very interesting passage in 2 Corinthians that provides a model for what this day-by-day lifestyle looks like.

> For Christ's love compels us, because we are convinced that one died for all, and therefore all died. And he died for all, that those who live should no longer live for themselves but for him who died for them and was raised again. So from now on we regard no one from a worldly point of view. Though we once regarded Christ in this way, we do so no longer. Therefore, if anyone is in Christ, he is a new creation; the old has gone, the new has come! All this is from God, who reconciled us to himself through Christ and gave us the ministry of reconciliation: that God was reconciling the world to himself in Christ, not counting men's sins against them. And he has committed to us the message of reconciliation. We are therefore Christ's ambassadors, as though God were making his appeal through us. We implore you on Christ's behalf: Be reconciled to God. God made him who had no sin to be sin for us, so that in him we might become the righteousness of God. (5:14–21 NIV)

This passage is a call to a particular way of thinking about and living in our relationship to God. What it calls us to in our relationship with God is a wonderful model for our relationship with one another in marriage. This is always true. The first great commandment always defines the second great commandment.

Paul understands that we have been reconciled to God by an act of his grace. He knew that there is no way for us to earn God's love or deserve his favor but, having said that, he was also quick to remind us that reconciliation to God is both an event and a process. Notice the words of verse 20: "We implore you on Christ's behalf: Be reconciled to God." Who is the "you" that Paul is addressing? (The "you" is not in the original, although it is surely implied.) The "you" is the Corinthian church. Now, maybe you're thinking, "Paul, if these people are believers, haven't they already been reconciled to God?" The answer is yes and no. Yes, they have been reconciled to God in the advent sense of God's acceptance of them in Christ. But there is another reconciliation that is still going on. To the degree that we continue to live for ourselves (v. 15), to that degree we still need to be reconciled to God. Since, in some way, we live for ourselves every day, we need to be reconciled daily to God in confession and repentance. What a perfect model this is for our marriages!

Yes, you've already made that one-time decision to live in love with one another, but you don't always live as if you have. To the degree that you daily, in some way, continue to live for yourself, to that degree you daily need to be reconciled to God and to one another. You don't just coast along, hoping somehow, someway to avoid the bad stuff. No, you live with *reconciliation intentionality*. You live with humble hearts and eyes wide open. You are ready to listen and willing to hear. You examine and consider. You take on habits of reconciliation that become the daily lifestyle of your marriage. And you make those habits a regular part of your daily routine.

Sadly, I think there are few couples who actually live this way. How many couples do you know who say that their relationship is the best it has ever been and that it is getting better all the time? How many couples say that they are now experiencing a deeper level of unity, understanding, and love than they have ever known? How many couples say that their spouse is their deepest, closest, and most precious friend? These things are not like a romantic cloud that you happen to wander into. No, they are the rich, relational blessing of living the way God, who created marriage, intended us to live. They are not relational luxuries for the romantically inclined. No, they are the essentials of a truly healthy and happy marriage, one that not only makes you smile but makes God smile as well.

Marital Reconciliation as a Way of Thinking

I remember that as a young pastor (just a few years ago!) my brother Tedd said that 95 percent of what couples need to know, understand, and do is clearly written in the Bibles that they say they hold dear. When he said it, I thought it was a huge exaggeration by a frustrated pastor who just happened to be my brother, but I have come to see the accuracy and insight in what he said. There is no collection of wisdom principles more stunningly insightful than what can be found in the pages of Scripture. Of course this would be true, since the book was written by the hands of men who were guided to write what they wrote by the one who created everything about which they wrote. It is only the Creator who could have such a powerfully insightful and practically transformational origin-to-destiny perspective as the one found in the Bible. Only he is able to have a perspective not limited by time and space and the bias of sin. Only he is able to speak from the vantage point of creation intention. Who could possibly know more about the world he created and the people he designed?

God's Word really does open up to us the mysteries of the universe. It really does make us wiser than we could possibly ever be without it. Yet, having said all this, it is important to reflect on how sad it is that we don't take more advantage of the wisdom God has given us. It is sad that we don't think his thoughts after him. It is sad that we don't require ourselves to look at life always through the lens of his wisdom. It is sad that we swindle ourselves into thinking that we are wiser than we are. It is sad that we aren't more irritated by our foolishness and more motivated to seek his wisdom.

Why have I reminded you of all this? Because the marriage reconciliation lifestyle, which is the focus of this book, is rooted in three essential wisdom perspectives that together must become the mentality of a healthy marriage. Let me lay these out for you.

1) *You must live in your marriage with a harvest mentality*. Paul captures this mentality with these very familiar words: "Do not be deceived:

God is not mocked, for whatever one sows, that will he also reap" (Gal. 6:7). If you are ever going to live with daily awareness of little-moment needs that propel you to live with habits of reconciliation, you have to carry this mentality around with you. You have to buy into the principle of consequences. Here it is: there is an organic relationship between the seeds you plant and the fruit you harvest. In the physical world you will never plant peach pits and get apples. If you plant peach pits and get apples, run fast and run long, because something has happened to the universe! In the same way, there will be organic consistency between the seeds of words and actions that you plant in your marriage and the harvest of a certain quality of relationship that you will experience as you live with one another. Every day you harvest relational plants that have come from the seeds of words and actions that you previously planted. And every day you plant seeds of words and actions that you will one day harvest. Most of the seeds you plant will be small, but one thousand small seeds that grow up into trees will result in an environment-changing forest.

2) *You must live in your marriage with an investment mentality.* We are all treasure hunters. We all live to gain, maintain, keep, and enjoy things that are valuable to us. Our behavior in any given situation of life is our attempt to get what is valuable to us out of that situation. There are things in your life that you have assigned importance to, and once you have, you are no longer willing to live without them. (These principles are laid out in Matt. 6:19–33.) Everyone does it. We live to possess and experience the things upon which we have set our hearts. We are always living for some kind of treasure.

Every treasure you set your heart on and actively seek will give you some kind of return. An argumentative moment is an investment in the treasure of being right, and from it you will get some kind of relational return. If you aggressively argue your spouse into a corner, it is not likely that the return on that investment will be her appreciation for you and a desire to have one of those conversations again! If you invest in the treasure of willing service, you will experience the return of appreciation, respect, and a greater friendship intimacy in your marriage. If it is more valuable to have your house immaculately clean than it is for your partner to be comfortable, then you will live with the return of that in the quality of your relationship.

Investment is inescapable; you do it every day, and you are seldom able to escape the return on the investments you have made. Ask yourself, "What are the things that are valuable to me right now, the things I work to experience every day and am unwilling to live without? And how is the return on those investments shaping my marriage?"

3) *You must live in your marriage with a grace mentality.* When I got married, I didn't understand grace. I had a principle-istic view of Scripture that caused me to bring a law economy into my marriage. The central focus of the Bible is not a set of practical-life principles. No, the central theme of the Bible is a person, Christ. If all you and I had needed was a knowledge and understanding of a certain set of God-revealed principles for living, Jesus would not have needed to come. I think there are many Christians living in Christless marriages. Without knowing what they have done, they have constructed a *law-based* rather than a *grace-based* marriage, and because of this, they are asking the law to do what only grace can accomplish.

The problem with this is that we are not just people in need of wisdom; we are also people in need of rescue, and the thing that we need to be rescued from is *us*. Our fundamental problem is not ignorance of what is right. Our problem is selfishness of heart that causes us to care more about what we want than about what is right. The laws, principles, and perspectives of Scripture provide the best standard ever for our marriages to quest for. They can reveal our wrongs and failures, but they have no capacity whatsoever to deliver us from them. For that we need the daily grace that only Jesus can give us.

So, we must not simply hold one another to the high relational standards of God's Word, but we must also daily offer the same grace that we have been given to one another so that we may be tools of grace in the lives of one another. Our confidence is not in the ability we have to keep God's law but rather in the life-giving and heart-transforming grace of the one who has drawn us to himself and has the power to draw us to one another. When we live with this confidence, we look at the difficulties of marriage not so much as hassles to be endured but as opportunities to enter into an even deeper experience of the rescuing, transforming, forgiving, empowering grace of the one who died for us and is always with us.

Three mentalities—each an essential building block of a reconciliation lifestyle, each requiring the honesty of personal humility, and each encouraging us to be reconciled to one another and to God again and again, and again.

Daily Commitments of a Reconciliation Lifestyle

You can have a marriage that is mutually satisfying while being honoring to God. You really can! Accepting who you are, resting in who God is, and living as he calls you to live will produce a harvest that is far better than the small-vision dreams that you are able to come up with on your own.

Here are the daily commitments that become the daily habits of the kind of marriage that God's design intended and his grace can make possible.

1) *We will give ourselves to a regular lifestyle of confession and forgiveness. We will come clean and deal honestly with our sin, weakness, and failure.* There is only one way that a marriage grows. There is only one way that a marriage changes. There is only one way for your marriage to be what God designed and has enabled it to be. What is this one way? Confession and forgiveness. It is only when we commit ourselves to daily patterns of humble confession, coupled with the willingness to quickly and completely forgive, that a marriage can exceed our limited expectations.

These two things always need to be held together. Regular patterns of forgiveness give us the courage to continue to confess, and regular patterns of confession allow us to experience the joy of the restoration of forgiveness. Why is this so hard for us? Why is this not a regular pattern in every marriage? What will this actually look like in the business of daily living?

2) *We will make growth and change our agenda.* We will pull weeds. You would tend to think that dissatisfaction is the enemy of marriage, but, in fact, the opposite is true. As sinners, we have the perverse ability to be all too easily satisfied. We tend to be willing to live with a human second-best that falls tragically short of God's wise and beautiful plan. We tend to settle for marital détente instead of striving for real love. We tend to be satisfied with low-grade bitterness and disappointment rather

than working toward a pattern of real confession and forgiveness. We tend to settle for a relationship that is all about negotiating rights instead of one that loves to give and to serve.

What does it look like to commit to daily change? How do you go about identifying weeds of wrong that need to be uprooted? How do you know for sure what needs to be planted in their place? How can you work to make dissatisfaction a good thing, something that actually deepens your love and the functional quality of your marriage? How do you keep from being stuck in patterns that fall way short of God's plan and fail to rely on the resources of God's grace?

3) *We will work together to build a sturdy bond of trust.* Trusting and entrusting, we will build a strong foundation. We simply cannot have a healthy, God-honoring, mutually satisfying marriage without trust. In a fallen world, trust is the fine china of a relationship. It is beautiful when it is there, but it is surely delicate and breakable. When trust is broken, it can be very hard to repair. It is trust that allows a husband and wife to face all the internal and external threats to their unity, love, and understanding. It is trust that allows couples to weather the differences and discouragements that every marriage faces. It is trust that allows couples to talk with honesty and hope about the most personal and difficult things.

There are two sides to trust. First, you must do everything you can to prove yourself trustworthy. Second, you must make the decision to entrust yourself into your spouse's care. What does it look like to engender a marriage where trust thrives? What does it look like to rebuild trust when it has been shattered? What are the characteristics of a relationship where trust is the glue?

4) *We will commit to building a relationship of love.* We will incarnate Christ's love. I sit in the balcony of my church on Sunday mornings and look down on the crowd, and I wonder how many of the couples are living in loveless marriages. You may be shocked at this, but I am convinced there are many marriages devoid of real love. Yes, there may be some respect and appreciation, and, yes, the couples may have learned how to avoid daily battles. They may enjoy doing things with one another every once in awhile, but the practical and personal sacrifices that define love are simply not there.

These couples do not respond with mercy and grace in the face of one another's weakness and failure. They don't willingly sacrifice their agenda and their comfort for the good of the other. They don't look for ways to help and encourage. They don't jump in and help the other bear the burdens of life in this fallen world. What does real love in marriage look like? What are the daily sacrifices that love makes? What does it mean to respond to your spouse with mercy? What does it mean practically to be willing to lay down your life for another person? What are the characteristics of a loving marriage?

5) *We will deal with our differences with appreciation and grace.* Celebrating the Creator, we will face our differences with hope. God places lilies next to rocks. He places trees next to streams. He causes bright sun to follow a dark night. He made the muscles of a lion and the delicacy of the wing of a hummingbird. One way God establishes beauty is by putting things that are different next to each other. Isn't this exactly what God does in marriage? He puts very different people next to each other. This is how he establishes the beauty of a marriage. The moon would not be so striking if it hung in a white sky; in the same way, the striking beauty of a marriage is when two very different people learn to celebrate and benefit from their differences and to be protected from their weaknesses by being sheltered by the other's strength.

6) *We will work to protect our marriage.* Watching and praying, we will work to protect our relationship. There are few things more dangerous to a marriage than the feeling of "arrival." When a couple loses a healthy sense of need, patterns of laziness and inattention grow. No longer does the couple carry around the sense of the enormity of the task they have undertaken. No longer do they live with a shared sense of need for God's help and protection. No longer are they looking down the road for potential difficulties that may threaten their union. No longer is their marriage protected by humble prayer.

Every marriage requires divine intervention. Every marriage needs divine wisdom. Every couple will be pushed beyond the limits of their character. Every couple will need strength beyond what they have. No husband and wife can do what they were designed to do in marriage without assistance. One of the beautiful things that marriage is meant to do is drive each of us away from habits of self-reliance into patterns of dependency on God. What does it mean to have "watch and pray" patterns in your marriage? How should a couple measure their potential? How do we recognize signs of impending marriage danger? What role does prayer play in a healthy marriage?

These are the six commitments of a healthy marriage, and with practice they become daily habits. These define how you admit your daily need and make reconciliation the moment-by-moment lifestyle of your relationship. There are few things sweeter and more beautiful than a long-term marriage of unity, understanding, and love. There are few things more deeply discouraging and personally hurtful than a marriage of distance, coldness, and conflict. There are few things sadder than couples who settle for survival, or choose to coast, or stay together but have essentially given up on one another.

A Better Way

It doesn't happen very often, but this was one of those occasions. I cried as I listened to their story. The tension in the room was unbelievable. It was impossible for Chad and Mary to speak to and about one another without anger. Sitting far across the couch from Chad, Mary never did stop crying. She was hurt, but she carried in the file cabinet of her mind a detailed record of wrongs that only deepened her pain. Chad was clearly a man who had had enough. The amazing thing was that there had been no unfaithfulness, there had been no angry violence between them, and there had been no decisive moments of disagreement. Chad and Mary had simply quit working on their marriage. They had quit paying attention. They had none of the habits that this book will consider. This marriage of discouragement and acrimony was formed in a thousand little, mundane, almost unnoticeable moments.

Neither one wanted to be married anymore. They both dreaded getting up in the morning and facing another day. They both pointed their fingers and maintained their self-serving list of offenses. There was a time when they had adored one another, but that time seemed like ancient history. There was no peace now, let alone affection. But I was not without hope, because Chad and Mary had finally made a good choice. They had reached out for help. I knew God cared, and I knew he would never turn a deaf ear to their cries for help. Sure, there was a long way to go, but we would go it together and experience the fresh start that God has made possible in his Son, the Lord Jesus.

What about you? Maybe you haven't gotten to the place of Mary and Chad, but perhaps in your heart you know that things in your marriage are not what they should be. You know that you have settled for less instead of working for more. You know that in little moments things are said and done that do not draw you together nor deepen your love. You know there are places where you are disappointed. You know there are times when you wish things could be better. You know there are ways in which you feel stuck. You're not sure how change can take place, but you wish it would.

I invite you to sit down with me, as Chad and Mary did. Let me hold in front of your marriage the most accurate mirror ever made—the Bible. Let me help you see with new eyes and hear with new ears. Let me invite you to open your heart and humbly reach out your hands for help. Let me encourage you not to be satisfied but to be needy and hungry. I don't know for sure what you expected your marriage to be, but I can tell you for sure that whatever it now is, it can be better. God welcomes us all to a lifestyle of reconciling grace, where problems are faced and change really does take place and where we no longer repeat the same mistakes again and again. Sit down. Take time. God is with you, and he has something better.

We have left undone those things which we ought to have done; and we have done those things which we ought not to have done.

BOOK OF COMMON PRAYER

Since nothing we intend is ever faultless, and nothing we attempt ever without error, and nothing we achieve without some measure of finitude and fallibility we call humanness, we are saved by forgiveness.

DAVID AUGSBURGER

COMMITMENT 1: **We will give ourselves to a regular lifestyle of confession and forgiveness.**

COMMITMENT 2: We will make growth and change our daily agenda.

COMMITMENT 3: We will work together to build a sturdy bond of trust.

COMMITMENT 4: We will commit to building a relationship of love.

COMMITMENT 5: We will deal with our differences with appreciation and grace.

COMMITMENT 6: We will work to protect our marriage.

5

Coming Clean: Confession

They just never came clean. Oh, they were skilled at pointing the finger. They were good at leveling charges. They were good at self-serving excuses. They were good at keeping lists of wrongs. They didn't know it, but they were quite skilled at the habits of acrimony and division. It made sense that by the time they got to me, they were hopeless. You simply can't continually rehearse in your heart all someone's perceived wrongs against you and grow in affection toward him or her. You can't argue to yourself daily that the person you live with is the chief cause of the wrongs that you do, and want to move close to them. You can't carry with you the detailed evidence of what you have suffered at the other's hands and have hope for your future together. But this is what they did.

In a moment, which I have talked about many times, they revealed the basic lifestyle of their marriage, although they did not know they were doing it. I had prayed with them at the beginning of the first time we got together, and I was trying to find a way into talking about the tough things we needed to discuss. I don't think that either one of them had much hope that I could say or do much that would actually help them, but I launched in anyway. I asked them each to tell me what they thought was wrong with their relationship. It was a moment I will never forget. There was no moment of hesitation or consideration. The second the words were out of my mouth, both spoke and said just one word—each other's name!

At that point I was out of a job, because there were no seekers in the room. He was there only in a desperate attempt to get his wife fixed, and she was there only in a desperate attempt to get her husband fixed. Their eyes were firmly focused on one another, and they were completely persuaded that their biggest marital difficulty was next to them on the couch. There was little self-awareness. There was almost no commitment to self-examination. It would have been so encouraging to hear one of them say, "I know I'm not perfect, but . . . " They didn't even go that far, which explains why they were both stuck and hopeless. They were convinced that they had made the mistake of marrying a messed-up person; they were convinced that the other had made them do things they would not otherwise have done; and they were convinced that they had no power to make the other change, although they had tried. As I sat with them, I was reminded once again that hopelessness is a way of seeing, not a state of being.

I have wondered many times since how many marriages are somehow, someway, stuck in this same cycle. Perhaps the cycle of blame is more subtle, and maybe the hopelessness has not set in, but the system is in place. The couple is stuck in a cycle of repeating the same things over and over again. They repeat the same misunderstandings. They rehearse and re-rehearse the same arguments. They repeat the same wrongs. Again and again things are not resolved. Night after night they go to bed with nothing reconciled; they awake with memories of another bad moment, and they march toward the next time when the cycle will be repeated. It all becomes predictable and discouraging. They hate the cycle. They wish things were what they once were. Their minds swing between nostalgia and disappointment. They want things to be different, but they don't seem to know how to break free, and they don't seem willing to do the one thing that makes change possible—confess.

They tell themselves they will do better. They promise they will spend more time together. They promise they will pray together for a moment before they start their day. They decide to spend more time together outside the house. They promise they will talk more. But it is not long before all the promises fade away. It is not long before they are in the same place again. All their commitments to change have been subverted by the one thing they seem unwilling to do: take the focus off the other and put it on themselves. Here is the point: *no change takes place in a marriage that does not begin with confession.*

Confession is the doorway to growth and change in your relationship. It is essential. It is fundamental. Without it you are relegated to a cycle of repeated and deepening patterns of misunderstanding, wrong, and conflict. With it, the future is bright and hopeful, no matter how big the issues that you are now facing.

The Grace of Confession

1) *It is a grace to know right from wrong.* Change is all about measuring yourself against a standard, being dissatisfied with where you are because you see that you have fallen short of the standard, and seeking the grace to close the gap from where you are to where you need to be. James likened the Word of God to a mirror (James 1:22–25) into which we can look and see ourselves as we actually are. It is impossible to overstate how important this is. Accurate diagnosis always precedes effective cure. You only know that the board is too short because you can place it against a measuring instrument. You only know that the temperature in your house is too hot because you have a measuring instrument in your house (called a thermostat). You only know that your tires have enough air because you can use a gauge that measures their exact air pressure. The Bible is God's ultimate measuring instrument. It is meant to function in each of our lives as a spiritual tape measure. We can place ourselves and our marriages next to it and see if we measure up to God's standard. God's Word is one of his sweetest gifts of grace, and open eyes to see it clearly and an open heart to receive it willingly are sure signs of God's grace.

2) *It is a grace to understand the concept of indwelling sin.* One of the most tempting fallacies for us—and for every human being in this fallen world—is to believe that our greatest problems exist outside us rather than inside us. It's easy to fall into thinking this way, because we have a lot of material to work with. We do live in a broken world where things don't operate as was intended. Every day is filled with difficulties and obstacles of some kind. We live with flawed people, and our lives will be complicated by their brokenness. Despite this, the Bible calls us to humbly confess that the greatest, deepest, most abiding problem each of us faces is inside, not outside, of us. The Bible names that problem—sin. Because sin is self-focused and self-serving, it is antisocial

and destructive to our relationships. Here's where this goes: it requires each of us to say that our greatest marital problem exists inside us, not outside us.

You know that you have been gifted with grace when you are able to say, "My greatest marital problem is me." It is so easy to point the finger. It is so easy to blame. It is a blessing to acknowledge that you carry around in yourself your own personal Judas who will betray you again and again (see Romans 7), and it is comforting to know that you are not alone in your struggle with sin.

3) *It is a grace to have a properly functioning conscience.* Many marriages travel a one-way road in the wrong direction. It is the direction of a hardened heart. Let me explain. In courtship we are very concerned with winning the other person, so we work to be loving, kind, serving, respectful, giving, forgiving, and patient. We would never think of doing anything unkind or rude. We are always thinking of the other, what he or she feels, desires, and needs. We find delight in making the other happy. We look for ways of expressing our love. But after the ceremony, the marriage often turns and begins to move in another direction. Maybe it's because we now have the other person and don't need to win him or her anymore. Maybe it's because we begin to take the relationship God has given us for granted. Whatever the reason, we begin to let down our guard. We quit being so solicitous. Selfishness begins to replace service. In small ways at first, we allow ourselves to do and say things that we would have never thought of doing and saying in courtship. We become progressively less giving, less patient, and less forgiving. We begin to look out for ourselves more than we do for the other. Maybe it's something as small as expecting the other to clean up our mess or (yes, I'm about to say it) passing gas in bed. But these are not little things; they are signs of something happening that is destructive and dangerous. At first, when we do these rude and selfish things our conscience bothers us, but it won't be long before our heart gets hard and our conscience doesn't bother us anymore.

It's like the homeless guy on the street. You look at him and wonder how he can possibly live with himself being so dirty. You wonder why he is not afraid of mistreatment or embarrassed at his condition. You can rest assured that he once felt those things, but in his struggle to survive he has become hardened. It just doesn't bother him anymore. Many marriages travel a similar road. It is the sad highway of a progressively hardening heart. I have been shocked at the way couples treat one another with no apparent twinge of conscience or embarrassment as they sit with me seeking help. It is a perverse ability that all sinners have—to become progressively comfortable with things that should shock, grieve, and embarrass us.

It is a sign of God's grace when our consciences are sensitive and our hearts are grieved, not at what the other person is doing, but at what we have become. That sensitivity is the doorway to real and lasting change. Change always begins with being dissatisfied, and personal dissatisfaction always begins with a conscience that is sensitive to wrong. Out of this comes a desire for change and a restlessness that causes us to reach out for the help, from God and others, that change requires.

4) *It is only grace that protects us from self-righteousness.* This is the other side of the coin. It is important to understand the dynamic that operates so subtly, yet so destructively, in our relationships. Because we all suffer from some degree of personal spiritual blindness—that is, we do not see ourselves with accuracy—and because we tend to see the weaknesses and failures of our spouse with greater accuracy, we begin to think of ourselves as more righteous than our husband or wife. When we do this, and in some way we all do, it makes it hard for us to think we are part of the problem in our marriage, and it makes it difficult to embrace the loving criticism and correction of the other person. This means that it is not only blindness that prevents us from change but assessments of personal righteousness as well. If we are convinced that we are righteous, we desire neither change nor the help that can make it happen.

First John 1:8 says, "If we say we have no sin, we deceive ourselves, and the truth is not in us." The deception of personal righteousness is a huge wall in the way of marital change. Here's how it works: the husband views himself as righteous and views his wife as a sinner in need of help, and the wife views herself as righteous and views her husband as a sinner in need of help. So, neither feels the need for personal change while being quite upset that the other sees no need for personal change. Each becomes more dissatisfied, impatient, and bitter, while the condition of the marriage worsens. But there is hope! Grace decimates self-righteousness. Grace opens our eyes and softens our hearts. Grace deepens our sense of need. Grace faces us with our poverty and weakness. Grace causes us to run after help and welcomes us with open arms when we come. When a husband and wife quit arguing about who is the more righteous and begin to be grieved over their respective sin, you can know for sure that grace has visited their marriage.

5) *It is a grace to see ourselves with accuracy.* To see ourselves with accuracy is the opposite of self-righteousness. I have been amazed to watch an angry husband angrily declare that he is not angry! I have been surprised to see a controlling husband and wife control a conversation in order to work to convince me that they are not controlling. I have watched a bitter spouse bitterly refuse the thought that she might be bitter. I have listened to self-righteous men and women self-righteously declare that they are not self-righteous. I have heard selfish people selfishly demand that they not be viewed as selfish. In each instance they would listen to what I had to say and then lay out for me the evidence that my assessment was wrong. It was not just that they were refusing to look at themselves (although that was also true). It was that, when they looked at themselves, they simply didn't see what I saw.

Here's what happens as a result. Because a husband is convinced that he is righteous and his wife is not righteous, he doesn't feel the need to look at or examine himself. That leaves him with only one conclusion, that the problems in the marriage are his wife's fault. So he watches her all the more hyper-vigilantly, and because she is less than a perfect person, he collects more and more "evidence" to support his view of the marriage struggles. Each day makes him more convinced that his wife is the one who needs to change, not him. Rather than being grieved at the weakness and selfishness of his own heart, he finds it harder and harder to deal with hers. He struggles to be patient with her and secretly wishes that she could be more like him. This posture is dangerous to any relationship but devastating to the health of a marriage.

Many married people are like the Pharisee in the temple who thanked God that he was not like the other sinners around him. They need the grace of an accurate self-assessment. Few things prevent change in a marriage more than a distorted sense of self. Few things are more needed than eyes to see ourselves with clarity and accuracy.

6) *It is a grace to be willing to listen and consider criticism and rebuke.* It is hard to see ourselves with clarity and hard to accept what we see when we do. It is so easy to be defensive. All of us carry inside ourselves an inner lawyer who is easily activated and quickly rises to our defense. We've all been in one of those moments when someone is pointing out some wrong in us, and although we are not speaking aloud, we have already begun a silent defense of ourselves against what they are saying. As they are pointing to evidence of a need for change, we are marshaling evidence that we are not, in fact, the person they contend we are. It takes grace to be ready to listen and willing to hear. It takes grace to quiet our mind, to focus our attention, and to settle our heart so that we can actually receive the help that God is offering us in that moment of unexpected confrontation.

Even the words we use for this kind of conversation carry with them negative connotations. Words like *rebuke, criticism, exhortation,* and *confrontation* tend not to paint a picture of situations we enjoy, yet these words point to something that is essential to a healthy marriage. It is something I have discussed in earlier writings. Healthy relationships have two essential character qualities. First is the *humility of approachability.* When both people step out from behind protective walls and open up to the perspectives and help of others, each individual—and their relationship—will be given an opportunity to grow and change. The second quality is equally important. In fact, these two qualities cannot live without one another. The second is the *courage of loving honesty.* Not only do we defend ourselves from the opinion of others, but we avoid uncomfortable moments by failing to say what needs to be said. In the fear of disagreement, tension, and rejection, we choose to be silent about things that, if addressed in love, could be used to bring new insight to one another and a fresh start to the relationship.

Only when our confidence is in the Lord, that is, in his constant help and forgiveness, are we able to step out into the light, unafraid of what we may be asked to face. When we really do believe that his grace has already covered anything we may have to confess and given us power for every change to which we may need to commit, we will not be afraid of living in marriages that are open and honest.

7) *It is a grace not to be paralyzed by regret.* I am persuaded that fear of regret is something that keeps us from facing things in ourselves that we need to face. Confession not only calls us to look at ourselves in the present, but it also calls us to access the past. If you are a husband who has been married for seven years and are now beginning to face the fact that you are an angry man, then you have to also be willing to look at the harvest that your anger has produced over those years. If you are a bitter wife who, in bitterness, has withdrawn into a protective shell, then you have to face not only your present state of withdrawal but how that bitterness has impacted the people around you during your withdrawal. It's hard enough to consider our present weakness and failure. It is even harder to consider the fruit that that weakness and failure has produced over the years. So, rather than giving in to the temptation to run and hide, we need to run to where help can be found.

Perhaps the brightest, most wonderful commitment of the Redeemer is captured in these words from Revelation 21:5: "Behold, I am making all things new." *New* is the operative word for what God is seeking to do in you and in your marriage. You are not stuck. You are not committed to the mistakes of the past. You are not cursed to pay forever for your errors. God's work is in the work of renewal. He sent his Son to earth in order to make real and lasting change possible. God has made fresh starts and new beginnings possible. Reconciliation can take place. Restoration really does happen. What was broken can be healed. The weeds of the old way can die, and flowers of a new, better way can grow in their place. God will not call us to face our harvest without giving us what we need to face it, and he will not call us to plant new seeds of a better way without giving us the wisdom and strength to do it. As we face regret, we bask in forgiveness and then turn to live in a new way, embracing the power that is ours as children of God.

8) *It is a grace to know that we can face our wrongs because Christ has carried our guilt and shame.* This point picks up on themes from above, but needs its own attention. It is telling to observe that the first two things Adam and Eve did after disobeying God was to cover themselves and to hide. For the very first time, they experienced shame and

guilt. They feared discovery and judgment, and although they worked to shift the blame to someone else, they were playing a fool's game. The blame-shifting did not quiet their hearts. It did not bring them peace. What they had done brought shame upon them and guilt in relation to God. It is important to understand that the shame and guilt were not just psychological or emotional experiences; they were real, and they had to be dealt with.

Dealing with our guilt and shame is what the whole Bible is about. It is about redemption, that is, the paying of a debt of guilt and shame that needed to be paid. That payment was made on the cross. Jesus took our shame, hanging in public, numbered with the criminals. He took our guilt by taking our sin on himself and paying the price for it—death. He did this even though he had no reason for either shame or guilt, because he was a perfect man. He did not do these things for himself; every action in the whole process was substitutionary. It was done for us. Why? So guilt and shame would not hold us; so that in the courage of celebratory faith we would quit hiding, quit excusing, quit blaming, and quit rising to our own defense. So that we could be unafraid of saying, "You are right, I was wrong, and I need your forgiveness." So that we could say, "I know I blew it last night, but I am committed to doing better." So that we could say to one another, "I need your help. I don't always see myself accurately. If you see something wrong in me, I welcome you to help me see it as well." So that we could look at our marriages and not declare that they are perfect but celebrate the fact that, over the years, we have taken many important steps closer to what God has called us to be and has designed our marriages to become.

You see, confession shouldn't be this scary thing we do our best to avoid; and sin, weakness, and failure should not be the constant elephant in the room that husbands and wives know is there but cannot talk about. Confession should be seen as a wonderful gift that every marriage needs. It should be liberating. It should be freeing. It should not be seen as a moment of personal loss but as an opportunity for personal and relational gain. Our confession should be propelled by deep appreciation and gratitude toward God, who has made it possible for us not to be afraid any longer of being exposed. Because of what Jesus has done for us, we do not have to hide or excuse our wrongs. We are freed from posing as if we are perfect, when in our heart of hearts we know we are not. We have been liberated from having to deny our difficulties. We can stare problems in the face with hope and courage, because Christ has made real, lasting, personal, and relational change possible. Fresh beginnings and new starts really do happen, and they can be ours! Is your marriage benefiting from the freedom of confession?

The Daily Habits of a Confession Lifestyle

So, what does it look like to take the grace of confession seriously, to get the elephant out of the room and make honest admission of wrong the regular habit of a marriage? Well, here are the daily habits of a confession lifestyle.

1) *We will be lovingly honest.* Confession requires honesty. It requires a willingness to approach the other when he or she has acted or spoken in a way that God says is wrong. We must be committed to deal with such issues in a way that is driven by Christlike love. This means that before we can speak to the other's heart issues, we first need to deal with the hurt, anger, and bitterness of our own heart. Remember, truth not spoken in love ceases to be helpful because the message gets twisted and distorted by other human emotions and agendas. When we approach our spouse, we are seeking to help her see what God wants her to see. Remember, we cannot confess to that which we do not see.

2) *We will be humble when exposed.* Humility, when we are approached by the other, means willingness to consider. It means quieting that background noise of our inner defense system. It means remembering that we have not yet arrived, that we are still sinners in need of daily grace, and that at this moment we are being loved by our Redeemer. Humility means the willingness to look in the mirror of God's Word and being glad that whatever we see there has already been covered by the blood of Jesus.

3) *We will not excuse.* It is such a typical impulse for us all: someone points out a wrong and we are immediately filled with an alternative view that places us in a very different light. Refusal to excuse means resisting the urge to build arguments for our righteousness. It means

refusing to turn the tables on the other, making sure he or she knows that we are not the only sinner in the room.

4) *We will be quick to admit wrongs.* There are few things that contribute more to the health of a marriage than the commitment to keep short accounts. We refuse to pout. We refuse to live in the silence of hurt, anger, and vengeance. When we have done wrong, we will be quick to seek forgiveness and reconciliation. If we have been wronged, we will be quick to approach the other and lovingly help him to see what he has said and done. We will make our approach in a spirit of forgiveness and hope. We will refuse to let the "sun go down on our anger" (Eph. 4:26).

Now, when you commit to doing this, you begin to experience the beauty of a relationship that has no reason to keep a record of wrongs and has no closets filled with the emotional baggage of yesteryear. So, whereas you used to wait days to talk about wrongs in your marriage, you now move quickly to resolve issues, because you have experienced the beauty of the forgiveness, reconciliation, and tender love that a confession lifestyle produces.

5) *We will listen and examine.* Each of us has to work to quiet our emotions and the self-righteous tendencies of our hearts. When approached, we all need to require ourselves to hear clearly and to think carefully. This means working to understand and consider. It means taking the light that is handed to us by the words of the other and shining it on ourselves, being willing to see things about ourselves that we have never seen before. Change is not only about admitting wrong; it is about progressively growing in self-knowledge. It is about developing a greater and greater grasp of the themes of strength and weakness in our marriage. It is about being ready, willing, and waiting to learn new things about ourselves and our marriage that will lead to lasting growth and change.

6) *We will greet confession with encouragement.* Few things crush a confession lifestyle more quickly than judgment. It is a tendency in every sinner to want the person who has hurt us to hurt in the way that we have been hurt. We want the other to feel the sting as well. Nothing encourages the courage of confession more than grace. If God were only a judge, nobody would confess anything to him. It is his goodness that leads us to repentance. His love draws us. His grace encourages us. His

patience gives us hope. So we run to him, not away from him. When we greet the confession with the same grace that we have been given by the Lord, we give the other courage and hope to confess all the more.

7) We *will be patient, persevering, and gentle in the face of wrong.* The fact of the matter is that change is most often a process and seldom an event. Change happens chaotically. It comes unannounced, in fits and starts. We don't wake up and say, "Hey, I think I'll create all kinds of change today." Change is pushed upon us by a persevering Redeemer, who will not walk away from the work he has begun in both husband and wife. He will put the need of change before us in the most inopportune moments. He will not submit to our schedule or agenda for our day. He has not promised that change will be enjoyable each time or a comfortable process over the long haul. He has promised to stay near us, giving us everything we need, and he has guaranteed that we will be more than we ever thought we could be. (He will not cease working until we are like Jesus. Now, how's that for a goal!) So, he calls us to be patient. He calls us to be willing to wait. He calls us to continue when continuing is hard, and as we are continuing, to look for any way we can to incarnate his transforming love.

8) We *will not return to the past.* Sadly, many marriages are held hostage by the past. Every current discussion of wrong gets kidnapped by the failures and hurts of the past. Without really realizing it, couples fall into a hopeless and discouraging pattern of having the same conversation over and over again. Eventually they reach the point where they simply do not want to talk to one another anymore; it's just too painful. The conversations don't move toward resolution; each conversation is just a reminder of how bad things are and of how long they have been that way.

So, we establish a pattern of short accounts where a daily cycle of confession, forgiveness, and reconciliation settles issues, alleviating any need to address them again. And we will resist, in moments of hurt and anger, resurrecting what has already been resolved.

9) We *will put our hope in Christ.* Confession is all about hope. First, confession unavoidably leads us to give up hoping in ourselves. It calls us to abandon our trust in our own wisdom, righteousness, and strength. It welcomes us to admit how weak, selfish, needy, fickle, and

rebellious we actually are. It faces us with the reality that we are still people in deep and daily need of rescue. Yes, we have grown, but sin still lives within us, diverting our desires and distorting our actions. So, we lay down the hope that we had in ourselves, and we take up a new, brighter hope. This hope is at the cross of Jesus Christ. He came to earth and lived the perfect life that we could not live. He became the perfect sacrificial lamb, taking our sins on himself, satisfying the Father's wrath and purchasing our forgiveness. He suffered the rejection of his Father so that we would be accepted. He walked out of his tomb, defeating death and making the hope of eternal life a reality. What does this have to do with marriage?

Everything!

When the shadow of the cross hangs over our marriage, we live and relate differently. We are no longer afraid to look at ourselves. We are no longer surprised by our sin. We no longer have to work to present ourselves as righteous. We say good-bye to finger-pointing and self-excusing. We abandon our record of wrongs. We settle issues quickly. And we do all these things because we know that everything we need to confess has already been forgiven, and what is needed for every new step we will take has already been supplied. We can live in the liberating light of humility and honesty, a needy and tender sinner living with a needy and tender sinner, no longer defensive and no longer afraid, together growing nearer to one another as we grow to be more like him.

Now, who wouldn't want a marriage like that?

COMMITMENT 1: **We will give ourselves to a regular lifestyle of confession and forgiveness.**

COMMITMENT 2: We will make growth and change our daily agenda.

COMMITMENT 3: We will work together to build a sturdy bond of trust.

COMMITMENT 4: We will commit to building a relationship of love.

COMMITMENT 5: We will deal with our differences with appreciation and grace.

COMMITMENT 6: We will work to protect our marriage.

6

Canceling Debts

We were so burdened. We took our debts very seriously. Luella had just delivered our second son, and we had no means of paying the enormous bill. Our little church was struggling to pay us, and we had encountered unexpected auto and home expenses. Times were so tough that we wondered if we would have sufficient food for our children to eat. Then we got the call from the hospital. I didn't want to answer it, but I knew I should. As I walked to the phone I was anticipating what the caller would say to me. I was anticipating the threats and the guilt. The only thing that gave me peace was that I knew they couldn't repossess our infant son!

The caller's voice was friendlier than I had anticipated. She asked me how I was doing. "How am I doing?" I thought. "How do you think I'm doing? I'm about to face my economic execution, and you're asking me how I'm doing!" But, instead of saying what I was thinking, I mumbled some kind of non-answer. She then said, "We have an assistance program for families like yours; we have decided that you qualify, and we have decided to cancel your debt. (We did have to pay some minor expenses.) I couldn't believe what I was hearing! It felt like a boulder had been taken off my chest. I can't express the joy and gratitude that flooded into my heart. After weeping together, Luella and I began to realize that not only had the cancelation of the debt lifted a burden from the past, but it had changed our financial future. Now we could struggle through without the burden of this debt hanging over us every day.

Why have I told you this story of God's grace and provision? Because it speaks so powerfully to the marriage of everyone reading this book. Healthy marriages are healthy because the people in those marriages find joy in canceling debts. I cannot think of a more essential ingredient in marriage than forgiveness. Yet forgiveness is not always attractive. Forgiveness is difficult and costly. It will push you to the borders of your faith. It will tempt you to fear and doubt. But when forgiveness is granted and debts are canceled, the return is much greater than the cost.

"I Don't Think I Will Ever Be Able to Forgive Him"

"I don't think I will ever be able to forgive him"—these were the first words I ever heard her say. She choked them out through her sobs, and she was convinced there was no way that she would ever be able to forgive him for what he had done. I thought I was about to hear a story of serial abuse or betrayal, but that is not what I heard. What I heard surprised me.

Sally said, "Jeb is basically a good man. He works very hard, provides for us well, and loves our children." I was a young pastor, and I was confused, not only because of their story, but because I didn't really understand the importance and dynamics of forgiveness. In the years to come, I didn't learn the essentiality of forgiveness from counseling couples; no, I learned it in moments of pain and grace in my own marriage.

I tried to graciously assist Sally to tell her story. She and Jeb had met in college, fallen madly in love, and married between their sophomore and junior years. They decided that they needed to finish school, so they could only work part-time. Before the first year was over, they had had their first child. Neither one was emotionally or spiritually mature enough to deal well with the things on their plate. Not only was a sinner married to a sinner, but an immature sinner was married to an immature sinner. They struggled to be on the same page with one another, and they expressed their irritation all too readily. Jeb began accusing Sally of being self-centered and perennially dissatisfied. Sally saw Jeb as distancing and demanding. They didn't have knock-down, drag-out fights, but their communication was largely negative and their low-grade tension was almost always in the air. Day after day there were problems between them that were not resolved. Day after day there were little moments of misunderstanding, hurt, and anger. Again and again they would end the day in disappointed silence, then fall to sleep rehearsing the wrongs of the other. The list got longer and the burden got heavier.

Over the months and years, the moments morphed into patterns of sin and judgment that neither one seemed to have the interest or skill to break. They both held onto their record of the other's wrongs as if it was a valuable family heirloom. What had hurt them in the beginning they now found scary to let go of. Jeb and Sally defended themselves against accusations of wrong by pulling out their precious list of the years of wrongs the other had done. These confrontations never moved toward reconciliation. Each conversation seemed to increase the weight of the burden and to thicken the walls of their defenses.

But something else happened that was devastating to their marriage. No, there wasn't a moment where things became physical, and neither one of them was unfaithful. No, what took place was progressive and subtle, but it sucked the life out of their marriage. Jeb and Sally had once liked one another, and they would tell you that they still did; but they didn't. There were many more things about Jeb that Sally disliked than things she liked. In fact, when Sally talked in any kind of positive way about Jeb, it was about ancient history. And it was hard for Jeb to say anything good about Sally without diminishing it with negative stories and irritated qualifications.

Why had this happened? Because the patterns of sin and failure were not accompanied by patterns of confession and forgiveness; what was left was the compilation of the wrongs of the other. So, what they meditated on with regard to one another was largely negative. In their minds they daily saw one another through a lens of wrongs and progressively forgot what was good in the other. The gentle and patient acceptance of love gave way to dislike and disrespect. Yes, there I've said it. Jeb and Sally tried their best to deny it, but they didn't like one another anymore. This simply made anger and irritation all the easier. They were a couple at war, and they were both overwhelmed with the daily carnage of the battle.

It was a friend of Sally's that begged her to get help. The way out would be simple, but the cost would be great.

The Harvest of Unforgiveness

The Bible is very clear: what you plant, you will harvest (Gal. 6:7ff). In a marriage, every day you harvest what you previously planted and plant what you will someday harvest. Jeb and Sally weren't experiencing mysterious difficulty. Sadly, they were harvesting what they had sown over the years. Let me lay out for you the marriage-damaging stages of the harvest of unforgiveness. I am deeply persuaded that the marriage of countless couples is in some way following this path.

1) Immaturity and Failure

Not only are all people who get married sinners, but most enter their marriages quite young, naïve, and immature. Typically, in the early years of marriage they do dumb, selfish, sinful things—things that neither one thought they would do. In their surprise and hurt, they give way to accusation, blame, judgment, and punishment rather than to honest confrontation, confession, and forgiveness. What they fail to realize is that not only are they responding poorly to the present moment, but they are beginning to set the direction of their marriage. Each selfish act followed by a bitter response damages the affection they have for one another and the unity they are meant to enjoy.

2) Falling into Comfortable Patterns

Since confrontation, confession, and forgiveness are all hard work, it is easier to give way to lower urges. It is easier to *harrumph* and walk away, to rehearse in your mind the other's wrongs, to compile your list, to yell in anger, and to level a threat. So many couples fall into comfortable but relationally destructive patterns. Meanwhile, the affection between them is weakening, and the distance between them is widening.

3) Establishing Defenses

Rather than growing as the result of a healthy lifestyle of honesty and forgiveness, many couples learn early in their marriage to build up walls of defense against each other's irritated accusations. Couples soon learn that the best defense is an offense, so they tackle the increasing criticism of the other by reaching into the list they have compiled and reminding the other how imperfect he or she is and, therefore, how difficult to live with. This combination of self-righteousness (convincing ourselves that we are not the problem) and accusation (telling our spouse that he or she is the problem) precludes relationship. We are not standing together seeking to defend our marriage against attack. No, we are viewing each other as adversaries and throwing up walls of defense against one another.

4) Nurturing Dislike

Because both husband and wife are allowing themselves to meditate on what is wrong about the other rather than celebrating the good God has done in and through him or her, their perspective becomes increasingly negative. Since human beings do not live by the facts of their experience but by their interpretation of the facts, this globally negative assessment becomes the interpretive lens through which they see their spouse. So what they once would not have seen as negative, they now interpret as negative. I have counseled many couples that simply don't like one another very much anymore. If fact, I have had husbands and wives say to me that it is hard for them to remember what attracted them to the other person in the first place!

5) Becoming Overwhelmed

At some point, living with someone you don't like very much and feeling the need to daily defend yourself against attack becomes very exhausting and discouraging. The same offenses are taken and the same accusations are leveled over and over again. The same debate over who is the harder to live with happens again and again. You come to the point of dreading getting up in the morning. You walk on eggshells, wondering when the next bomb will drop and shatter what little peace you have left.

6) Envy of Other Couples

It's hard when you live like this not to look over the fence or across the aisle and envy couples that seem to have everything you don't. It's tempting to wonder what it would be like to be married to that other woman or that other man. It's tempting to doubt God's love and wisdom when you feel that you have been singled out for difficulties that others aren't facing. It's tempting to throw other couples in one another's faces. Comparing your marriage to the airbrushed public persona of another couple is always dangerous but particularly destructive to a couple who are already not giving themselves much reason to continue.

7) Fantasies of Escape

It always seems to lead here. You are angry, hurt, and overwhelmed. You don't really like the other very much, and you don't look forward to the times you have together. You feel overwhelmed and smothered. You tell yourself that you are the daily victim of the other's sin. You can't imagine that your spouse is really going to change. It all seems so impossible, so you begin to fantasize about escape. At first, it's just the unrealistic daydreams of the tired, but it becomes more than that. The road between fantasy and obsession or fantasy and resolve is often not very long. You are in a place of being very susceptible to taking a means of escape that is not really escape but only troubles the trouble that you are already overwhelmed by.

You may be thinking, "Wow, Paul, that is a very bleak picture!" Well, I would ask you this: what is the journey you have taken as a couple? Do you have deeper respect, more tender affection, and greater appreciation than you had when you first got married? Are you more able to lovingly confront and graciously forgive? Has your friendship grown and your unity been solidified? Or has your marriage taken the opposite journey? Remember, Jeb and Sally had no "major sins" between them. Their marriage rusted into brokenness by the daily rain of the little drops of unforgiveness.

Then Why Don't People Just Forgive?

Why don't people just forgive? That is a very good question. If forgiveness is easier and more beneficial, why isn't it more popular? The sad reality is that there is short-term, relationally destructive power in refusing to forgive. Holding onto our spouse's wrongs gives us the upper hand in our relationship. We keep a record of wrongs because we are not motivated by what is best for our spouse but by what is expedient for ourselves. Here are some of the dark "benefits" of unforgiveness.

1) *Debt is power.* There is power in having something to hold over another's head. There is power in using a person's weakness and failure against him or her. In moments when we want our own way, we pull out some wrong against our spouse as our relational trump card.

2) *Debt is identity.* Holding onto our spouse's sin, weakness, and failure makes us feel superior to our spouse. It allows us to believe that

we are more righteous and mature than our spouse. We fall into the pattern of getting our sense of self not by what God has called us to be and do but by comparing ourselves to our spouse. This pattern plays into the self-righteousness that is the struggle of every sinner.

3) *Debt is entitlement.* Because of all our spouse's wrongs against us, he or she owes us. Carrying our spouse's wrongs makes us feel deserving and therefore comfortable with being self-focused and demanding. "After all I have had to endure in relationship with you, don't I deserve . . . ?"

4) *Debt is weaponry.* The sins and failures that our spouse has done against us that we still carry around with us are like a loaded gun; it is very tempting to pull them out and use them when we are angry. When our wife has hurt us in some way, it is very tempting to hurt her back by throwing in her face just how evil and immature she is.

5) *Debt puts us in God's position.* It is the one place that we must never be, but it is also a position that all of us have put ourselves in. We are not the judge of our spouse. We are not the one who should dispense consequences for our spouse's sin. It is not our job to make sure he feels the appropriate amount of guilt for what he has done. But it is very tempting to ascend to God's throne and to make ourselves judge.

This is nasty stuff. It is a relational lifestyle driven by ugly selfishness. It is motivated by what we want, what we think we need, and by what we feel. It has nothing to do with a desire to please God with the way we live with our spouse, and it surely has nothing to do with what it means to love her in the midst of her struggle to live God's way in this broken world. It also is scarily blind. We are so focused on our spouse and all his failures that we are blind to ourselves. We forget how often we fail, how much sin mars everything we do, and how desperately we need the grace that we are unwilling to give to him. This way of living turns our lover into our adversary and turns our home into a war zone.

Yet, we have all been seduced by the power of unforgiveness. We have all used the sin of another against him or her. We have all acted as judges. We have all thought we are more righteous than our husband or wife. We have all used the power of guilt to get what we want when we want it and in so doing have done serious damage to the fine china of our marital love.

It seems almost too obvious to say, but forgiveness is a much better way. It is the only way to live in an intimate, long-term relationship with another sinner. It is the only way to negotiate through the weakness and failure that will daily mark your marriage. It is the only way to deal with hurt and disappointment. It is the only way to have hope and confidence restored. It is the only way to protect your love and reinforce the unity that you have built. It is the only way not to be kidnapped by the past. It is the only way to give your marriage the blessing of fresh starts and new beginnings.

The cost of forgiveness is great, but the harvest of forgiveness is a beautiful thing, so it is vital to understand what forgiveness is and does.

What Is Forgiveness?

Here is what you have to understand: forgiveness is a *vertical commitment* that is followed by a *horizontal transaction*. Both aspects of forgiveness are essential in the order that I have presented them.

When you have been wronged in word or action by your husband or wife, your response must be shaped by an immediate commitment that you make before God. Forgiveness begins by your giving the offense to the Lord. This does not mean that you act as if something wrong is right. It means that you do not carry the wrong with you (bitterness), and that you do not treat the other in light of the wrong (judgment). You entrust yourself to God's mercy and justice, and you give yourself to overcoming evil with good (see the principles laid out by Paul in Rom. 12:9–21). You commit to respond to your spouse with the same grace that you have been given. You do not insert yourself into God's position and mete out punishment for his or her offenses.

Now, this does not mean that you eat the offense and act as though nothing happened. It does not mean that you pretend you were not affected, offended, or hurt by what your spouse said or did. In fact, the Bible actually calls the one who has been sinned against to go to the person who committed the offense and present him with it. Are you confused? Does it seem that this is a contradiction of what I said above? This is where the order of the two parts of forgiveness is essential. The reason you must start with giving the offense to God is so that when you come to your spouse, you come with the right attitude (grace) and the right goal (reconciliation). *Vertical forgiveness* clears your heart of the baggage of bitterness and condemnation so that you can face her with her wrong in a way that is kind, patient, loving, humble, and encouraging.

Something important needs to be said here. Husbands, it is not spiritually helpful for you, or loving toward your wife, to act as though what is not okay is okay. Wives, it is not good for you or kind to your husband to act as if a sin committed against you is all right. The Bible nowhere calls us to grin and bear it for the sake of the relationship. In fact, I am persuaded that our silence in the face of wrong is not motivated by a desire to love the other well but by not wanting to hassle through the difficult process of kind and loving confrontation. We are silent not because we love our spouse but because we love ourselves, and we do not want to put ourselves through something uncomfortable. When we fail to bring such things into the light, they fester in the dark of our own sinful heart, and the other does not benefit from the conviction and confession that would help him grow and change.

You see, while the first part of forgiveness is *judicial*, that is, entrusting the offense to God who alone is able to judge, the second part of forgiveness is *relational*. It is a transaction of grace between the person who has committed the offense and the person who has been offended. Now, pay careful attention to what I am about to say: you cannot relationally forgive someone who has not asked for it. The biblical pattern is this: someone confesses, you forgive. That is why you go to her. You go as God's instrument, with the hope that her eyes will be opened, that her heart will be grieved, and that she will respond by confessing her sin and asking for your forgiveness (which you are ready to give because you are not harboring bitterness in your heart.)

Often, forgiveness is a process, not an event. You may find yourself returning to old, bitter thoughts and getting angry once again, and you need to confess that to the Lord and seek his help. You may have succumbed to treating your spouse judgmentally, even though you had committed not to, and you need to confess that wrong to him or her. It may be that the one who committed the offense is having a hard time seeing and owning what he or she has done. This may mean that you have to go to your spouse more than once, reminding him or her that there is a sin between you that has not been dealt with, and because of that there is a breach in your relationship and the need for reconciliation. Your purpose is not to badger him into confession but to let him know that you love him so much that it pains you to have wrongs in the way of the unity and understanding that you should be experiencing. But it must be said again: you cannot forgive someone in the relational sense of what forgiveness means until he or she has sought your forgiveness.

When Is Forgiveness Needed?

There is another distinction that needs to be made here. The biblical call to confession and forgiveness is to be followed only in instances when one spouse has done something to the other that the Bible calls sin. You do not need to ask forgiveness when you have done something out of human weakness, like forgetting in the busyness of the day to pick up something at the store. It is right to communicate to the other that you are sorry for forgetting and for any hassle it might have caused. You do not have to ask forgiveness for accidents, like tripping on the rug and dropping a piece of fine china. Again, it is right to express remorse for your spouse's loss, but in such cases you do not need his or her forgiveness.

You do not need to ask forgiveness for differences in personality or perspective. It is not wrong that you see things differently from your husband or wife. God has authored your story. He determined the influences that have shaped you. He brought you together in the intimate community of marriage. Differences are not wrong, but what we do with them might be.

You do not have to ask forgiveness for attempting to do something and failing. Perhaps you told your wife that you would fix something, but you were not able to. This is not a sin against your wife and does not require confession and forgiveness. It is loving, however, to let her know that you are sorry for the hassle caused her by your inability to get the job done.

Forgiveness is a vertical commitment and relational transaction that is to occur in moments when sin has gotten in the way of the unity, love, and understanding that God welcomes us to enjoy as his children in marriage. It lifts the burden off our shoulders of bearing wrongs and restores what has been broken. The more you are willing to forgive, the more you experience its blessings. The more you experience its blessings, the more you are quick to give yourself to the cycle of commit-confront-confess-forgive. You start living in the benefits of short accounts between you and your mate. You love the fact that there are no big and open issues between you. You have no closets to empty, and you are thankful, and in your thankfulness you appreciate one another all the more and also the one—God—who calls you to forgive.

What Forgiveness Requires and Returns

Forgiveness is an investment in your relationship with God and in your relationship with one another. As with all investments, there is cost involved. In any investment you make, your concern is that the return will be greater than the cost. So, it is important that we consider the requirements and returns of forgiveness for you and your marriage.

Forgiveness requires *humility*. It is only when we really do believe that life is bigger than us, that there is something more important than our wants, needs, and feelings, and that we have been given life and breath for the purposes, plans, and praise of another, that we will be willing to forgive. When we stand in the center of our own universe with nothing more important to us than ourselves, we find nothing more offensive than a sin against *us*. Or when pride allows us to think of ourselves as righteous—surely more righteous than the person we live with—then it is hard for us to forgive. Forgiveness is much easier for the person who lives conscious of the reality of how much he also needs to be forgiven. Nobody gives grace better than someone who is convinced he needs it as well.

Forgiveness also requires *compassion*. Compassion is being moved by the plight of another, coupled with action to help him or her. Husbands and wives, does compassion ever grip you when your spouse sins against you? Are you touched by your spouse's struggle with sin? Do you feel for her when she faces the disappointing reality of her failure once again? Are you sad for him in those moments when he is easily entrapped? Do you stand alongside one another in the worst of moments doing anything you can to relieve the burden of your spouse's struggle with sin? You forgive her because you love her, and because you love her, you care about her and the struggle she is going through with sin. You know what it is like to commit to what is right and end up doing what is wrong (see Romans 7). You forgive him because, by God's grace, you look at him through tender, rather than judgmental, eyes.

Forgiveness requires *trust*. Forgiveness is not so much an act of faith in your spouse as it is an act of faith in God. You do believe that God is with you. You do believe that his Word is true. You do believe that what he calls you to is right and good. You do believe that he will give you what you need to do what he has called you to do. You do believe that your identity is secure, even if your spouse rejects you and doesn't seek your forgiveness. You do believe that there is blessing on the other side of the hard work of forgiveness. You do believe that when you fail and take up the offense once again that God will forgive you and give you the power to change. Because you trust God, you are willing to forgive your spouse.

Forgiveness requires *self-control*. If you are going to forgive your spouse for committing a sin against you, you must say no to yourself, exercising the self-control that only God is able to give you. To forgive, you have to say no to bitterness, which permits you to carry a wrong and not give it room to expand in your heart and shape your responses to your husband or wife. You have to say no to the desire to lash out with angry words and actions of vengeance. You have to say no to the impulse to share your anger with a relative or friend. Giving way to these things is never a prelude to forgiveness.

Forgiveness requires *sacrifice*. Earlier I said that we fail to approach our spouse when he or she has wronged us because we love ourselves more than we love our spouse. Perhaps that seemed harsh to you, so let me explain. Seldom is self-love a self-conscious thing. Perhaps what you are conscious of is that you're afraid of rejection, afraid of being drawn into a long debate, afraid of your spouse getting angry, or afraid your spouse will throw all your failure in your face. In short, you don't want to expose yourself to all the possible dangers of lovingly confronting your spouse with something he or she has said or done but hasn't acknowledged. Do you see what you are doing? You are opting for self-protection rather than for what would be helpful for your spouse and for your relationship and pleasing to God.

Forgiveness requires that we be willing to let go of our desire for safety and comfort and for the surface peace of silence, and, as an act of faith, that we endure what we do not want to face in order for the other to be helped and our relationship to be reconciled.

There is one thing that forgiveness requires that is more important than anything we have looked at so far. Forgiveness requires *remembering*. Why is it that we are so skilled at remembering the other's weakness, failure, and sin and so adept at forgetting our own? Why are we so good at seeing all the ways that another needs to be forgiven but forget how great our need for forgiveness is? When we are filled with the grief of our own sin and with gratitude for the amazing forgiveness we have been given, then we will find joy in giving to our spouse what we have received. Perhaps a lifestyle of unforgiveness is rooted in the sin of forgetfulness. We forget that there is not a day in our lives that we do not need to be forgiven. We forget that we will never graduate from our need for grace. We forget that we have been loved with a love we could never earn, achieve, or deserve. We forget that God never mocks our weakness, never finds joy in throwing our failures in our face, never threatens to turn his back on us, and never makes us buy our way back into his favor.

When you remember, when you carry with you a deep appreciation for the grace that you have been given, you'll have a heart that is ready to forgive. That doesn't mean that the process will be comfortable or easy, but it will mean that you can approach your needy spouse remembering that you are just as in need of what you're about to give to him or her.

A Better Harvest

Yes, you can choose to carry that list. You can choose to punish the other. You can choose for disappointment to become distance, for affection to become dislike, and for a desire for companionship to morph into a search for an escape. You can taste the sad harvest of marital détente that so many couples live in, or you can plant better seeds and celebrate a much better harvest. The harvest of forgiveness is the kind of marriage everyone wants.

Forgiveness stimulates appreciation and affection. When we forgive one another daily, we do not look at one another through the lens of our worst failures and biggest weaknesses. As we talk honestly, weep and pray, and repent and reconcile, our appreciation for one another grows and our affection deepens. We quit looking at the other person as the enemy. We stop protecting ourselves from him or her and begin to work together to build walls of defense against the many threats to a marriage that exist in this fallen world.

Forgiveness produces patience. As we respond God's way in a daily lifestyle of confession and forgiveness, we begin to experience things we never thought we would see in our marriage. We begin to see bad patterns break, we begin to see one another change, and we begin to see love that had grown cold become new and vibrant again. We experience hard moments when God gives us the grace not to give way to powerful emotions and desires that would take us in the wrong direction, and we see the practical help and rescue his wisdom gives us again and again. All this means that we no longer panic when a wrong happens between us. We no longer take matters into our own hands in the panic of hurt and retribution. We no longer try to be the other's conscience or judge. No, we are much more relaxed in the face of failure and willing to patiently follow God's commit-confront-confess-forgive plan. We have come to understand that his grace is bigger than any difficulty we will ever face in our marriage. So, we are able to rest and wait, knowing that God is at work, even when we are exhausted and discouraged, and that he will not quit working until his work in us and our marriage is complete.

But there is one more thing. Forgiveness is the fertile soil in which unity in marriage grows. When you are living every day in the confession and forgiveness pattern, you are forsaking your way for a better way. Your marriage is no longer a daily competition for who is going to get his or her way. You no longer see your spouse as a threat, wondering just when he will once again get in the way of what you want. You are not obsessed with your comfort, pleasure, and ease and with the fear of when your mate will interrupt it. No, forgiveness puts you on the same page with each other. You have both submitted your desires to the desires of Another. You no longer try to build your own little marriage kingdom. No, you now, together, live for God's kingdom. You now live with the same set of expectations and rules. You now have the same way of thinking about and addressing problems. And together you celebrate what God has given you, both aware that you could never have done it yourselves. You now experience unity like never before, because forgiveness has liberated you for a higher purpose and a better daily plan.

Remember Jeb and Sally? God put someone in their lives to show them a better way. Yes, Jeb and Sally are still making war, but it is no longer with one another. Together they are battling the one enemy that is after them and their marriage. As Jeb and Sally do this, they are very thankful that forgiveness has freed them from the war that they used to be so good at making.

We would rather be ruined than changed;
We would rather die in our dread
Than climb the cross of the moment
And let our illusions die.

W. H. AUDEN

Aim at heaven and you will get earth thrown in.
Aim at earth and you get neither.

C. S. LEWIS

COMMITMENT 1: We will give ourselves to a regular lifestyle of confession and forgiveness.

COMMITMENT 2: We will make growth and change our daily agenda.

COMMITMENT 3: We will work together to build a sturdy bond of trust.

COMMITMENT 4: We will commit to building a relationship of love.

COMMITMENT 5: We will deal with our differences with appreciation and grace.

COMMITMENT 6: We will work to protect our marriage.

7

Pulling Weeds

Marriage really is just a long-term exercise in gardening. If you've done any gardening you know there simply aren't any shortcuts. When you drive by that house festooned with gorgeous flowers of a wide variety of colors and kind, tell yourself that what you are looking at is hard work. Gardens begin with hard work. Clearing the land isn't fun, but it's essential. Digging holes for the seeds isn't enjoyable, but it, too, is a necessary step. The work of regular watering and weeding is also a necessity. Pruning off wilted flowers and dead leaves is necessary for plant heath, too.

Why is it that we don't expect our gardens to just grow by themselves—you know, from weedy land to lush garden—yet we expect our marriages to blossom beautifully without the daily work of pulling up weeds and planting seeds? I must confess that I just don't get it. I don't know why we think that the most comprehensive and long-term of all human relationships can stay alive and thrive without the same commitment we make to our gardens. Perhaps one of the fundamental sins that we all commit in our marriages is the sin of inattention.

Did you ever drive by that house (maybe it's yours) where the garden was planted by an impatient or lazy gardener? You can see some evidence of flower life, but the plants are not healthy, and the view is surely not pretty! I think there are many, many marriages just like that. They were not planted well, and they haven't been tended well since. Let me stop and ask you right here: is your marriage in some way a picture of neglect? Was it planted well? Has it been weeded and watered with regularity? Have you lacked the motivation to do the hard work of seeding and weeding and then stood back wondering why things don't look prettier?

This chapter and the next are a call to take a gardener's approach to your marriage. You have to be committed to pulling out weeds and planting seeds, or you will simply not have the marriage that grace makes possible.

Welcome to My Weed Garden

I couldn't help thinking, "How could someone live like this?" Sam and Sarah always seemed to be in a rush and to be too busy. Maybe the biggest weakness in their marriage was impatience. They seemed to want too much too soon; they both worked long hours so that they could acquire all the things they had decided they needed in order to enjoy the "good life." Their impatience ("got to have it now") kept them too busy. Sam seemed too busy to "romance" Sarah. No, I don't mean extravagant vacations to exotic destinations or once-in-a-lifetime gifts. He didn't do the little things—a daily morning hug before leaving the house, a silly card with an "I love you" note, an unexpected dinner out, a "for no other reason than I love and appreciate you" bouquet of flowers, or actually saying, "I love you"—on a regular basis.

They had little time for real look-you-in-the-eye conversation. Sarah knew that little things were becoming big things that could grow into huge, destructive things and that she needed to talk about them, but there never seemed to be time. Oh, she would drop hints; she was good at dropping hints, but Sam wasn't good at picking them up. More and more Sarah saw Sam as preoccupied and clueless. More and more it seemed that the kind of conversation they needed to have wasn't going to happen anytime soon.

All this made for a minefield of little conflicts. No, not "get the missiles out of the silo, this is war" battles, where there is more angry noise than actual communication. Sarah and Sam seldom screamed; they didn't have time for things to escalate to that level. But, because they weren't talking and because their relationship lacked unity-motivating tenderness, they disagreed all the time. They knew when going into their marriage that they got up on different sides of the universe each morning. These differences had the potential to make their relationship exciting, engaging, and mutually growth-producing. It also meant that theirs was a relationship that would need constant weeding. Disagreeing all the time made their life together complicated, discouraging, and exhausting, so they both developed habits of staying clear of conflict, which often meant staying clear of one another.

Their busyness constricted their shared spiritual life down to an hour and a half on Sunday morning. They didn't read or pray together. Conversations about matters of faith seldom came up. In fact, there was little Godward motion in the marriage at all. They almost never talked about the blessings and calling in their relationship with God. When spiritual things came up, the conversation was more institutional and schedule-oriented. They would look at their schedules and briefly discuss whether they could participate in an event or a ministry.

It was hard for them to make any long- or short-term plans with one another. There were some big decisions that they needed to think through together, but they never seemed to be able to find the time. There were decisions that needed to be made about Sarah's continuing to work and whether they were going to continue to live in their present house. Because they were not talking these things through with one another, they began to develop individual thoughts about them. As these differences began to seep out, discussing the important decisions became all the more distasteful.

As it always does, the distance and coldness in their relationship made its way into their sexual life. Going to bed at night wasn't typically done together, and when it was, it wasn't typically warm. They didn't end their day in a moment of tenderness or with expressions of love. In fact, going to bed was often quite silent. Sam would plop into bed, roll over, and begin to sleep, while Sarah was still sitting up reading. Or Sarah would close her eyes while Sam was still across the room writing Facebook responses.

Sex is not the fuel of a good relationship; it is the expression or fruit of one. So it is impossible not to drag the character and quality of the relationship into this moment of nakedness and vulnerability. Sam wasn't attracted to Sarah as he once was; she had become a distant friend. And when they had sex, Sarah battled with feelings of being used. As sex became more mechanical and unfulfilling, it became less frequent. Yet, their lack of good communication made it seem impossible to talk about this delicate topic.

Sam and Sarah were not in a disastrous marriage, but they were in a very weedy one, and the weeds were about to choke the life out of the love that was once there. But don't be too hard on them. We agreed we are all "weedy" people who need to pull personal and relational weeds daily so that the flowers of love and grace may grow. Sinners (which, in case you forgot, all of us are) always drag their sin into their marriages. Weeds of thought, decision, desire, motivation, word, and action cannot be completely avoided this side of heaven, so pulling weeds is the necessary commitment of any good marriage.

Jeremiah and Your Marriage

God's words of commission to Jeremiah have a powerful and practical application to your commitment to a daily lifestyle of marriage reconciliation. Yes, I know that God's call to Jeremiah is individual and specific, since he was being called as one of God's prophets. It is not God's call to Jeremiah that is interesting and helpful; it is the content of the call. Embedded in God's words is a model for how real and lasting change takes place. It is wonderfully helpful for diagnosing and correcting your marriage in the places where both are needed.

The words are brief but beautifully and accurately descriptive: "See, I have set you this day over nations and over kingdoms, to pluck up and to break down, to destroy and to overthrow, to build and to plant" (Jer. 1:10). If change was to take place in Israel (and it was desperately needed), God is saying that this is how it will have to happen: pluck up and break down, plant and build. God is saying that change always has two sides to it: *destruction* and *construction*. Change is needed because there are things in you, or in your situation or relationship, that need to be uprooted or torn down, and if change is actually going to be change, there are new things that need to be planted or built in the place of what was uprooted and torn down.

For your marriage to be healthy, you must have *destructive* and *constructive* zeal. I know that this sounds funny, but for your marriage to be what it was designed to be, there are things that need to be destroyed. But, like the problem of weeds that keep jutting their heads out of once-clear ground, this destructive agenda cannot be a one-time commitment. In some way, there are things, little and big, in the way of what our marriages should and could be. I am going to suggest what some of these may be, but it is important that you know that what I am giving you is a general, pump-priming list that you need to expand and apply to the specifics of your own marriage.

Selfishness

Maybe it's a leap for the best cookie, a quick movement toward the best seat in the TV room, or controlling the flow of the conversation with friends. Perhaps it is pouting so you get to go to the restaurant you want, arguing too hard to make sure you win, or doing something nice, but making sure that the other notices. Maybe it's being too busy to be bothered, not volunteering to help, or taking offense too easily. Perhaps it's wanting the one who hurt you to hurt as well, presenting yourself as more spiritual than your spouse, or taking your good old time when you know the other is waiting. Maybe it's refusing to forget what you say you have forgiven, manipulating a bit to get your own way, or being less than candid because you just don't want to have the conversation. Perhaps it's being so busy taking care of yourself that you have little time to care for the other, wanting from him or her what you are unwilling to give in return or making more demands than concessions.

It really is there in all of us—selfishness—because it is the DNA of sin. Perhaps nothing is more destructive in marriage than this. Perhaps it is the root of all the dumb and nasty little things we do to one another. Maybe it is the reason we make those big, disastrous choices that have the potential to end marriages. Doesn't Genesis 3 point us in that direction? At the bottom of it all, what is wrong is that we want our own way, and, in wanting our own way, we want to be sovereign over our little worlds, making sure that what we want is exactly what we get.

All this is a horrible reversal of God's design, so it will never work. We were constructed as social beings, made to live in vertical communion with God and horizontal communion with one another. Nothing works in life (let alone in marriage) when the human community is comprised of a bunch of self-appointed little sovereigns seeking to set up their own little kingdoms. That way of living precludes relationships and guarantees war. The other-centeredness that we were designed for and that God uses to rescue us from us is the only way of living that makes us able to live with one another in respect, appreciation, and peace.

Selfishness is like liquid clay; it will shape itself to the contours of whatever vessel it is poured into. You and I aren't necessarily less selfish than other couples around us; we are differently selfish. Since none of us is sin-free, we all need to look for evidences of the DNA of selfishness shaping the way we think, desire, act, and respond in our marriages. This is a weed with a huge root system and the vitality to suck the life out of marriage.

But don't be discouraged or overwhelmed. As I said earlier, the cross was specifically designed to free us from our slavery to ourselves. Grace is a can opener. It alone has the power to free us from the vacuum-sealed can of our selfishness. So where are the weeds of selfishness in your marriage? How are you doing at finding them and pulling them?

Busyness

There is no doubt about it: too many of us are trying to have hundred-dollar conversations in dime moments. Too many of us have left little time in our schedules for meaningful conversation, tender connection, and focused problem solving. Too many of us have little time for relational reflection and introspection in our marriages. Too many of us are doing marriage on the fly. Marriage, too often, is what we do in between all the other things we are doing that really determine the content and pace of our schedules. But marriage doesn't function very well as an in-between thing, and marriages surely don't tend to thrive when we leave them alone and ask them to grow on their own. A marriage that is going to grow, change, and become increasingly healthy needs cultivation. Like a garden, it doesn't do well when it is being neglected.

So, why are we so busy? There may be many answers to that question, but let me suggest one that is particularly true of Western culture. The answer may surprise you: *materialism.* I think we all have been influenced by the materialism of Western culture, which says that happiness and fulfillment are to be found in material things. If you are a Christian, you would say that is wrong and that you do not believe it. But that does not discount the fact that the influence is very powerful, and the evidences of its seduction are in all of our lives in some way.

The constant pursuit of bigger and better material things sucks away our time, energy, and relational vitality. We not only have to work way too much to acquire material things, but once we have them, we are enslaved to the responsibility to maintain them. And with all our acquiring, the things we have acquired don't satisfy the longings of our heart. So we go out and get more, as if we are running a race that has no finish line.

Many of us live in houses way bigger than we actually need. Many of us have closets that are stuffed with clothing we seldom wear. Many of us are spending way too much money on restaurants, entertainment systems, big vacations, and luxurious cars. And if that does not describe you, perhaps this will: almost all of us are living beyond our means in some way.

Again, because it is built on a lie (material things can make us happy), materialism can't and doesn't work. It leaves us empty, in debt, and addicted, while taking our time, attention, and energy away from the most important human relationship in all of life. I cannot tell you how many times I have had a husband or wife say to me, "I would love to do these things [things that keep a marriage healthy], but I simply do not have the time." Could it be that we work too much because we want too much, and we keep working and keep wanting because what we are looking to for satisfaction simply does not have the capacity to satisfy us? Meanwhile, the weeds continue to grow, and our marriages suffer as a result. Could it be that you are too busy? What keeps you too busy or too exhausted to address the struggles of your marriage and to do the good things that make your marriage grow?

Inattention

Think of your physical body. Healthy people are healthy because they pay attention to their bodies. They pay attention to what they eat. They pay attention to signs of illness or disease. They pay attention to the need for regular exercise. They don't expect to be healthy without paying attention and responding to what they see and feel. I am deeply persuaded that many marriages get to an unhealthy place simply because they have been neglected. Sadly, many of us are better at responding to crisis than we are at working on prevention. We are all guilty, in some

107

way, of taking our marriages for granted and, in so doing, taking one another for granted.

Here's how it tends to happen. Courtship is all about attention, because you are trying to win the other person. You pay careful attention to his or her likes and dislikes. You quickly learn what responsibilities he carries and what his schedule is like. You listen for the tone of her voice, and you examine the expression on her face. You study how he responds to various situations. You pay attention to what tends to upset her and what has the power to bring her joy. You learn where he needs support and encouragement. You learn what she finds comfortable and what she considers to be difficult. You become a student of his personality, tastes, politics, theology, family, history, and dreams for the future. You do all this because you are committed to know her and know her well, and you are committed to know her well because you want to win her.

Now, none of this is wrong in itself. True and lasting love is *knowing*; that is, it is a commitment to love another in ways that are specific to who he or she is and what God has called him or her to do. But it is very telling that this positive attention to the other and to the health of the relationship tends to wane once the person has been "won." This has more of the feel of a hunt than it does of a marriage. It is the sad dynamic of, "I don't have to pay attention to you anymore because I now have you." Sure, few people consciously say that to themselves, but it is the way many of us actually end up living with one another. We begin to relax too much and quit working as hard, so our marriage begins to suffer. There are not many couples fifteen years into marriage who would say that their relationship with one another is more understanding, more unified, and more loving, giving, and serving than it was when they first got married. Few would say that their marriage is more of a tender, intimate friendship than it has ever been. But many couples look back on courtship and wonder what happened. Remember: a healthy marriage is a healthy marriage because, by God's grace, the people in that marriage never stop working on it!

Is your marriage suffering from inattention? Have you become comfortable with taking one another for granted? Are you neglecting the work that is necessary to keep your relationship healthy?

Self-righteousness

Do you welcome those moments when your husband or wife approaches you with a criticism or concern about something you said or did? Are you glad that God has placed you next to someone who helps you see yourself with greater accuracy? Do you embrace and act on the thought that you could be a better husband or a better wife? When you are approached with a criticism or concern, do you ever redirect the conversation, working to convince the other that you're not the only sinner in the room? Have you actually invited your spouse to confront you in places where he or she thinks it is needed? Do you ever blame your words or behavior on your husband or wife? When you feel a twinge of guilt, do you work to relieve your guilt by self-atoning arguments for the rightness of what you said or did? How active is your "inner lawyer," internally arguing in your defense, even as the other person is speaking? Have you tended to think that all the weeds in your marriage were brought in by your spouse?

I was there—self-righteous—but I did not know it. I was an angry man, but I simply did not see myself with anything approaching accuracy. In fact, I was quite hurt when Luella would characterize me as angry, and I was quite convinced that she was a discontented wife. Once (and this is humbling to admit) I actually said to her, "Ninety-five percent of the women in our church would love to be married to a man like me!" Can you believe it? I was convinced of my own righteousness and, therefore, convinced of my innocence. Oh, by the way: Luella very sweetly informed me that she was in the five percent!

What about you? Has self-righteousness kept you from weeding your marriage? Have you failed to keep the soil of your marriage clean, so that good things may grow, because you don't think you have any weeds? What thoughts, desires, motives, goals, choices, words, or actions need to be uprooted if your marriage is ever going to experience what God's grace makes possible to experience?

Fear

You and I are probably more motivated by fear than we think. Fear is most often not an experience of trembling dread. It is most often not an experience of hand-wringing anxiety. Fear is most often a way of looking at your world that shapes the thoughts of your heart and, because it does, structures the way you respond. Perhaps your struggle is with the *fear of failure*. Perhaps you spend too much time thinking about the "what ifs." Perhaps you are all too skilled at conceiving the bad things that may result if this or that happens. Perhaps you have spent so much time meditating on and preparing yourself for potential difficulties that you unwittingly fulfill your own prophecies. Maybe you are not actually responding to your spouse based on what he is doing but on what you are afraid he might do.

Or maybe, for you, it's the struggle with *fear of man*. Perhaps you've attached too much of your inner sense of well-being, your security, and your hope to your husband or your wife. Maybe you are all too skilled at riding the daily roller coaster of his responses to you. Perhaps you work too hard to read his emotions. Perhaps what he thinks simply means too much to you. Maybe she is too able to make or break your day. Perhaps you work too hard to please her. Maybe her affirmation means more to you than it should.

I am persuaded that fear of man is a huge issue in the struggles of many marriages. I think that many of us are trying to get from our husband or wife what we will only ever receive from God—peace. Desires for acceptance and respect are not wrong in and of themselves. These desires remind us that God designed us to be social beings. We were made to live in community. Yet, it must be said that although the desire for acceptance and respect is not wrong, it must not rule our hearts. When these desires rule our hearts, they cause us to turn our husband or wife into our personal messiah, something that never results in good things in our marriages.

Is fear a weed that needs to be pulled out in your marriage? Is there a way in which your husband or wife has become your replacement messiah? Are you so afraid of failure that it keeps you from doing with courage the things God has called you to do in your marriage? Do the "what ifs" keep you from living in your marriage with joy in the here and now?

Laziness

It's hard to admit, but laziness is a big issue in our marriages. We know that we shouldn't go to bed angry, but it seems that it will take too long to solve our conflict. We know that we need to clear up this morning's misunderstanding, but it won't leave us much time to relax before bed. We know that we are not on the same page financially, but working it through simply isn't very exciting. We know we need to discuss what is happening in our sexual relationship, but we simply don't want to face the uncomfortable nature of that conversation. You know that you are bitter, but there just doesn't seem to be time in your schedule to examine and confess it. You know that things are not right, but you tell yourself you should wait for a better moment. You walk away from an argument, and you know you should go back and ask for forgiveness, but you don't know what you will get into if you do.

It's a fact: laziness is rooted in self-love. It is the ability to take ourselves off the hook. It is the willingness to permit ourselves not to do things we know we should do. It is believing that good things should come our way without our having to work to get them. It is opting for what is comfortable for ourselves rather than what is best for our spouse. Laziness is always self-focused and self-excusing. Laziness is undisciplined and unmotivated. Laziness permits us to be passive when decisive and loving action is needed. Laziness allows us to avoid when we should be engaged. Laziness expects more from others than we require from ourselves. Laziness demands good things without being willing to invest in them. I am persuaded that laziness is a much bigger deal in our marriages than we have tended to think. Check out these proverbs.

> I passed by the field of a sluggard,
>> by the vineyard of a man lacking sense,
> and behold, it was all overgrown with thorns;
>> the ground was covered with nettles
>> and its stone wall was broken down. (Prov. 24:30–31)

Isn't this exactly what we have been describing? Your marriage is inflicted with difficulty because you have failed to act to keep it what God intended it to be.

> The desire of the sluggard kills him,
>> for his hands refuse to labor. (Prov. 21:25)

Often, marriages are troubled by discontent and unfulfilled desire. Proverbs connects these to laziness. Because you are not doing the hard work of following the command principles of God's Word, the good desires that you have for your marriage remain unfulfilled. This heightens your discontent, adding more trouble to your marriage and making it even harder to deal with the things you must deal with for your marriage to be what God designed it to be.

> The sluggard will not plow by reason of the winter;
>> Therefore he shall beg in harvest, and have nothing.
>> (Prov. 20:4 ASV)

> The sluggard says, "There is a lion outside!
>> I shall be killed in the streets!" (Prov. 22:13)

These proverbs capture the excuse dynamic of laziness. We take ourselves off the hook by giving ourselves plausible reasons (excuses) for our inactivity.

> The way of a sluggard is like a hedge of thorns,
>> but the path of the upright is a level highway. (Prov. 15:19)

Where does laziness in marriage lead? It leads to disappointment, discouragement, discontentment, and future trouble. In a fallen world, very few things are corrected by inaction.

So, what about you? What about your marriage? When was the last time you looked for weeds? When was the last time you and your spouse sat down together and took an honest look at your life together? Are you paying the price in your marriage for neglecting the first step of good relational gardening? Have your unity, love, and understanding been choked by the weeds of selfishness, busyness, inattention, self-righteousness, fear, laziness, or something else that has gotten in the way? You don't have to be afraid of examining your marriage, no matter how weedy it may be, because God meets you in your difficulty with his amazing grace. He blesses you with the grace of wisdom, patience, strength, and forgiveness. If you are God's children, it is never just you and your spouse, somehow hoping that you can work your way through your problems. No, there is a third Person who inhabits every situation and location of your marriage. He is with you, he is willing, and he is able to come to your aid. In fact, in his grace, he has made you the place where he lives. Perhaps for too long you have let the weeds of sin choke the life out of your marriage. How about standing up and beginning to pull out the weeds? How about believing that, as you do, he will give you just the grace you need at just the moment you need it?

COMMITMENT 1:	We will give ourselves to a regular lifestyle of confession and forgiveness.
COMMITMENT 2:	**We will make growth and change our daily agenda.**
COMMITMENT 3:	We will work together to build a sturdy bond of trust.
COMMITMENT 4:	We will commit to building a relationship of love.
COMMITMENT 5:	We will deal with our differences with appreciation and grace.
COMMITMENT 6:	We will work to protect our marriage.

8

Planting Seeds

I don't know if you have thought about this, but your life is shaped by choice-points. No, I'm not talking about those huge moments of epic decision that we all know change our lives in some way. I'm talking about the thousands of little decisions in mundane moments of daily life that almost go unnoticed but are actually what shape and direct our lives. You see, the quality and character of a marriage isn't set in two or three grand moments of choice. You make only three or four big decisions in your entire life. No, the character of a marriage is formed in thousands of little moments of saying yes to one thing and no to another. It is the character developed in little moments that you carry into those big moments of decision.

The last chapter was about examining your marriage, searching for those little thoughts, attitudes, and actions that you must say no to, and this chapter is about considering the things that you must say yes to, and in so doing give them room to shape your marriage.

If I could go back to the garden metaphor, cleared ground doesn't stay clear for very long. If you weed a patch of ground and leave it bare, in a few days you will see the shoots of weeds pushing their way through clods of soil. You will wonder where they came from, and you'll be irritated that they are already taking over the patch that you so laboriously cleared! What you must quickly do, after you have cleared the ground of weeds, is plant flowers in their place. Weeds don't just go away, and flowers don't just grow in their place unless someone is pulling weeds and planting seeds. The application to marriage is obvious. It is not enough to identify the weeds in your relationship that need to go; you must also think about what God is calling you to put in their place. That is what this chapter is about. I want to talk about pulling and planting in a way that may surprise you, but it is just the way the Bible talks about it.

The Weeds and Seeds

I'm constantly amazed at how helpful the Bible is in diagnosing the human struggle but how little use we actually make of it when we are trying to understand the things all of us go through in marriage. Because our Creator knows and loves us and knows how terribly broken we and our world are, he wants us to know how what is wrong goes wrong and how it can be fixed. Galatians 5 is one of those incredibly helpful biblical passages. Here, the Creator-Savior speaks to us as a loving Father, helping us to understand relational mysteries that we would never understand without him. Even though this passage sets the bar high, it should not leave us burdened or depressed, because Jesus perfectly did all the things that we have failed to do, and he did them for us so that we can stand before God in weakness and failure, confessing our need without fear. Because of Jesus, we know that God will not turn his back on us when we fail. Rather, he willingly gifts us with the grace we need to do, in our marriages, what he has called us to do.

Let's look at Galatians 5 and see how it gives us a ground-level way of looking at the specific pulling and planting that must be part of every marriage. It amazes me to think about the fact that for years I looked at Galatians 5:13–26 as being about spiritual character growth but failed to see that it is a relationship passage from beginning to end. Look for the relational implications as you read the apostle Paul's words:

> You, my brothers, were called to be free. But do not use your freedom to indulge the sinful nature; rather, serve one another in love. The entire law is summed up in a single command: "Love your neighbor as yourself." If you keep on biting and devouring each other, watch out or you will be destroyed by each other.
>
> So I say, live by the Spirit, and you will not gratify the desires of the sinful nature. For the sinful nature desires what is contrary to the Spirit, and the Spirit what is contrary to the sinful nature. They are in conflict with each other, so that you do not do what you want. But if you are led by the Spirit, you are not under law.
>
> The acts of the sinful nature are obvious: sexual immorality, impu-

rity and debauchery; idolatry and witchcraft; hatred, discord, jealousy, fits of rage, selfish ambition, dissensions, factions and envy; drunkenness, orgies, and the like. I warn you, as I did before, that those who live like this will not inherit the kingdom of God.

But the fruit of the Spirit is love, joy, peace, patience, kindness, goodness, faithfulness, gentleness and self-control. Against such things there is no law. Those who belong to Christ Jesus have crucified the sinful nature with its passions and desires. Since we live by the Spirit, let us keep in step with the Spirit. Let us not become conceited, provoking and envying each other. (NIV)

The best place to begin mining the riches of the wisdom of these words is to start with the warning in verse 15. One thing we are all tempted to do is back away from the power and influence of the things we do and say. A husband will yell at his wife, but he will tell himself that it was just a little moment and comfort himself with the thought that despite his anger, she knows that he loves her. A wife will be nasty in the morning, punishing her husband for what he did the night before, but she'll tell herself that it's a new morning, and he really does know that she loves him. We all tend to forget that these little moments are important precisely because they are little moments. Since we live in days that are filled with little moments, it is precisely here that the character and quality of a marriage is formed.

Here is the point: you cannot escape the influence of what you do and say on the person you live with and on your relationship to him or her. Paul says, "If you keep on biting and devouring each other, watch out or you will be destroyed by each other" (v. 15). God has made you a person of influence in the life of your spouse. You will always be influential in some way. You cannot escape the implications of Paul's words. And notice what he says will be destroyed—*you*. You can rob your wife of her hope. You can crush your husband's faith. You can damage one another's heart. You can cloud your spouse's view of God's presence, goodness, and grace. You can tempt the other to believe that he or she is alone and without help. Husbands and wives, you and I must ask, "How do I daily influence the way my spouse thinks about God, him- or herself, and life?" Your response to the rest of this amazing passage will be determined by the degree to which you have embraced the warning of verse 15.

Now, notice the first principle in this highly relational passage: "Do not use your freedom to indulge the sinful nature" (v. 13). There is no bigger struggle for any of us. There is nothing that complicates our marriages more. A healthy marriage is all about knowing what to say no to. What we are being called to here is both insightful and practical, and it is a protection for your marriage, but I'm convinced that most of us don't have a clue what it means. Let's unpack these potentially marriage-changing words.

"Live by the Spirit, and you will not gratify the desires of the sinful nature" (v. 16). Because there is sin still inside all of us, there are thoughts, desires, motives, choices, and decisions that we must fight internally. We will never gain ground in our relationships starting by addressing wrong behaviors, because the real battle of relationships lives at a much deeper, more profound level. It is this level that Paul is addressing here. You can only understand this deeper battle when you understand the fundamental nature of sin.

The DNA of sin is selfishness (see 2 Cor. 5:15). Sin turns all of us in on ourselves. It reduces our circle of hopes and concerns to things that touch and involve us. It makes us all focused on and driven by our wants, needs, and feelings. Sin can so fill our eyes with our needs that we become functionally blind to the needs of others. We can be so focused on our interest that we have little interest in the interest of others. Now, think about this: if the DNA of sin is selfishness, then sin in its fundamental form is antisocial. The needs of the individual trump the needs of the other person or the needs of the relationship. Think about when and where you got angry last week. Would it not be safe for me to conclude that little of your anger came from concern for the other person or concerns for your marriage? Most often, we are angry because the other got in the way of something we wanted. You will never understand the struggles of your marriage until you begin to face the reality that something lives inside you that is destructive to relationships. The Bible gives this thing a name: *sin.*

But there is more to say. Because sin is self-focused and therefore antisocial, it dehumanizes the people in our lives. They cease being the objects of our affection. They get reduced to either vehicles or obstacles. If they are vehicles helping us get the things we want and think we need, we are excited about them and thankful that they are in our life. But if they become obstacles in the way of what we want, we get spontaneously irritated and impatient with them and want somehow to move them out of our way. Although our anger tells us that they are the problem, the problem really has its genesis in the self-orientation and self-obsession of our own sinful hearts.

This is why Paul says, "Don't go there!" Think about it: what does it mean to *indulge* something? It means to go where it is drawing you to go. It means to feel its cravings. If I go to the local Chinese buffet and indulge my appetite, I do not have one plate. Thirty-seven plates later I tell myself that there are still edible delights that I need to enjoy! Healthy marriages are healthy because the people in those marriages have learned to recognize and say no to selfish instincts that lurk in their hearts and in the heart of every one of us.

Selfishness is one of the big weeds that choke the life out of a marriage, and we must continually recognize that selfishness is first a condition of the heart before it is ever a set of choices, words, and behaviors. Having said that, it is important to recognize that selfishness expresses itself in a catalog of behaviors. Paul lists these as "acts of the sinful nature" (v. 19). When you think of the trouble that troubles all our marriages, this list is stunningly accurate. Most of the words on the list picture with specificity the things that tend to infect all our marriages, not just in those big moments of difficulty but more regularly in the mundane moments of daily life. Check out these words: hatred, discord, jealousy, fits of rage, selfish ambition, dissensions, factions, and envy. Think about it: has your marriage been free of discord? Have you lived without jealousy? Have you been free of instances of rage? Has selfish ambition ever gotten in the way? Have you ever had dissension in your marriage? Has an otherwise nice day ever been kidnapped by envy? Be humbly honest; in some way all these things have troubled all our marriages.

Consider how selfishness can shape a marriage. If you are not fighting the internal battle, but rather you are permitting your wants, needs, and feelings to be the driving force of your relationship to your spouse, not only will you not say no to things you should say no to, but you will work to get the other to somehow, someway deliver to you the things you have set your heart on. I know this is hard to accept, but you and

I must. This means that the basic style of our actions, reactions, and responses to the other is *manipulation*. I don't mean a preplanned, intentional swindling of the other person. No, I mean that, in ways in which you will be unaware, you will work to get your spouse to participate in what you want, to deliver what you are convinced you need, and to submit to what you feel.

The three most familiar tools of marriage manipulation are *threat, payment,* and *guilt.* A wife will say, "I don't know what I'm going to do if have to live with this living room any longer!" A husband will say, "Sometimes I wonder if we just made a big mistake!" In each instance, the husband and wife are using the threat of something to rein in their spouse and get him or her to acquiesce to their agenda. We also will use something we know our spouses want, need, or enjoy as an incentive to get them to do what we want them to do. For example, a husband may give his wife a luxurious weekend away, not so much because he wants to be with her but so that when she next complains, he can say, "I do and do for you, and this is the thanks I get?" Or a dissatisfied wife may say to her husband, "I remember when I was a happy woman. It was before I got married. I never thought it would be this way. I never thought we would end up this way." What is she doing? She is inflicting guilt, hoping that her husband will feel guilty, and because of his guilt he will do what she wants him to do. There is much more manipulation going on in our marriages than we tend to think. The very nature of manipulation is that it is propelled by love of self, not love for the other.

The Common Thread

What do all these actions that Paul lists have in common? What is the single strand that holds them all together? Selfishness. That one thing that lurks in every heart is the enemy of the unity, love, and understanding that we all say we want in our marriages. Sure, you've married a less-than-perfect person. And, yes, your life will be complicated by his or her weaknesses and failures. Your husband or wife will have bad days. He will make regrettable choices. She will not always be as lovable as she was in courtship. It is true—you just don't get to be married to perfection. But even with all this being true, your biggest problem is not the imperfection of your spouse. No, it is this antisocial thing that lurks in the recesses of your heart. Your biggest struggle is with the selfishness that tempts and seduces us all. We must all pull this weed again and again, along with all the weeds of destructive words and actions that attach themselves to it.

Planting Seeds

Planting seeds is really what Paul is calling us to. We are to commit to intentionally planting the good seeds of a healthy relationship into the soil of our marriages. This will take understanding, commitment, discipline, and perseverance. Paul delineates the contrasting relational lifestyle this way: "Serve one another in love" (v. 13). Then he says something startling: "The entire law is summed up in a single command: 'Love your neighbor as yourself.'" If you had written the words, "The entire law is summed up in a single command," what would you have written next? I think I would have written, "Love God above all else." But, shockingly, that is not what Paul writes. Instead he writes, "Love your neighbor as yourself." How is it that love of neighbor summarizes all that God calls us to? The answer is both simple and profound. It is that those who love God above all else will love their neighbor as they love themselves. It is hard to hear these things, but there is the hope of lasting change found in these words.

The problem in our marriages is not first that we don't love one another enough; no, the problem is that we don't love God enough, and because we don't love God enough, we don't love one another as we should. Could it be that we are so busy loving ourselves and making sure that our spouse "loves" us in the way that we want to be loved, that we have little time and energy left to love our spouse as we should? Could it be that we are so busy working to co-opt the other into the service of our wants, needs, and feelings that we are too distracted to notice all the opportunities to love that every day gives us, and too busy making sure that we are loved to do anything about these opportunities even if we noticed them? Why does all this happen? It happens because we have replaced love of God and rest in his care with love of self and the anxiety of "neediness."

Again, what this means is that you don't fix a marriage first horizontally; you fix it vertically. It's only when we have confessed our lack of love for God—his plan, his purpose, and his call—and it is only when we admit that we have replaced his agenda for us with our selfish agenda that we will then be free to begin to love one another in the way that his grace makes possible. It is then that manipulation gets replaced by *ministry*. Rather than working to co-opt your spouse into your service, you find joy and satisfaction in discovering ways to serve him or her. You want to look ahead for impending needs. You want to do things that bring him joy. You want to share her griefs and carry her burdens. When these desires are mutual, your marriage does not become perfect, but it becomes a place where real unity, understanding, and love have room to live, breathe, and grow.

Attention: Help Needed

We have already said that this kind of service is not natural to us because we all still have the residue of sin in us and because the DNA of sin is selfishness. So, if we are going to live this way, each of us needs the rescue, intervention, and enabling that only God's grace can give. It is here that we need to hear these words: "My grace is sufficient for you, for my power is made perfect in weakness" (2 Cor. 12:9). Be honest: it's your tendency to argue to yourself that you are the strong one in your marriage and that in some way you are burdened with the weakness of your spouse. But sin leaves pockets of weakness in all of us. No one reading this book is proud of everything he has said in his marriage. No one reading this book is proud of everything she has done in her marriage. No one would defend everything he has thought or desired. So, change is not found in defending our righteousness but in admitting our weakness and crying out for help, and the apostle Paul is reminding us that help is available, and it is up to the task.

Enough of pointing the finger. Enough of listening to your inner lawyer defend your cause. Enough of carrying around a record of your spouse's wrongs. Enough of judging, criticizing, and blaming. Enough of holding the other to a higher standard than the one you hold for yourself. Enough of complaining, arguing, withdrawing, and manipulating. Enough of the self-righteous standoff that never leads to change. Enough of hurt and acrimony. Enough of painting yourself as the victim and your spouse as the criminal. Enough of demanding and entitlement. Enough of threat and guilt. Enough of telling the other how good you are and how thankful she should be to live with a person like you. Enough of going to bed in angry, self-righteous silence. Enough of hyper-vigilantly watching him to see if he is delivering. Enough of riding the roller coaster of her ups and downs. Enough of looking to him to be your personal messiah, satisfying the longings of your heart. Enough.

It is time to quit pointing the finger and to start confessing how deep and pervasive your weakness is. Change in your marriage begins with confessing your need. It is time to say, "Lord, there are times when I get it right, but so often I get it wrong." So often I let impatience and irritation get the best of me. So often I am jealous and unforgiving. So often I fail to find joy in serving and satisfaction in giving. So often I would rather win than have unity and peace. I tell myself that I will do better, but I fall into the same old traps. Lord, won't you strengthen me by your grace so that I can love as you have called me to love?"

What does it look like to live this life of love? What does it mean practically to plant new seeds of love in your marriage? Well, there is another list in Galatians 5 called the "fruit of the Spirit." There could not be a better catalog of the character qualities of a good marriage than this list. If you want to pull the weeds of manipulation out of your marriage and give yourself to an agenda of love, then this list is for you. Consider these words: love, joy, peace, patience, kindness, goodness, faithfulness, gentleness, and self-control (vv. 22–23).

What does a commitment to serve your spouse in love look like? Well, it looks like getting up in the morning and committing to searching for concrete ways to *love* your husband or your wife. Where does he tend to be discouraged or overwhelmed? What are the daily tasks in which she could use assistance? In what special way can you communicate your affection? Perhaps an unexpected card in a lunch bag, or a delivery of flowers, or a call in the middle of the day just to say, "I love you." Maybe you communicate love by not turning on the flat-screen and being willing to talk instead. Maybe love gets communicated by fixing something broken, just because fixing it would make the other's life easier. Maybe it would be best communicated by your willingness to take over a duty that has usually fallen to the other. There is no want for opportunities to love; the issue is, do we see them and are we committed to respond to them when we do. *Would your spouse call you a loving person?*

Serving in love means being committed to *joy*. What is joy about? It means looking for reasons to be thankful. It means being better at counting your blessings than you are at calculating your complaints. It is about communicating appreciation. It is about letting her know how much the things she does for you mean to you. It is about daily thanking God for your marriage, even though it is less than perfect. Joy means looking for the good in the other and encouraging it when you find it. Would your husband or wife characterize you as being thankful?

Serving in love requires being committed to *peace*. Let's admit it: there is a shocking amount of conflict in each of our lives. Almost every day we are angry, impatient, irritated, resentful, or disappointed in someone. Sin makes it easier to make war than to make peace, and most of our fights are over issues of little long-term consequence. Sure, there are moments when the stakes are high and we are struggling over something of life-altering significance, but those moments are rare. Sadly, many of us have a short fuse, a quick intolerance for any failure of others and a quick irritation at anyone or anything that gets in our way.

So, if we are really committed to peace, we will gladly overlook minor offenses. We will be quickly willing to forgive. We will work to restore relationship when something has separated us. We will find unity more attractive than winning and peace more compelling than power. We will be willing to listen and committed to think well before we speak. We will not allow ourselves to resurrect offenses that have already been forgiven, and we will be willing to quickly confess when we have been wrong. We will never go to bed while we are still angry, and we will seek to protect our marriage from anything that may interrupt our peace. Would your spouse say that you are a peacemaker?

Serving our spouses in love also means being committed to responding to them in ways that are *kind* and to do to them only what is good. Think with me for a moment: being kind and doing what is good are the commitments of everyone in courtship. Why? Because each is trying to win the other. But after they are married, both tend to let down their guard. In your case, maybe that means not being as polite and patient as you were when you were dating your spouse. Maybe it means being more critical than you ever would have been when you were trying to win her. Maybe it means failing to put him first the way you did before you got married. Perhaps it means doing things that are rude, things you would never had considered doing when you were still attempting to win your spouse's affection. Would your husband or wife say that you are a kind person?

Serving in love also means that you are *faithful* to the vows you made when you got married. Faithfulness is surely one of the essential character qualities of a good marriage. Faithfulness begins with your thoughts and desires. Do you allow yourself to fantasize about leaving your marriage or about being married to another person? Do you ever look at or think about another man or woman in ways that you shouldn't? Are you still on task, loving your spouse just as you promised you would when you publicly made your vows? Are there other things that have gotten in the way such as work, personal pursuits, children, general busyness, inattention, laziness, forgetfulness, bitterness, or self-interest? Would your spouse say you have been faithful in every way to what you promised?

Serving in love means being committed to *gentleness*. What is gentleness? It means that something doesn't get damaged in the process of being handled. A child makes his mommy a card, but he lacks gentleness, so when the card is finally delivered, it is wrinkled, torn, and stained. Often we permit way too much harshness, rudeness, and angry talk in our marriages. In our disappointment and hurt, our responses lack gentleness, deepening the difficulty with which we are already struggling. A quiet heart and a soft answer are very powerful tools in the hands of a God of transforming grace. Gentleness should not be confused with weakness; gentleness is a quiet confidence in the power of God to change what needs to be changed. It is the recognition that if we could change another person by the volume of our voice, the power of our vocabulary, and the force of our personality, Jesus would not have had to come! Would your husband or wife describe you as gentle?

Serving in love means being committed to the daily exercise of *self-control*. A good marriage is always the result of saying no, not to the other person but to yourself. If you want to damage your marriage, go wherever your desires and emotions lead you. In heated moments of disagreement, in painful moments of disappointment, and in disheartening moments of hurt, you will be tempted to do and say things that are not only wrong but will also add to the trouble you are already experiencing. Disagreement is hard, but it does not have to degenerate into personal war. Disappointment is hard, but it does not have to give way to personal attack. It is painful when you have been hurt, but to lash back is never a step toward reconciliation. There may be no more needed character quality in marriage than self-control. It is the constant willingness to critique your thoughts, edit your words, and restrain your behavior out of love for your spouse and love for what is right. Self-control means you simply won't give yourself permission to get down and dirty. You will take the time that you need to be in a place where you can speak and act with love, wisdom, grace, and gentleness, and be committed to unity, understanding, and peace.

Planting Good Seeds Requires Help

The memories of our very first garden are still alive and well in my brain. I was a garden novice; naïve in every way. I walked out to the chosen spot: rocky, hard, and untouched soil. All I was carrying were a few hand tools and a dream of vegetables to come. Was I ever in for a shock! My first dig with the shovel wasn't really a dig at all. The shovel didn't even penetrate the sod. It just slid across the surface and out of my hands. I moved a few feet and tried again, but that spot was just as hard. I went to look for a pickax. (What was I thinking?) Back at the future garden spot I took a mighty swing with the pickax and made a small hole, a hole not at all commensurate with the force I had exerted! Luella watched. I think she was trying her best not to laugh. My neighbors were probably enjoying the free entertainment while thinking, "He'll learn." The next garden tool I used was a phone! I called my brother-in-law to see if I could borrow his gas-powered, earth-eating rototiller. I had been humbled by the soil's resolve, and I was ready to admit that I needed help.

If you are going to pull out the deeply rooted weeds of a selfish heart and plant new seeds of self-sacrificing love into the soil of your marriage, you need help. Your instincts of self-orientation are as sturdy as the sin that still remains there. When you combine this with the fact that you won't always see yourself accurately because sin is deceitful, guess who it deceives first? You'll have no trouble identifying the weaknesses and failures of your spouse, but you won't see yours with equal clarity. All this is further complicated by artifacts of the self-righteousness that are still inside you. We all tend to be skilled self-swindlers, making ourselves feel good about what God says is not good.

I know you are like me. You want to think that the change that needs to take place in your marriage is being inhibited by your spouse. Yet, the reality is that all of us defend what we do and say, and all of us get in the way of what God is doing. Therefore, we all need more than the "hand tools" of spiritual gardening. The strength and wisdom we have in our hands does not have the power to break through the hard soil of wrong patterns so that new and better seeds can be planted. I don't know if you face this fact or not, but here it is: if your marriage is ever going to be what it was designed to be, you need divine intervention. Let's consider for a moment what that looks like.

Have you ever had a moment in your marriage when you didn't know where to turn? You know that, as a couple, you are not in a good place, and you know you have tried to initiate change, but it either didn't happen or didn't last. You seemed to have tried everything; nothing has worked. Well, in Galatians 5 we are told where to look.

Listen to these words: "So I say, live by the Spirit, and you will not gratify the desires of the sinful nature. For the sinful nature desires what is contrary to the Spirit, and the Spirit what is contrary to the sinful nature. They are in conflict with each other" (vv. 16–17 NIV).

I have said this and will continue to return to it throughout this book: the big battles in marriage are not the ones you fight with your spouse. No, the big battles are the ones being fought in your heart. All of the horizontal skirmishes between a husband and wife are the result of this deeper battle. Remember, there is still sin remaining in your heart, and the DNA of sin is selfishness. Since sin in its fundamental form is selfish, then sin is essentially antisocial. This means that you and I must recognize there is something that still lurks inside us that is destructive to marriage. It is important to notice that after Galatians calls us to a lifestyle of loving service, it turns to remind us of this ongoing, daily, moment-by-moment war.

If you are ever going to have a marriage of unity, understanding, and love, you have to be willing to fight daily, but not with your spouse. You need to be committed to fighting with yourself. You need to be committed to fighting against the powerful draw of your self-focus. You need to fight the instinct to indulge those boiling emotions and powerful cravings. You need to exegete your desires, corral your motives, critique your thoughts, and edit your words. You need to battle until your litany of "I wants" becomes a joyful list of "I would be glad to's."

Let me say it this way: the spiritual gardening that will make for a beautiful marriage (pulling and planting) must largely be done within your own heart. There are self-centered thoughts, attitudes, desires, motives, choices, and goals that must be uprooted from the soil of your heart, and new seeds of other-focused thoughts, attitudes, desires, motives, choices, and goals must be planted in their place. And you need to remember that this pulling and planting is not a one-time thing, but something that must become the lifestyle of your union.

But there is something even more powerful that the words I quoted above point you to. It is hope for your marriage and mine. The words above give us more than insight into the inner dynamics of the marriage struggle. They give us the best hope ever for our marriage, no matter what condition it is presently in. In fact, I am convinced that it points us to the only place where real hope for lasting transformation can be found. These words remind us of something that many husbands and wives are ignorant of or have forgotten along the way. Here is real hope. As you commit to the daily inner battle of pulling and planting, *you are not alone*! Right here, right now, wife, say it to yourself: "I am not alone!" Right here, right now, say it to yourself, husband: "I am not alone!"

God knows how big our struggle is. He knows how deep the war inside us runs. He knows how weak and blind we all can be. He knows how fickle our hearts can be. He knows how easily we lose our way. So, to help our marriage he didn't just give us a set of principles; no, he gave us *himself*!

Immanuel has invaded your marriage with an initiative of warrior grace. He is not standing outside your marriage, giving you principles to live by and judging you if you don't. No, he has literally gotten inside your heart, so he can battle for you at the very place where the war for marriage takes place—your heart. He knows that you and your spouse are not perfect. He knows that sin will again and again get in the way of what a marriage can and should be. He knows that rules, principles, and perspectives are not enough. He knows that your marriage needs more than information; it needs transformation, so he has taken residence inside you. This means that he battles with the dark instincts of sin that are still within you, even when you don't!

If you are God's children, then your marriage isn't just a union of two; it is more accurately a union of three. Think about this: the same Spirit that now lives inside you, wife, also now lives inside your husband. His presence provides the best platform for marital unity and love that you could ever wish for. He brings you the wisdom and strength you need to be what you are supposed to be and to do what you have been called to do in your marriage. And his sweetest gift, in an agenda of grace, is that he daily rescues you from *you*, which is just what you need but are unable to do for yourself.

Hope for your marriage is not to be found in your spouse. No, it is to be found in that third invisible Person, who has made himself part of your union. He has come to you so that you would have everything you will ever need to pull what needs to be pulled and to plant what needs to be planted so that your marriage can be everything that God designed it to be.

Able to Get Unstuck

Jodie and Wesley were stuck and very discouraged as a result. Jodie was a reader and made Wes a reader by proxy. She had dragged Wes's brain through almost every marriage book that hit the shelves. Her bookcase was a museum of marriage hope that had turned yellow on the page. It wasn't that they had a horrible marriage. There had been no adultery, and they weren't in the heat of conflict all the time. But their marriage just wasn't a marriage. They lived and parented together, but that was about the extent of their union. Their sexual relationship was the only barometer necessary to understand the weather of their marriage. Neither Jodie nor Wesley was able to remember for sure when they had last had sex. It wasn't that they stopped suddenly. It wasn't that one was refusing the other. It was that sex had long ago quit being tender, exciting, and satisfying. It felt as though they were having sex because they thought they were supposed to. Jodie said it was like being naked in the arms of a stranger, and Wes said that Jodie's disinterest made it very hard for him to perform. What had become boring was now painful, so painful that they silently made a pact to stop (even though there never was an actual conversation about it).

The sexual relationship is a good barometer for every couple. The character and quality of the marriage relationship will determine the character and quality of their sexual union. You don't leave disappointment and division at the bedside. You don't escape misunderstanding and hurt simply because you are in one another's arms. Because, in this most intimate of human relationships, you are actually physically disrobed and in the arms of another to whom you are offering your physical self, most if not all of the layers of self-protection are gone. You are in a place of exposure and vulnerability. This is what makes the sexual relationship so beautiful. You can be exposed and vulnerable in the arms of your lover and be unafraid, because you know he or she will care for you, and you know that the result will be mutual satisfaction.

But this was not at all the experience of Jodie and Wes. Jodie confidentially shared with one of her friends her dismay at the demise of her sexual life. Her friend suggested she read one of those Christian, "body-part," sexual manuals, as if Jodie and Wes's problem was that they didn't know where stuff was and what it was designed to do. Pay attention to what I am about to say, because I think this applied not only to Jodie and Wes but to thousands of other couples as well. Jodie and Wes did not need a course in *physiology*; no, they needed a course in *theology*. They needed to know the truth about the struggle inside their own hearts, and they needed to know that hope was not to be found in principles alone but in the presence of the warrior Spirit living inside them.

Wes and Jodie weren't stuck. They began to do the daily work of pulling and planting, and they learned to cry out in weakness and receive the strength they needed to go on. This didn't mean that they instantly had a good marriage; they actually had a long road of change before them. But they were no longer pointing the finger at one another, they were no longer fighting against one another, and they were no longer giving way to discouragement and giving up. They were not only now facing the war within, but they were also helping each other to see where the battle was taking place and encouraging one another as they worked to fight it. And together they celebrated the fact that they were not alone as they began to pull the weeds of an old way and plant a garden of better things in their marriage. God hadn't left them alone with only the hand tools of their own wisdom and strength; no, he had given the most powerful tool of transformation that they could ever have—himself. And he offers the same help to you!

To be trusted is a greater compliment than to be loved.

GEORGE MACDONALD

It is better to suffer wrong than to do it, and happier to be sometimes cheated than not to trust.

SAMUEL JOHNSON

COMMITMENT 1:   We will give ourselves to a regular lifestyle of confession and forgiveness.

COMMITMENT 2:   We will make growth and change our daily agenda.

COMMITMENT 3:   We will work together to build a sturdy bond of trust.

COMMITMENT 4:   We will commit to building a relationship of love.

COMMITMENT 5:   We will deal with our differences with appreciation and grace.

COMMITMENT 6:   We will work to protect our marriage.

9

Sticking Out
Your Neck

Crista and Will got married young. It was hard for them to make ends meet, with Will in school full-time and Crista working long hours to support them, but they made it work. They had known each other from just about day one. They had lived down the street from one another and seen each other just about every day. Their families were not close, but both participated in the neighborhood activities. They went to grade school and high school together. Somewhere in high school a spark was lit. Crista and Will began to hang out with one another, and both sets of parents were delighted. When it came time to graduate, they couldn't bear the thought of being separated, so they decided to enroll in the same college. It wasn't what they had planned, but they just couldn't wait any longer to get married, so they got married between their sophomore and junior years. It took about six weeks for Will and Crista to realize that it wouldn't work for both to go to school, so Crista dropped out and secured her first of many jobs.

Perhaps it was because they had known each other for so long, or maybe it was just garden-variety immaturity, but Will and Crista seemed to take their relationship for granted. No, they weren't mean to one another, and they remained faithful, but there was something missing. Their marriage seemed more like the location where both of them lived rather than an investment that both of them were making. For Will, this meant he was too busy, too unpredictable, and too willing not to follow through. For Crista, this meant she was too critical and too committed to her outside friendships. What neither of them knew was that during the very period when they should have been building a sturdy foundation of trust in their marriage, they were unwittingly eroding what little trust they had brought into it.

Will insisted that he had to take a full load of courses. He said he couldn't deal with the thought of stretching his program to five or six years. It was a lot for a newly married man to take on. He spent way too much time away from home. He did way too much of his study in the university library. He kept his nose in his books way too much at home. Crista would say, jokingly, that she had lost a husband and gained a student; but she meant it. The Will she had come to love was silly and romantic. She had been captured by his goofy sense of humor, his tender attentiveness, and his clear love for God. There were moments when Will would be Will, but they were fleeting moments. Most of the time he seemed to have little time for Crista and no time at all to do nothing whatsoever with her simply because he loved to be in her presence. There was no quiet time between them. They shared no down time. They conversed on the fly. And Will seldom stopped studying long enough to be either goofy or romantic. Sure, on her birthday weekend Will took her away, but she was crushed to discover that he had brought his books with him, and she was angry that she spent much of the weekend watching him study, just like she did at home. Crista soon got tired of chasing Will; she got tired of begging for his attention and of his perfunctory displays of affection followed by recycled excuses for their lack of time together.

Will's busyness was not the only thing Crista struggled with; his unpredictability bothered her even more. Will would promise to pick up something for her, but he seldom remembered. He would assure Crista that he would fix something around the house but only got around to it when he thought that he could push her no further. Will promised that he would schedule time for them to be together, but there always seemed to be an interruption or some reason for rescheduling. Time-wise Will was even more unpredictable. He rarely kept to his announced schedule; he was rarely home when he promised to be, and when they were going somewhere together, Will always seemed to make them late. Each week Crista felt she was confronted with plenty of evidence that she simply could not rely on Will. And when she attempted to talk to Will about his unreliability, he would accuse her of not being understanding.

To Crista, it seemed that Will was willing to follow through only on things that were important to him. It seemed he regularly put off things that were important to her. Being on time was not important to Will, and he didn't seem to care that it was important to Crista. Will was a bit of a pioneer and a plan-B guy, so he didn't mind making do. A toilet that didn't flush properly or a drawer that no longer rode on its tracks didn't bother Will at all. Will didn't pay much attention to his watch; in fact, he wore it only because Crista had given it to him for his birthday. Will argued that *what* you do is way more important than the speed at which you do it.

Crista had known Will long enough before they got married to know that he was not perfect, and she knew that there were places where they looked at life differently. She wasn't surprised that they weren't always on the same page. But there was something happening inside herself that scared her—she felt herself withdrawing from Will. No, not because he was a malevolent man, but because he was an unreliable man. Crista reasoned that if she could not entrust the little things in her life to Will, how could she entrust big matters of heart and life? And what distressed her even more was Will's unwillingness to hear her concern. She wondered if she would ever have the bond with Will that she had always dreamed she would have.

They didn't fight. They managed to get along, but their marriage was far from being a case study in unity, understanding, and love. Few people who knew Will and Crista would have known that a foundation stone of a healthy and lasting marriage was crumbling under them.

Will's experience was very different from Crista's. He saw himself as a dedicated and busy guy who just needed to be cut a little slack. It seemed to him that Crista was much more demanding than she was understanding. He wasn't an irresponsible guy, he would tell himself; just a very busy one. He was tired of coming home at night to Crista's pointing at her watch. He was tired of Crista's pouting because some job around the house was going to have to be done on Will's schedule, not hers. He was tired of Crista's laying guilt on him because they didn't have time together, when she knew that he had no time. He was tired of being accused of not caring, when he had inflicted himself with his tough schedule precisely because he cared about Crista and their future together.

Will felt that there was no way to measure up to Crista's standards, and that even if he could, she would raise the bar higher. Will said he began to spend more time in the university library because Crista's constant jabs made it impossible to concentrate on his studies. And he had long since quit sharing much with her about his academic life because, when he did, she would say that it was the only thing they talked about because it was the only thing that was important to Will.

Crista didn't realize it, because it wasn't done with self-conscious intentionality, but she had withdrawn into a circle of friends she had made at their church. She shared more of her thoughts and feelings about life by text message to her friends than she did with Will. And while Crista was withdrawing into her circle of friends, Will simply withdrew into himself. They didn't trust each other enough to place themselves into the other's hands. Crista was plagued by wondering if she had made a huge mistake in marrying Will. She would see a young couple together and wonder what it was like to be married to that man. She would see couples at church and wonder if they could rely on one another as she had always dreamed she and Will would be able to. And she wondered how she could live this way for the rest of her life. She simply didn't trust Will anymore, and there would be moments when she wondered if he had someone else in his life who had taken his attention and captured his heart.

Will protected himself with non-answers and physical distance. These things kept him from having to deal with Crista's dissatisfaction but only made things worse. He felt that the only way they could live together was to live separately. He no longer trusted Crista to care about him and the things he was investing in for both of them. He found other places to talk about his joys and disappointments, but most of the time he talked to himself; the problem was that he always agreed with how he was seeing things.

Their marriage was no longer a marriage in the real sense of what marriage means. No, there had been no adultery. No, there had been no physical violence. No, they weren't screaming despicable things at one another. No, neither of them was a liar or a manipulator. Their trust wasn't destroyed in an explosion of unfaithfulness but through the drip, drip, drip of relational laziness and personal selfishness. And because it happened this way, they did not see it happening and work to avert it.

I am convinced that the story of Will and Crista is mirrored thousands of times by couples all around us. Perhaps you are one of them. Let me encourage you to look into the mirror of the following questions.

A Trust Questionnaire

1) Is there more unity, understanding, and love in your marriage now than there has ever been?

2) Do you both do what you promise in the time that you have promised?

3) Are you attentive to what your spouse sees as important?

4) Do you make excuses for failures to do what you have promised, or are you ready to confess?

5) Do you listen well to your spouse and act on what you have heard?

6) Do you follow through with mutually agreed-upon plans?

7) Do you work together on planning and scheduling priorities, or do you demand that the other do it your way?

8) Do you share with your spouse your thoughts, desires, hopes, dreams, and concerns, or is it easier for you to be quiet or to share with someone else?

9) Is there any evidence that you have withdrawn from the other in protective distance?

10) Would your spouse say that you are good for your word and faithful to your promises?

11) Do you carry wrongs around with you, or do you trust one another to confront and confess?

12) Do you ever wonder what the other is doing when not with you?

13) Are you conscious of editing your words and withholding your feelings because you can't trust your spouse to deal with them properly?

14) Is your marriage partner the best friend in your life or has your dream of this kind of companionship evaporated?

15) Is your sexual relationship mutually satisfying, or is it hard for you to give yourself physically to your spouse?

16) Do you say things to other people about your spouse that you have not communicated to him or her?

17) Do you look forward to sharing times together, and when you have these times are they peaceful and enjoyable?

18) Are there problems between you that remain unsolved because you don't have the bond of trust necessary to work together on a solution?

19) Are you comfortable with the vulnerability that a good marriage involves?

20) Do you ever wonder if you made a mistake in marrying the person who is your spouse?

21) Do you ever fear that you are being manipulated or taken advantage of in any way?

22) Do you ever wonder if your spouse cares for him- or herself more than for you?

No Escaping the Need for Trust

So, look over your answers. What do you think? Is trust solid in your marriage? Maybe you're wondering. Perhaps you want to know more about what trust is and what trust looks like before you make your assessment. What is this thing called *trust* that is so essential to any good, sturdy, and healthy relationship? Let me give you a street-level definition and then unpack it for you. *Trust is being so convinced that you can rely on the integrity, strength, character, and faithfulness of another that you are willing to place yourself in his or her care.*

Now, think about this definition in the context of marriage. When you say those vows in front of God, your family, and your friends, you are making a commitment to place yourself in the care of the other person and to care for him or her in return. One of the essential foundation stones of marriage is trust. No trust, no marriage—at least, not the kind of marriage that God designed when he created this lifelong relation-

138

ship. You can have cohabitation without trust. You can have relational détente without trust. But you cannot have the intimate, vulnerable, mutually cooperative, one-flesh union that marriage is intended to be without trust.

You must be able to take the other at face value. You must be comfortable when he or she is not in your eyesight. You must not worry whether he is being honest or will be faithful to his promises. You must not fear that she cares for herself more than she cares for you. You must never wonder if there is someone else who has captured his interest and/ or affection. You must never worry for your well-being or safety. You must not be afraid to stick out your neck and be vulnerable. You must not fear that you will be taken advantage of or used in any way. Trust is about rest, peace, security, and hope. Trust allows you to face the worst and hope for the best. Trust makes you willing to take risks and allows you to risk being willing. Trust makes you feel safe and makes it safe for you to share your feelings. Trust allows you to speak honestly and to listen to the honesty of the other. Trust lets you know that you are cared for and causes your care to be known. Trust causes you to look out for the other's interest while resting in the fact that she will look out for you. Trust is about mutual care but is committed to care even when it is not mutual. Trust is about being good for your word and about being committed to do only what is good. Trust means doing anything you can to let your spouse know that she can be confident in entrusting herself to your care.

Perhaps you're thinking, "All that is helpful, Paul, but can you be even more concrete in terms of what trust looks like and what and how trust functions in the context of marriage?" To be even more concrete, let's return to the questionnaire and let me unpack each question for you and how it is an indicator of the quality of trust in your marriage.

Where the Rubber Meets the Road

1) *Is there more unity, understanding, and love in your marriage now than there has ever been?* Perhaps this is the best indicator of all. When there is a strong bond of trust, the intimacy of marriage grows. Trust allows a couple to work through differences and build unity. Trust allows you to work to understand your spouse and to know that he

or she will work to understand you. When your spouse proves that he cares about you enough to demonstrate to you that he can be trusted, your respect and affection for him will grow. This does not mean that your marriage will be free of difficulty. Remember, you do live in a fallen world, and you do live with a flawed person. Trust won't alleviate all of your problems and differences, but it will give you a means of dealing with them.

2) *Do you both do what you promise in the time that you have promised?* Like it or not, you must face the fact that the way you follow the promises you make will function as a barometer of your trustworthiness to your spouse. And this is how it should be. If you love her, you will take your promises to her seriously. If you love him, you will enjoy the fact that he is able to rest in the assurance that whatever you have committed to do for him, you will do, and you will do it in the time that is best for him.

The problem here is that most of the promises we make in marriage are little-moment promises. They are promises that have to do with the daily needs, duties, and schedule that make up the lifestyle of any couple anywhere. Because these promises are not promises of consequence, it is very tempting not to take them seriously and to fail to consider the consequences of not following through. Remember what we have already considered: the character of a marriage is not built on three or four significant moments. No, the character of a marriage is established through ten thousand little moments. It is the character that is built in the little moments that you carry into the big moments of life. So trust is not built in two or three significant moments of promise (although those moments are formative as well), but trust is built moment by moment and day by day. It is the degree of your daily reliability that tells your spouse that you are a person who can be trusted or not. Loving your spouse means you love to serve her, and you love to gift her with the rest that comes from knowing that you will be faithful to the promises you have made, no matter how small.

3) *Are you attentive to what your spouse sees as important?* Because of the selfishness of sin, it is easy to be self-absorbed and self-focused. It is easy to be captured by your own schedule and interests. Perhaps there is no more dangerous force in marriage than garden-variety selfishness.

Perhaps there is no greater marital mistake than to somehow give your spouse a reason to wonder if you really do care about your interests more than you care for hers. Love is about opening yourself to your spouse and her interests. Love means committing yourself to care about what he cares about; to be interested in a thing simply because it interests him. Love is about acknowledging, anticipating, and meeting your spouse's needs. Love is about sharing your sorrows, joys, and concerns. And when you love someone this way, you are building a bond of trust. It is hard to trust a person who cares so much for himself that he fails to care for others. However, you will entrust yourself to the person who loves you enough to trouble his life with what troubles you.

4) *Do you make excuses for failures to do what you have promised, or are you ready to confess?* Self-righteousness, inapproachability, defensiveness, and self-excusing are all toxic to trust. You will not entrust yourself to your spouse if he is defensive and unapproachable. You will not trust your spouse if, in time of failure, she is unwilling to look at herself. You will not trust your spouse if, when it is time to humbly listen and humbly confess, he fails to be willing to do either. Trust doesn't demand perfection. Trust demands humility. In your heart of hearts, you know you will never marry a perfect person. In your heart of hearts, you know that you will both fail. So, in your heart of hearts you want to live with your spouse with the assurance that when he has failed you in some way, he is willing to face it and deal with it. Patterns of self-excusing tell you that your spouse is more interested in herself than she is in you. Self-defensiveness tells you that he is more interested in being right than in forging with you a relationship of unity, understanding, and love. Humble openness, coupled with the commitment to admit to and confess wrongs, is an essential ingredient of a bond of trust.

5) *Do you listen well to your spouse and act on what you have heard?* If you are living with someone who just does not listen, sooner or later, confronted with the futility of getting the person to listen, you will quit talking. You and I are drawn to people who listen. One of the most amazing things that God promises to you and me is that he will never turn a deaf ear to our cries. You can run to God with no fear whatsoever as to whether he will ignore you. Yet, there is probably no

marital pain that I have heard expressed more frequently than the pain of not being heard.

"She just doesn't listen."

"Talking with him is like talking to a brick wall."

"I can't believe that you won't give me this one thing; just be quiet and listen to what I'm trying to say."

"It took me a while, but it finally became clear: he quickly checks out when I begin to talk. No, he doesn't walk out of the room, but when I am finished there is no response whatsoever."

"I am so tired of hearing her say, 'Do we have to talk about this now?'"

"The time doesn't ever seem right, so we seldom talk about anything that matters."

I cannot tell you how many times I have sat with couples and heard words like those. The one being ignored quits talking, but not only that; he does something even more debilitating to their marriage—he quits trusting. You tend to trust people who care about you enough to listen to what you have to say and who have demonstrated to you that they are committed to respond to what they have heard with words and actions.

6) *Do you follow through with mutually agreed-upon plans?* Planning together in things large and small is what marriage is about. It is the life-plan of two people coalescing and becoming one plan. Marriage is the most comprehensive form of shared life that a human being can ever experience. God's goal for marriage is that a husband and wife would live in a relationship so deeply blended and unified that it could only be called "one flesh." So, the work of every husband and wife is the work of unity. Because you desire life together, you need to plan together. It is no longer his and hers. Therefore, you need to do the give-and-take work of discussing and planning together. And you need to rest assured that when you have agreed together upon a goal with a plan of action, the other will remain loyal to the plan and follow through as you have agreed. When this happens, trust is strengthened, but when you agree to a plan and then go out and do it your way, rather than the mutually decided way, you present yourself as a person who cannot be trusted.

7) *Do you work together on planning and scheduling priorities, or*

do you demand that the other do it your way? Let's be humbly honest here; we all want our own way. The instinct to be sovereign over your little world and to get what you want and what you tell yourself you need doesn't leave when you are publicly mouthing your vows. God is working right now on you so that you would live for something bigger than yourself, but there will be artifacts of the instincts to live selfishly in your heart until you cross over to the other side. Demand and entitlement destroy trust because, as you live with your spouse, she soon comes to understand that no matter what commitments you have made to her, what you really want is your own way. You have vowed to cooperate with her, but what you really want is for your wife to participate in supporting the desires and plans of your little kingdom of one. When she sees you operate this way, she knows that you cannot be trusted to work with her and to care for her.

8) *Do you share with your spouse your thoughts, desires, hopes, dreams, and concerns, or is it easier for you to be quiet or to share them with someone else?* Has your life together encouraged greater and greater levels of trust? Have you learned that you can say anything to your spouse because he approaches you with a heart that is gentle, kind, understanding, and patient? Have you experienced starting at opposite ends of an issue and watching honest and patient communication bring you together? Or has your spouse not taken your concerns seriously? Have you been dismissive of your spouse's thoughts, hopes, and dreams? Are you better able to communicate with one another today than you were earlier? Do you go into a conversation assured that you will get a patient ear? Or do you find it easier to talk candidly with someone other than your husband or wife? When someone outside of the house has become a replacement confidant for your spouse, it is a sure sign that trust has been broken.

9) *Is there any evidence that you have withdrawn from the other in protective distance?* Are you afraid to be honest with your spouse? Are you afraid to disagree with him? Are you afraid to lovingly confront or contradict her? Are you afraid of what would really happen if you told him what you really think? Are you afraid to stick your neck out and be vulnerable? Do you ever feel that you are walking on eggshells? Do you feel the need to measure your words? Do you ever feel that you need to

protect yourself from her? Have you withdrawn in some way? There is no getting around it: withdrawal is a sure sign of a lack of trust. Yet, there are many, many couples out there who have no intention of divorcing, which is a good thing, but they live in self-protective distance from one another, which is a bad thing.

10) *Would your spouse say that you are good for your word and faithful to your promises?* The Bible holds out the real possibility that your view of yourself may be less than accurate. Yes, I know we all tend to think that we know ourselves better than anyone does. But is that actually true? The Bible teaches that sin blinds, and because it blinds, we do not know ourselves as well as we think we do. I like to say it this way: sin blinds, and guess who it blinds first? We have no problem seeing the weaknesses and failure of others, but we can get surprised when ours is pointed out. So we actually need people in our lives who will help us to see ourselves with accuracy (see Heb. 3:12–13).

This is one of the benefits of marriage. Because you are actually living with your spouse 24/7, he or she has a comprehensive view of who you are and how you operate. No, your spouse's view of you will not be perfectly without bias, but it will tend to be more objective than your view of you. So take this question and the others to your spouse. Ask your spouse if he has come to consider you to be trustworthy and why or why not. Open your heart to see what you could not see by yourself and commit yourself to respond to what your spouse helps you to see with humility and a commitment to change.

11) *Do you carry wrongs around with you, or do you trust one another to confront and confess?* Choosing to be bitter is choosing what feels good to you but not what is best for your spouse or for the relationship to which you have committed yourself. When you are unwilling to go through the difficulty of helping your spouse to see how she has hurt you and the tension of disagreement, you love your comfort more than you love her. When you are not sure that it is safe either to confront or to confess to your spouse, then you are saying that you are not sure that your spouse is a person who can be trusted. Silence is a sign of the lack of trust.

12) *Do you ever wonder what the other is doing when not with you?* Trust means you have no concern whatsoever about what your spouse is

doing when he is out of your presence. The need to follow him, check up on him, and to cross-examine him when he returns are sure indicators that you do not trust him. Trust means that you know that your spouse would not think of doing anything when she is away from you that she would not do in front of you. Being trustworthy means you never feel the need to look over your shoulder to see if you're being seen, and you never feel the need to cover your tracks or rehearse your story. Trust means living with the rest that comes from knowing that neither one of you has anything to hide.

13) *Are you conscious of editing your words and withholding your feelings because you can't trust the other to deal with them properly?* The nature and style of your communication with your spouse is a very good indicator of the degree of trust that exists between you. If you are withholding your thoughts and feelings from the other, it means either that you don't love him enough to share yourself with him, or you don't trust him enough to place yourself in his care. I don't know how many times I have heard a husband or wife say, "I had no idea you felt that way about . . ." Have you experienced situations in which you have shared something with your spouse and he used it against you? Have you ever shared secret things told to you by your spouse with someone else? When you're not sure that you can place the fine china of your life in the other person's hands, then you are being confronted with a weakness in trust in your marriage.

14) *Is your marriage partner the best friend in your life, or has your dream of this kind of companionship evaporated?* Marriage really is a human covenant of companionship. God wasn't so much giving Adam a physical helper for the work in the garden as he was giving him a companion. God knew that he had created a social being, and because of Adam's social hardwiring, it was not good for him to live without the companionship of one made from him and made like him. You could argue that this *is* the most basic reason for marriage. God created a life-long companion for Adam, and his relationship with Eve would exist on earth as a visible reminder of God's love relationship with people and as the God-ordained means by which the earth would be populated as God designed. So the character and quality of the friendship between a husband and wife always functions as an accurate measure of the health

of their marriage. It is also an accurate barometer of trust. When trust is present between two people, their appreciation and affection will grow, and as these things grow, friendship flourishes.

15) *Is your sexual relationship mutually satisfying, or is it hard for you to give yourself physically to your spouse?* What does good sex have to do with trust? Everything! I must be honest here. I am a bit tired of Christian marital body-part books. I don't think that the problem for most couples in the area of sex is that people don't know where stuff is! I don't think the average couple needs sexual maps and charts. Now, a little education can be helpful, but I don't think biology is the solution to the overwhelming sexual dysfunction that is the plight of many Christian marriages. I think that this particular dysfunction is directly related to trust. It is important to understand that you do not leave the character and quality of your relationship at the side of the marital bed. You drag the nature of the relationship right in the middle of this naked and vulnerable moment. If you have experienced the selfishness of your spouse in a variety of ways, why would you not conclude that he or she will be selfish in bed as well? If your spouse has been demanding, critical, and vengeful in other times and places, wouldn't it be logical to assume he or she will be the same during the act of sex? On the other hand, if you have been able to entrust yourself to your spouse's care in other situations, would it not be safe to conclude that your spouse will care for you in this most vulnerable of all marriage moments? There is a direct relationship between joyful, mutual, marital sexual satisfaction and trust.

16) *Do you say things to other people about your spouse that you have not communicated to him or her?* Exchanging honest marital communication for marital gossip is a clear sign of the breakdown of trust. Now, I do not mean talking about your marriage with another person when you have come to the realization that there are things you are facing together that you will not be able to solve together. When you seek out external help, you do it because you have talked, and you now know you need help. No, I'm talking about giving up on your spouse and giving in to releasing your steam by talking about him without his knowledge. Our churches are riddled with women's gatherings, formal and informal, that are not so much times of healthy fellowship but

unhealthy times for complaint against the men in their lives. If you are trustworthy, you would not think of saying anything to others that you hadn't first said to your spouse, and you wouldn't say it to others unless they were part of the problem or positioned to be part of the solution. And if you know that you can trust your spouse, you know that you can speak to him with candor, and he will hear and respond. There are too many marriages out there where the husband or wife has been replaced, when it comes to communication, by a friend who functions as a replacement spouse.

17) *Do you look forward to sharing times together, and when you have these times are they peaceful and enjoyable?* Joyful anticipation of time together is a good indicator of the health of a marriage. Actually being able to have peaceful and mutually satisfying times together is an even better indicator. Longing to be together is a sign that you know you can trust the other to share of him- or herself and to care for you. Experiencing peace between you is a sign that you are both willing to make the sacrifices that need to be made in order to experience unity, understanding, and love. Here it is: you anticipate being with people you trust.

18) *Are there problems between you that remain unsolved because you don't have the bond of trust necessary to work together on a solution?* The inability to solve problems is a sure sign of the breakdown of trust. It takes patient love and persevering humility to work together to solve problems. It takes loving the other person more than you love yourself. It takes a willingness to make concrete sacrifices. It takes exchanging a demanding attitude for servanthood. It takes ears that are ready to hear and a heart that is ready to receive. It takes a commitment to not walk away until the problem is solved. When you gift the other with these things over and over again, your spouse comes to understand that he can trust that, in a moment of difficulty, you won't run over him and do it your way. He knows that you will love and care for him as you are working with him to solve whatever needs to be solved. The more your spouse experiences this, the more she knows she can trust you, and the more she knows she can trust you, the more she will be willing to hang in with you and work toward a solution to the problem of the moment.

19) *Are you comfortable with the vulnerability that a good marriage involves?* You can't have a relationship without vulnerability, and the reason vulnerability is called vulnerability is that it requires risk. Are you still willing to stick your neck out and be vulnerable because you know that your spouse will care for you when you do? Or have you long since quit putting yourself in any situation of personal vulnerability in your marriage? Think about the fact that marriage without vulnerability is not marriage. Even the most basic of marital acts, cohabitation, requires vulnerability. The degree to which you are comfortable with emotional, physical, and spiritual nakedness in front of your spouse is a sure indicator of the quality of trust that exists between you.

20) *Do you ever wonder if you made a mistake in marrying the person who is your spouse?* It is probably blatantly obvious, but I will say it anyway: marital regret is a powerful indicator of the breakdown of the relationship and the breakdown of trust. If you are there, I have two words for you: seek help. If there is a fundamental breakdown of trust between you, then you probably do not have the bond that it takes to reconcile and restore your marriage. Let the pain of your regret not tempt you to run but motivate you to seek God's help. Go to your pastor or a mature brother or sister and begin to share your dilemma. Look for someone mature who takes God's Word seriously. Don't wallow in regret. Remember, Jesus died for what you are now facing. He is with you, and he is for you, and he will not leave your marriage, no matter how bad it gets!

21) *Do you ever fear that you are being manipulated or taken advantage of in any way?*

If you have come to the place where you actually fear the other person, then you are in a situation where there has been a complete breakdown of trust. You simply don't fear someone who loves you. You don't fear someone who takes your best interest to heart. You don't fear someone who has treated you with kindness and gentleness. If your companion has become your adversary, then trust is gone and the marriage cannot work. No, that does not mean it is over; it simply means it needs fundamental change and healing. You cannot let yourself or your spouse live with the status quo. You can't allow yourself to be content with learning how to avoid danger. You must commit to doing everything in your power to rebuild what has been broken. God will honor your commitment to do what is right by giving you strength as you go.

22) *Do you ever wonder if your spouse cares for him- or herself more than for you?*

Remember our definition of trust at the beginning of this chapter: *Trust is being so convinced that you can rely on the integrity, strength, character, and faithfulness of another that you are willing to place yourself in his or her care.* Don't be willing to live in a marriage where trust has died. Believe that God will never call you to do a thing without giving you the wherewithal to do it. His grace will take you places you hadn't intended to go, but it will also produce in you things that you could never produce on your own.

Restoring Grace

Thankfully Will and Crista got tired of the distance and the pain. They got tired of walking on eggshells. They got tired of living in a marriage that was not a marriage. So they reached out for God's help and the help of his people. It was not easy for them to rebuild what had been broken, but they did, and in so doing they experienced the truth that God's grace really is sufficient and his strength really is made perfect in our weakness. That same grace is available to you as well. Reach out for it and don't let go until it has transformed you and returned trust to your marriage.

COMMITMENT 1:   We will give ourselves to a regular
                lifestyle of confession and forgiveness.

COMMITMENT 2:   We will make growth and change our
                daily agenda.

**COMMITMENT 3:   We will work together to build a sturdy
                bond of trust.**

COMMITMENT 4:   We will commit to building a relationship
                of love.

COMMITMENT 5:   We will deal with our differences with
                appreciation and grace.

COMMITMENT 6:   We will work to protect our marriage.

10

Someone to Be Trusted

It is one of the most beautiful things you can see. It is even more beautiful to experience it. It is a sweet thing to watch a couple who are totally at rest with one another. It is wonderful to watch the respect and affection flow between them. It is a beautiful thing to watch them negotiate their way through difficulty as if they were one person. It is sweet to see how relaxed they are with one another, how comfortable they are in one another's care. It is a beautiful thing to see what happens in a marriage when trust grows and thrives. I wish my marriage had begun that way, but it didn't.

I think I made the mistake that many people entering into the life-long relationship of marriage make—I took trust for granted. We loved one another and our relationship was pretty comfortable and easy, so I simply did not think about trust. Little did I know that not only was I not building a sturdy bond of trust, but I was eroding what little trust there was between us. I look back, and it is hard to believe that all of this was going on and I did not have clue one. No, I wasn't a mean or violent man; I was a selfish and immature one. I wanted my own way and I didn't deal well with difference. I didn't so much want unity; I wanted uniformity, and when I didn't get it, I did all the wrong things.

Luella was very patient, but she would not acquiesce. She knew that my attitude and responses were wrong. She was not going to declare war and respond in kind, but she also was unwilling to live in a relationship with someone whom she could not trust. Change needed to take place. What was going on could not continue. Trust needed to be built like it had never been built before. I am deeply grateful for Luella's resolve. She would not call wrong right. She would not melt into the shadows. She was not willing to give in or give up. She kept calling me to what was right, even though she knew I would get angry when she did. As you know, we are still together. There is remarkable trust between us. Luella is not only my hero, but she is also my best friend. We have remarkable peace and unity between us. We love to be with one another, and we are both grateful for the years we have had together. All this would have been impossible without the building of a beautiful bond of trust between us. For that, I am thankful to Luella, to others who God used to show me the light, and to the transforming grace of a relentless Redeemer.

Trust—it's readily given, easily broken, and costly to restore. You are usually willing to grant someone trust at the beginning of a relationship. Most of us don't enter a relationship cynically. You are willing to take someone's words at face value and willing to give him the benefit of the doubt when he does something you do not understand. You are willing to listen to explanations and graciously receive confessions, but you are looking for her to prove herself worthy of the trust you have willingly granted her. At some point, you will realize that you are in a relationship with someone either predictable and reliable or not faithful or true to his or her word. Here is the point: trust is inescapable in any relationship, particularly in marriage, and although it is temporarily granted, trust is something that must always be built for any relationship to be healthy. This is true of marriage even more. If your marriage is going to be what God intended it to be, trust must be built, maintained, and protected, and restored when broken. This is what this chapter is about.

Trust: Marriage's Construction Project

I made the big mistake that many of you have made. I took trust for granted. We liked one another; we seemed to get along well, so it didn't seem that trust would be a problem. Trust wasn't a practical, daily goal that I carried around in my brain. I didn't evaluate my actions, reactions, words, and responses from the vantage point of how they would build or weaken Luella's trust in me. Consequently, I did things that damaged trust, and I didn't even know it.

Now, it is true that you will have some level of trust between you as you enter marriage. If you didn't, you probably wouldn't have gotten married. But there is a real way in which the early years of a marriage are a trust internship. You are watching one another, learning the degree to which you can rely on one another and entrust yourselves to each other. You are also learning the things that you need to do to demonstrate to the other person that you are someone who can be trusted. These things are going on in every young marriage. The problem is that most couples aren't aware of them, and because they aren't aware, they are not as focused and intentional as they should be.

Because of the love you have for one another and your desire for your marriage to work, you will grant one another probationary trust, but you will not continue to entrust yourself to someone who has demonstrated in a variety of ways that he or she cannot be trusted. This brings up something else that needs to be considered. You are a sinner, married to a sinner. You will not always do and say things that engender trust. You will have moments of selfishness or needless irritation. You will get angry and say things that you shouldn't. You will have times when you want to be right more than you want to have peace. You will have moments when you are more demanding than you are giving. You will resurrect an offense that you said you had forgiven. You will be critical when you should be encouraging. Look at this list. None of these things encourages trust. No, they do the opposite. They challenge and break down whatever bond of trust you have been taking for granted.

You see, the comprehensive cohabitation of marriage will expose you. It will reveal your true heart and your true character. The pressures, opportunities, and responsibilities of marriage will shine a light not only on your strengths but also on your weaknesses, failures, and sins. What you really want, what you truly value, and what you think and do when you do not get these things will be exposed. This means that your husband or wife will see you for who you really are in marriage. This is why it is so important to be intentional, so important not to take trust for granted. You want to build such a strong foundation of trust together that when you sin against one another, you have established enough trust to deal with the sin in a way that doesn't further erode trust and do lasting damage to your union.

It's hard for me to think about how different the first period of my own marriage would have been if I had known that the early years of a marriage are building years. Now, if you didn't know that either, and although you lived together you didn't build together, don't panic. The bright message of Scripture is that change really is possible. God sent his Son to live, die, and rise again to give us new life and with that new life the promise of reconciliation and restoration. Your marriage is not encased in concrete. You are not stuck. God not only calls you to change, but he has already given you everything you need to make the changes to which he has called you. Remember, you are not alone in your struggle. He has invaded your marriage with his powerful love and transforming grace. Confess the things that have broken the trust between you and get to work building trust once again.

I've seen it again and again—husbands and wives trying to live together without trust. It is an exercise in futility. You simply cannot have a relationship with someone whom you do not trust. Such a marriage is a cycle of doubt, accusation, conflict, recrimination, hurt, disappointment, and withdrawal. I've listened to people who have so little trust between them that they literally debate everything the other says. But I've been able to be there when they have finally become desperate, when they finally refuse to live that way anymore. I have been able to be there when they quit pointing the finger at one another and begin owning personal responsibility. I have been able to be there when they begin to confess their wrongs to God and one another. I have been able to be there when they begin to get serious about trust and begin to be intentional about building it. And I have been there with them to celebrate fresh starts and new beginnings.

Here's what you need to understand: the building of trust between you begins vertically before it ever begins horizontally. This means that because of your confidence in God's presence, love, power to change you, forgiveness, wisdom of what he calls you to do, his empowering grace and unwillingness to forsake what he has begun before it is done, you are able to step out and build a trust relationship with your spouse.

You see, as you are doing that, you are not placing your eggs in your spouse's basket and hoping that she will not drop them. No, you know that she is less than perfect, and you know that he will fail. Rather, you have placed all your eggs in God's basket, and you know that even if your spouse fails you, God will not. You know that he will give you what you need to deal with the danger and disappointment that comes with building a life of trust with someone who is still flawed. Because of your confidence in God, you can move toward your spouse and not be afraid to do this because, although you love your spouse, you don't get your identity, purpose in life, and inner sense of well-being from him or her. You get that from the Lord, and because you trust him, you can build trust with your spouse.

Play It Straight

Straightforward, clear, and transparent communication that is without manipulation, deceit, or subtext is essential to building a relationship of trust. No matter what the location or situation, your spouse needs to be able to take your words at face value. She must not be in a position where she is left wondering if you really meant what you said or said what you meant. He must not be in a situation where he is required to read between the lines or to figure the hidden meaning behind the words that you spoke. That is what is being addressed when the Bible calls us to let our yes be yes and our no be no.

This is where I think that the words of Paul about communication with one another are so helpful. He says, "Let no corrupting [unwholesome] talk come out of your mouths, but only such as is good for building up, as fits the occasion, that it may give grace to those who hear" (Eph. 4:29). What is Paul's definition of wholesome communication? He doesn't reduce, as we have done, wholesome communication to the avoidance of certain words. For Paul, wholesome communication starts with the intention of the heart. Wholesome communication is *other-centered, other-regarding* communication. You say something to your spouse not because you want something *from* him but because you want something *for* him. You want your words to consider him, to consider the moment, and to consider how you may grace him (build him up) with what you are about to say. There's no subtext, hidden meaning, or manipulative intent that you need to fear. You love him and want the best for him, and your hope is that your words will benefit your spouse in some way. This kind of communication will always build trust. *Is your communication free of hidden agenda, and is it motivated by the needs of your spouse?*

Be Good for Your Word

Keep the promises you make. It is just that simple. You want the person you live with to know that what you commit to do, you will do, in the time that you have promised to do it. Now, as I stated earlier, most of your promises will be small, but you can't let yourself minimize the importance of the little promise. Remember the theme that runs throughout this book: you do not build a marriage of unity, understanding, and love in a few big moments of life, but in ten thousand little moments. Little promises are important precisely because they are little, and the cumulative effect of your little moments of faithfulness will convince your husband or wife that you can be trusted with the greater matters of life. Your spouse will know that she has been blessed to live with someone upon whom she can rely and who will not let circumstances, contingencies, or excuses get in the way of his doing what he has promised to do. *Are you serious about your promises, even when they are little, and do you do everything in your power to follow through?*

Face Up to Your Wrongs

Self-righteousness and self-defensiveness do not encourage trust. Humble approachability does. Again, it really is that simple. The person you live with has empirical evidence that you are not perfect, so she needs to know that in situations where you have failed, she can come to you with the knowledge that you will listen and humbly consider what she has said to you. She has to know that you have an accurate view of yourself, that you know that you are still in need of growth and change, and that you are willing to examine your thoughts, desires, choices, words, and actions. Without this, when your spouse has been wronged, she has no place of appeal and therefore no realistic hope of change.

You see, in marriage you are not trusting that your spouse will be perfect, but you are trusting him to be willing to deal with his failures with honesty, humility, and the commitment to change. The building of trust always requires admission of wrongs and a commitment to change. This requirement is essential, because marriage, being this side of heaven, is always between two flawed people living in a fallen world.

In fact, in our hearts we long for something even more encouraging. We long for a marriage where confrontation isn't regularly needed, because when we do or say something wrong, we are unsettled in our hearts (the convicting ministry of the Holy Spirit), and without being confronted with the wrong we did or said, whichever one of us was wrong comes to the other and owns the wrong and seeks forgiveness and a restoration of the relationship. Who wouldn't want to live in this kind of relationship, and who wouldn't be drawn to trust such a person? *Do you quickly admit your wrongs and seek forgiveness?*

Watch Out for the Other Person

Genuine, heartfelt, self-started, and regular nurture of the other person is another important seedbed of trust. You tend to feel safe moving toward someone who has demonstrated in a variety of ways that he really does think about you, watch out for your welfare, and look for ways to care for you. I have had many husbands and wives say to me, "I'm just not on my husband's radar," or, "He doesn't seem to know that I am around," or, "She's in her own little world." You don't tend to entrust yourself to someone who gives you the impression that she is so busy caring for herself that she has little time to care for you.

Now, this is war. No, I don't mean a battle between you and your spouse about how well you care for one another. No, I am talking about a battle that rages in your own heart. It is the battle of kingdoms that we have already talked about. It is a battle over which kingdom will rule your heart and control the way you respond to your spouse. Will you be ruled by the kingdom of self and allow your responses to your spouse to be controlled by no larger concern than your wants, your needs, and your feelings? Or will you joyfully give yourself to the kingdom of God and live for something bigger than yourself? Remember, the kingdom of God is a kingdom of love. The centerpiece event of this kingdom is a radical sacrifice of love—God giving up his own Son to death so that we might have life. Remember, too, that the central call of the kingdom of

God is a call to love; love God above all else and love your neighbor as yourself. It is a call to step away from me-centric living and give yourself to other-focused living.

But this is war. Sometimes you get it right. Sometimes you actually find joy in giving up what you want for the sake of the other:

"I'll go to her movie."

"I'll buy the house that she likes."

"I'll opt for peace rather than doing anything I can to prove that I am right."

There are other times when we get it wrong:

"I don't care how much she moans; I am going golfing."

"I know we can't afford it, but I need a vacation."

"I know she is uncomfortable with some of the things I ask her to do, but she is my wife."

If you are going to live a consistent lifestyle of caring for one another, you have to be aware of this war and seek God's grace to fight it. *How well do you care for one another?*

Keep Short Accounts

For us, it was a stunning little piece of practical wisdom that kept the struggles of the early years from completely destroying our marriage. We took it seriously, and we acted on it with resolve. It was hard because it called us to do things that were uncomfortable and didn't fit well with the emotions, desires, and schedule of the moment. But it made sense to us, and we determined that we were going to live in light of its call. Do I have you intrigued? It came to us as an unremarkable phrase in a very theological portion of Scripture, but when we read it over again, it jumped off the page. There it was in the fourth chapter of Ephesians: "Do not let the sun go down on your anger" (v. 26). It is a call to keep short accounts so that you do not give the Devil an opportunity (v. 27).

Consider how practically wise this directive is. Bad things tend to happen when you give offenses time to marinate in your heart. You've experienced this. As you carry the offense around with you, it tends to grow in size and magnitude. As it grows, your hurt and anger grow as well. As this is happening, you begin to rehearse the things you would like to say to the other person in defense of yourself and to help them understand what a heinous crime they have committed against you. Without knowing it, you are troubling your own trouble and heading to a marital explosion rather than a sweet reconciliation. Because you have given the offense time to expand, you will talk about it in ways that are inflammatory and over the top. This will cause the other to be defensive rather than open, because you are making the situation much bigger than it was. As your spouse responds defensively to you, you are hurt at his unwillingness to face what he has done. Now, you have added a hurtful impasse to the original offense. Both of you now feel justified in your anger, and each is waiting for the other to give in first.

Not allowing the sun to go down on your anger allows a little offense to remain little, it allows big offenses not to collect more and more hurt, and it protects you from the nasty whispers of the enemy, who is a deceiver, a divider, and a destroyer. For us, this meant that we would not go to sleep angry at one another. Sometimes that meant lying in bed, propping our eyes open, and hoping that the other person would ask for forgiveness first! But over the years we learned the protection and benefit that comes from keeping short accounts. So now it is but a few minutes after something wrong has been said or done before we approach one another seeking forgiveness and reconciling once again. We know that we will need to do this until sin no longer remains in us.

When the love relationship you have with the other is so important to you that you are pained when there are problems between you, and you work quickly to make things right, you are building a bond of trust in the relationship. The commitment to keep short accounts tells you that your spouse takes you seriously, tells you that your relationship is important to your spouse, and tells you that your spouse is willing to examine herself out of love for you. This gives you confidence that you can move toward your spouse and not be afraid of what will happen as you entrust yourself to his care. *Do you quickly deal with wrongs and quickly settle your differences?*

Remember That Trust Is War

Why does the Bible warn us not to give way to "enmity, strife, jealousy, fits of anger, rivalries, dissensions, divisions, [and] envy" (Gal. 5:19–21)? Here is the humbling answer to that question. The Bible again and again calls us away from these things because they are all too natural for all of us. As people with sin still living inside us, we are better at making war than we are at making peace. We are better at anger than we are at understanding. It is easier to demand than to forgive. It is easier to live with divisions than it is to reconcile with one another. It is easier to be envious than it is to be grateful.

The call to run from these things reminds us that there is something that still exists inside us that is destructive to relationships. There is something dark inside us that makes us crave our own way. There is something in us that makes "I" more attractive than "we." That something is sin. God's repeated warnings remind us how much we are still in need of help. And, husband, you don't first need to be rescued from your wife. No, these warnings in Scripture remind you that you need to be rescued from you, because if you give way to the sin that still lives inside you, you will never live in a marriage of unity, understanding, and love. And, wife, you don't need to be first rescued from your husband. No, you need to be rescued from you, because if you let the sin inside you have its way, you will destroy any possibility of having a relationship of lasting love with your husband.

The Bible doesn't simply warn you away from these things; it calls you to a new and better way of living together as well. Words such as these picture that new and better way of living: "love, joy, peace, patience, kindness, goodness, faithfulness, gentleness, [and] self-control" (Gal. 5:22–23). These things are hard for us because they pull us beyond the comfortable borders of our strength and wisdom. They ask us in faith to do what is not natural. They call us to take our eyes off ourselves and to focus them on God and others.

Acknowledging the war between these two lists does something very important in your heart. It produces in you a deep need for God's help. It causes you to reach out for the grace that only he can give. It pushes you to seek the grace of rescue, the grace of forgiveness, the grace of wisdom, the grace of enablement, the grace of perseverance, and finally the grace of deliverance. Your need of grace changes the way you respond to your husband or wife. Because you are needy, you aren't judgmental and impatient in the face of your spouse's weakness and failure. No one gives grace better than the person who knows he needs it, as well. The self-righteous person, who thinks he has arrived and has little need for change, tends to look down on the person near him who is weak and failing, and he tends to be quickly irritated and quick to judge.

There is no better seedbed for trust than a humble sense of personal neediness. This creates a lifestyle of understanding and gentleness in your marriage and a desire to change and grow together. *Do you respond to your husband or wife out of a sense of your own heart need?*

Trust: Homeland Security

Trust not only needs to be built, but it needs to be protected. How do you protect the trust that you have built and ensure that the relationship between you and your spouse remains safe and secure? Well, again, the agenda here is pretty simple. First, you need to be committed to talk, talk, and talk. I have been amazed over the years at how little consistent and honest communication goes on between married couples. I think there are many, many couples who simply do not talk. Sure, they discuss the schedule and logistics of their life together, but they do not talk with one another in a heart-disclosing, relationship-protecting way. Sinners living in silence do not produce unity, understanding, and love.

There are also many couples who attempt to talk, but they do it at the wrong time or in the wrong place. The mall is not the place to have a serious conversation about defects in your relationship. Just before your husband leaves the house in the morning is not the optimal time to tell him that you don't think he really loves you. Blurting out one of your wife's foibles when you are hanging out with other couples will probably not result in a productive conversation later.

Constant conversation is the model each of us needs to pursue in our marriage. There is probably never a day free of the need for us to communicate about something that has happened in us or between us. The commitment to communicate tells your spouse that you love her, that you take your relationship seriously, and that you are committed to being open to examine yourself and willing to change. All these things protect the trust that is growing between you.

Second, you must listen, listen, and listen. There are ways in which it is much easier to talk than it is to listen. When your spouse is speaking to you about you, it is very easy to listen more to your inner lawyer than it is to listen to her. You know how it works. The moment you realize that your spouse wants you to look at something you have said or done, it is very easy to slip into defensive mode. As your spouse is speaking, you have already begun to defend yourself against what she is saying, even though you haven't yet said anything in return. Because your mind is occupied with self-defense, you are not hearing her well, even though it may appear like you are listening. When you are doing this, the content you are left with is not so much what she has said to you but your self-defensive twist on what she has attempted to get you to hear and see.

So, listening is not about being passive. Listening is an active commitment. In order to hear your spouse well, you have to fight the battle with your self-righteousness, your tendency to excuse what you have done, and your skill at shifting the blame. Listening is something you have to fight to do.

Along with talking and listening, you need to pray, pray, and pray. In prayer, you thank God for what he has given you (reminding yourself to look around and be grateful), and you reach out for God's help (reminding yourself of your ongoing need for his grace). It is also wonderful for your spouse to hear you pray for him and for God's helping hand for you. I have committed myself to pray these three prayers every morning even before I get out of bed:

"God, I am a man in desperate need of help today."
"I pray that you would send your helpers my way."
"Lord, give me the humility to receive the help when it comes."

So when it comes to that bond of trust between you, there is no room to take it for granted, no room to let things slide, and no room to passively hope for the best. No, you get up every day and you work to protect the good things that God has enabled to grow between you.

Trust: Restoring What's Broken

Sadly, trust is the fine china of a marriage and so it is capable of shattering. Sometimes it is shattered by years and years of small-moment neglect. Sometimes it is shattered by one huge moment of unfaithfulness or betrayal. Whatever the case, you need to know what to do when the trust between you is broken. Here are some vital steps.

1) Admit Your Need

Some couples seem more committed to protecting the reputation of their marriage outside their home than dealing with the real brokenness that exists inside it. When it is clear that trust has been broken, don't allow yourself to deny that it is. Don't compare yourself with other couples who you think are worse off than you. Don't give way to discouragement and allow yourself to be tempted to give in or give up; admit your plight to God and to one another. Honesty about what is broken is the first step to seeing it rebuilt.

2) Get Help

When trust is broken, you are going to need to reach outside your marriage for help. Why? Because you don't trust one another enough to work together and do the things that are necessary to get from where you are to where you need to be. You will need someone to hold you accountable for your commitment to change. You will need someone to help you listen well and speak in a way that is productive. You will need someone who can help you negotiate those places where change is costly, and you will need someone who will work with you in faith, even when your faith is weak.

3) Don't Give Up

When your emotions are frazzled, when your strength is weak, when your hope is dim and your resolve is just about gone, it is very easy to be tempted to cut and run. It is very easy to tell yourself that there is no way out. It is very easy to be cynical, refusing to believe that the other is willing and able to change. It is very easy to begin fantasizing about life on the other side of marriage. It is very easy to go into your shell and turn your home into a motel where two people live, but live without meaningful relationship to one another. There are many people who live in marriages that have long since died. There are husbands and wives who have closed off their feelings and live lonely lives while sharing the same address. There are couples whose relationship has been reduced to perfunctory phone calls, quick text messages, and brief e-mails. There are many couples who have gotten to the point where they don't like one another very much and don't really want to be together but haven't done anything to change the state of their marriage. In a word, most of the people who have given up still live together. It is a painful and discouraging way to live. If your marriage is sick, refuse to let the patient die. Don't give up! Get angry! No, not at your spouse but at the sin, weakness, and failure that has broken your union, and fight these things as the enemies they are.

4) Stick Your Neck Out

Restoring trust means you have to be willing to take risks again. You can't have a relationship without being vulnerable, and you can't be vulnerable without taking risks. Don't say to yourself, "I've been taken once and it won't happen again," but, rather, participate in the restoration of the trust between you. You cannot hide from your spouse while you are working with him or her to rebuild what has been broken. The privacy fences you erect to protect yourself also preclude you from relationship to the person from whom you are seeking protection. At some point, if trust is going to live in your marriage once more, you have to be willing to step out of your bunker into the open and take steps toward your husband or wife. You don't have to do this all at once. Change is more often a process than it is an event. But you must be willing to stick out your neck for trust to be restored.

5) Get Back Up Again

You can be sure that the trust-rebuilding process will not go perfectly. There will be moments of failure. There will be disappointments along the way. There will be moments when you will think that you have made a mistake. There will be times when you will feel that your greatest fears have been realized, that you will never have trust between you again. So, you need to go into rebuilding with realistic expectations. You know you are going to fail at some point, but you also need to know that that failure does not mean you are wasting your time. It simply means that the trust between you is still new and fragile. You need to get back up, address the failure with honesty and grace, and continue to do the good things you have been doing to restore what has been broken.

6) Remember Jesus

When you are working on rebuilding trust, you need to place your hope not in your husband or wife but in the third person in your marriage, the Lord Jesus. He is in with you and for you. As the designer of marriage and the one who brought you together, he has more zeal that your marriage would actually be what he created it to be than you will ever have. He has the wisdom you need. He has the strength you need. He offers the forgiveness you need. And he will not leave you when the going gets tough. Cry out to him; he will never turn a deaf ear to you. Listen to his Word; there is wisdom there that has the power to restore. And when you are discouraged and feel that you are all alone and no one understands, remember Jesus. He suffered rejection and mistreatment. He was not even able to trust his closest companions. On the cross, as he bore our sin, even his Father forsook him. He knows what you are going through, and he is the only one who is ready and able to give you the grace you need as you seek to put the shattered china of your trust together again.

Trust is a beautiful thing when it is the glue that holds a husband and wife together, and it is a sad thing when it is what keeps them apart. Where are you when it comes to trust, and how is God calling you to get from where you are to where he can enable you to be? Don't be willing to live with shattered trust. Your Lord is in the business of restoration and is ready to help you.

Love never dies a natural death. It dies because we don't know how to replenish its source. It dies of blindness and errors and betrayals. It dies of illness and wounds; it dies of weariness, of witherings, of tarnishings.

ANAIS NIN

Love at first sight is easy to understand; it's when two people have been looking at each other for a lifetime that it becomes a miracle.

AMY BLOOM

COMMITMENT 1: We will give ourselves to a regular lifestyle of confession and forgiveness.

COMMITMENT 2: We will make growth and change our daily agenda.

COMMITMENT 3: We will work together to build a sturdy bond of trust.

COMMITMENT 4: We will commit to building a relationship of love.

COMMITMENT 5: We will deal with our differences with appreciation and grace.

COMMITMENT 6: We will work to protect our marriage.

11

All You Need Is Love

When I saw her in the lunch line I was captured right away. For me it was love at first sight. For Luella, it was just first sight! She was not so taken. I spent the next month trying to maneuver my way to a date with her. She finally agreed to go out with me, but she warned me that she was not interested in a relationship. I heard the words, but I didn't really listen to the meaning. We had a wonderful time together; I made her laugh, which was important because she was dealing with a broken heart. Although she told me not to, I asked her out again. She repeated the warning but agreed to go out again. Each time I would ask her to see me again, she would issue the warning but would agree to go. Before long we were seeing one another consistently. In a variety of ways she seemed to be everything I had ever hoped for in a person I would choose to spend my life with. No, we never talked about the future. We were just enjoying one another in the present.

As the weeks and months progressed I became convinced that I loved Luella. I had never felt this way toward anyone before. So I began looking for an opportunity to say those amazing, life-altering words, "I love you." I wanted the moment and the location to be just right. I knew that this was an important moment, and I didn't want to blow it. I finally found what I thought was the perfect moment, and I ventured out and said what I had wanted and waited to say. I looked into Luella's eyes and said, "Luella, I love you." I thought I would hear birds sing and violins play. Luella's response was swift and pointed. She said, "You love me? What do you know about love? Don't ever say that to me again!" I heard birds dying! I heard violins breaking! I couldn't believe it! After all my waiting and planning, she had thrown the words right back at me.

It is humbling to admit, but that evening Luella was right. I was the deeply mature age of seventeen, and I knew little about love. What I thought was love, I would not call love today. It should be obvious since Luella is now my wife that she didn't give up and walk away from me. Our affection for and commitment to one another continued to grow. I will never forget the night when she looked at me and said, "I want to say something to you, Paul: I love you." I responded in kind, and things have not been the same since.

Where Is the Love?

What I am about to say will surprise some of you, but I am convinced it is true. There are many more loveless marriages out there than you and I would tend to think. As a young man, I was very attracted to Luella. I had begun to think of what it would be like to spend my life with her, but I didn't really know what love was. There are many relationships that end in marriage that seem founded on love but really aren't. There is a *love drought* that is causing marriages to dry up all around us. This love drought makes it impossible to have a marriage that is a lifelong relationship of unity and understanding. When it comes to love, we have two problems. First, there are many things we call love that simply do not rise to the level of what love is. And we lack a clear definition of what love is and what love does.

Many couples think it is love that keeps them together, but there are signs that they may be living in the middle of a love drought, and they don't know it. The dynamic is much the same as what happens in your physical body. Perhaps you've had a car accident, and a few days later your knee begins to stiffen. At first, the pain in your knee greets you every morning and distracts you during the day, but before long you get used to it. The stiffness alters the way you walk, and at first you are very aware that you are limping, but before very long your limp just becomes the way you walk. In fact, at some point you are not aware that you are limping at all. What was once pain has morphed into the normal way your knee feels, and what was once a limp morphs into your normal gait. You don't feel hampered or crippled by your knee, and you seem to get around quite well. Then an old friend whom you haven't seen in ages visits you and immediately says, "You're limping; what happened to your leg?" It is then that you realize that your normal isn't actually normal.

We are all rocked to sleep by the regularity. The things you see and experience over and over again tend to be the things that at some point you quit noticing. If you drive to work the same way every day, I imagine there are sights and sounds that you no longer see and no longer hear. You have been lolled into inattention by the daily regularity of what you are seeing and hearing. If you live in the city, at some point you quit being distracted by the people and the traffic that is on the other side of your walls. Maybe the first few nights in your city house were sleepless because of all the noise, but now you don't feel that you live in a noisy neighborhood. Now, you know that your block hasn't suddenly become very quiet. No, you have changed. The regularity of the noisiness has made noisy your normal, so much so that you do not hear the noise anymore. You're not irritated or distracted by the noise anymore for one significant reason: you don't hear it anymore. Someone comes to spend a weekend with you in your loft in the city, and in the morning they say, "Is it always this noisy at night?" You're thinking, "I don't really think it's that bad." What is abnormal has become so normal to you that you live right smack-dab in the middle of it, and you neither see nor hear it.

There are many couples in the same situation in their marriages. They think their marriage is okay. They would say they think they have a pretty normal marriage, but they think this because what should be abnormal to them became so regular that it became the new normal, and when it did, they quit seeing and hearing it. The problem for these couples is not that they are dissatisfied with their marriage. No, their problem is that they are all too satisfied with something that falls way short of what God designed a normal marriage to be. They are limping through the noise of a broken marriage, and they don't even know it.

Many of us are way too skilled at living with plan B. We are all too good at painting over cracked walls, at working around broken plumbing, and at rigging dysfunctional wiring. We are all too good at getting along, making do, and hoping for the best. We are all too good at talking ourselves into the belief that things will get better, that our problems aren't really that big, and that we are better off than many couples. We are all too skilled at living with less and thinking it's more. When we do this, we don't look for help and we don't work for change. Rather than fixing what is broken, we have learned to live with it as if it's not. We are not moved to seek help because we don't really see the places where help is needed anymore. We are comfortable when we should be concerned. We are passive when we should be active. We are satisfied when we should be dissatisfied. We get up each day and make things work the best we can, but our best falls way short of God's best.

That is the value of a book like this one. Perhaps this book will help you hear again, see again, hunger again, and hope again. Perhaps this book will give you windows to look through that will help you to see your marriage with clarity and accuracy. Perhaps you will see things that you have not seen for a long time, and God will use that to ignite new desire and a renewed commitment to change. Perhaps this will begin a process of redeeming the realities of your marriage.

So, what are the markers of a lack of living, active love in your marriage? Let me give you several things that are indicators of a love drought.

Disunity. Jacob and Erin could not have been more different from one another. It was simply a fact of their married life. But those differences were what attracted them to one another and initially made their relationship exciting, personally enhancing, and complete. Jacob was a straight-down-the-middle Midwestern boy—no compromises, no deals. Erin was raised in Hawaii by back-to-earth, counterculture parents. Jacob and Erin woke up on different sides of the universe each morning, yet they had contributed to substantial growth and change in one another. But now, theirs was a house divided. It didn't take much for them to disagree, for the disagreement to escalate into an argument, and for the argument to result in another stalemate. It was frustrating and exhausting for them both.

Now maybe you're thinking, "Of course they disagree, Paul; they have nothing in common!" But an important point needs to be made here. It is that unity is not the product of sameness. Remember, the God who made lilies also made rocks. As creator, God has invested his world with difference; all things are not the same. He has made people widely

170

different from one another. All this reflects his glory. And as sovereign, he chooses to bring different people into intimate relationship with one another for his honor and their good. Unity is not the result of sameness. Rather, unity results when love intersects with difference.

It is self-love that hates difference. It is self-love that makes you impatient. It is self-love that makes you want your own way. It is self-love that convinces you that your way is the right way. It is self-love that makes winning more attractive than unity. Love celebrates who God has made the other person to be. Love celebrates the process of working together to become one. Love celebrates the grace of change that operates in the middle of the difficulty of difference. Love prizes unity and is willing to make sacrifices to achieve it. Love turns difference into an opportunity to experience a deeper and fuller unity. Love isn't impatient, and it does not walk away. Love perseveres. Love stays active until what God has planned becomes your actual experience. Love listens, works, and waits. Unity happens when love intersects with difference. *Is the unity of your marriage growing?*

Misunderstanding. Melissa and Randy lived a lifestyle of misunderstanding. They had so many "But I thought you said . . ." "No, I didn't" conversations that they had gotten to the place where they dreaded talking to one another and expected misunderstanding when they were finished. Little things became big, confusing things. Plans that looked simple became convoluted and complicated. There was so much misunderstanding between them that even their moments of agreement turned out to be disagreements. No, Randy and Melissa didn't need a course in communication; they needed a functional commitment of love. You see, a lifestyle of misunderstanding is a sure sign of a lack of love.

It is self-love that makes you more committed to what you understand than to understanding your spouse. It is self-love that causes you not to listen well. It is self-love that makes you unwilling to wait until you are sure that you have understood your spouse. It is self-love that keeps you from viewing your spouse's words, perspectives, desires, and opinions as valuable. It is self-love that fills your brain so full of what you think and know that you have little room for your spouse's thoughts. It is self-love that makes you value your own way more than you value real functional understanding existing between you and your mate.

Love longs for the two of you to be on the same page. Love is willing to pay the daily sacrifice that it takes to reach real understanding. Love values the words of the other person. Love celebrates the process of understanding, as much as the result. Love prizes a lifestyle of peace because it not only honors God, but it honors the person that he designed to journey with you. *Do you live together in the joy of street-level understanding?*

Separation. It was more 1960s Cold War for Jimmy and Gayle than actual peace. No, they hardly ever disagreed and they hardly ever fought. Jimmy was content with the way things were. Gayle left him to himself, and he was not about to trouble trouble until trouble troubled him. Gayle enjoyed the lack of conflict, but she was far from being satisfied. She knew that what she and Jimmy enjoyed was not really a marriage in the true sense of what that means. Sure, they could have logistical planning and scheduling conversations. They could handle getting something to eat and going to a movie. But they didn't really have a relationship. They had détente. They hadn't grown closer and more unified. They hadn't worked to forge a relational lifestyle. No, they had become tired of the little skirmishes and the all-out wars. They got tired of going to bed angry and waking up with acrimony. So, they forged a silent conspiracy. They conspired to live together, but separately. They became masters at giving one another a wide swath of space, and they studiously avoided any topic that would take them down the pathway of potential difference. From the outside it looked as though they had a good marriage, but a marriage is exactly what they didn't have. What they had was a peacefully avoidant lifestyle of cohabitation.

Love will always find this kind of separation unacceptable and painful. Love is motivated by what a deep privilege it is to have someone to love and to receive love. Love thrives when the call is to build the relationship even stronger. Love is willing to make the painful sacrifices that togetherness always demands. Love understands that cohabitation is a location, not a relational goal. Love will not rest until we can rest in one another's arms and experience rest. *Is your marriage more a picture of cohabitation than it is of relationship?*

Physical dysfunction. Any real sexual relationship between George and Jeanne had long since died. They had guilt-ridden, obligatory sex every couple of months, and even that was beginning to die. Jeanne wanted to be excited about being with George, but she wasn't. She dreaded the cold and impersonal sex that lacked true intimacy and was over quickly. There were times when Jeanne felt that George was having sex with her but using it as a tool of masturbation. She felt guilt when she thought this way, but she knew for sure that what they experienced in the bed had nothing to do with love. She knew that George did not find her attractive and alluring, and she didn't find herself physically drawn to him either. It is a tragedy when sex has little to do with love.

As I told their story, you knew that Jeanne and George needed something more than a better understanding of physical sexuality. I must admit, once more, that I am tired of Christian, body-part books. It's as if we think that the many, many couples who are experiencing sexual dysfunction are doing so because they don't know where their body stuff is. Seldom is the problem as simple as a lack of understanding of physical sexuality. No, what diverts and destroys physical sexuality is a lack of love. If your spouse hasn't loved you outside the marriage bed, why would you think that she would love you when you are in the marriage bed? If she has been impatient and selfish with you on a regular basis, wouldn't it make sense for you to expect that she would do the same when you are having sex? If your relationship isn't a daily act of love, there is little chance that sex will be.

Love lives in awe of the holiness of the sexual relationship in marriage. Love finds joy in your comfort, satisfaction, and safety. Love will serve you and not use you. Love finds more excitement with giving than receiving. Love enjoys the unique vulnerability of the nakedness of the marriage bed and takes care that this vulnerability is never demanding or dangerous. Love sees sex as an act and celebration of the relationship of self-sacrificing love that the marriage is all about. Love knows that you never escape the true quality and character of your relationship when you are naked and in one another's arms. Love turns sexual difficulty into an occasion to give and share a deeper love. Love celebrates the Creator's design and in so doing is respectful of your body and the way it operates. Love seduces you in a way that honors you and does not turn you into an object of autoerotic satisfaction. Love is willing to wait so that together you can be fulfilled. Love gives and serves even when the heart is excited and the body stimulated. In the marriage bed, love loves. *Is your sexual relationship a picture of patient, self-sacrificing love?*

Conflict. Selena and Jose knew how to fight. They did it with frequency and skill. They knew what weapons to use against one another, and they used them well. Selena was susceptible to carrying around way too much guilt, so Jose knew he could win his battles with her by making her feel guilty. Jose was a romantic, so Selena would withhold romance in order to win the latest battle. No one could spend much time with Selena and Jose without watching them skirmish. It didn't take much for conflict to explode, and each of them seemed committed to whatever was necessary to win. It wasn't always this way. There had been a time when both of them would be upset that they had allowed themselves to get into a fight. Now, it seemed conflict was more typical than peace and division more regular than forgiveness.

Peace is a beautiful and sought-after thing for a person committed to a lifestyle of love. When you love someone, you are pained when things separate and divide you. When you love someone, you are willing to overlook minor weaknesses, irritations, and offenses, because you do not want anything to interrupt your life together. When you love someone, real lasting peace is more valuable to you than being right or being in control. When you love someone, you are willing to forgive, serve, wait, listen, consider, examine yourself and your motives, and make personal sacrifices—all things that create and build peace in a relationship. If conflict between you and your spouse does not cause you grief, what is being exposed is a failure to love. Love loves peace and hates conflict. *In your marriage, do you hate conflict and do you work in whatever way you can to create peace?*

Watch Out for Faux Love

When you commit to examine the quality of the love in your marriage, it is important to realize that counterfeit love wears convincing masks.

Physical attraction is an amazing thing. God displays his creative glory in ten thousand different forms of human beauty. God displays his creative glory in giving us an endless variety of tastes when it comes to beauty. We all don't look the same, and we all don't look at each other the same way. We see beauty in different ways and are attracted to different people as a result. Physical beauty is a powerful attraction because it is physical. We live in a material world, so physical beauty is one of the things we all care about in some way. Physical attraction is not in itself wrong or dangerous. Perhaps it is the first thing that connects us. If someone is physically repulsive to you, the relationship will probably not last very long. The initial buzz of physical attraction has a very short shelf life.

Yes, it is scary but true that people do get into serious relationships and even marriage based on physical attraction. You are drawn to someone because of her beauty. You want to be near her and with her, just like you want to own the beautiful painting you saw at the art fair. You may even be fantasizing about life with her before you have gotten to know her. This is how powerful the draw of physical attraction can be. You may even have allowed yourself more physical contact with her than is appropriate before marriage, thereby deepening the physical attraction. You may think you love this person, but you don't really. No, what you love is her physical beauty. What you think is love is self-love in the mask of true love. You want to be with her not because you love her, but because you love yourself and you want to decorate your life with her physical beauty. Now, I know this sounds harsh, but I think many couples have fallen into this trap.

Physical beauty gets normalized in marriage. You wake up that first morning to a person with baboon breath and rat's-nest hair and you wonder what attracted you so. He falls out of bed and puts on rumpled and stained sweats and stumbles to the bathroom and makes sounds you'd rather not hear. Then it hits you: you married a fantasy, but you got the real person. Real people have imperfect bodies. Real people grow warts, gain weight, and get old. Marriages built on physical attraction always lead to disappointment.

An emotional connection with a man or woman is an exciting thing. To find someone that you can relate to, talk to, and feel comfortable with is fun and fulfilling. Who wouldn't want to experience this? It's fun to be able to talk without ever feeling one of those uncomfortable periods of silence while you're searching for the next possible topic. It's enjoyable to be able to relate to what the other one is experiencing and feeling. It is nice to have your personalities complement one another. It's nice when you think and feel the same way about things. It's enjoyable when you are in a relationship relatively free of stress and tension. It's good to be able to anticipate how the other will respond and react to something that you will share together.

In marriage this emotional connectivity is important. You cannot have a long-term relationship with a person who is never on the same emotional page as you. But you can have all of this and not have love. The opposite could be said as well. You can have a relationship where the emotional connection between the man and woman was not natural and spontaneous, where it took much more work to connect in that way, but where a solid relationship of true love developed. Emotional connection is powerful and enjoyable, but the powerful thing you are experiencing may not be love.

Here is the point: like physical attraction, emotional connection can actually be self-love wearing the mask of true love. Could it be that you are powerfully attracted to someone because he is easy and enjoyable to be with? Being with him doesn't take a lot of commitment or effort because you are so emotionally alike. Maybe you are attracted to him not because you have come to love him, but because you love yourself, and he is comfortable to be with, and you are drawn to the effortlessness of the relationship. Let's be honest. Most of us don't enjoy hard work and will avoid it if possible. I think this tendency to work-avoidance and ease-attraction has gotten many marriages off on the wrong foot by convincing couples that they are experiencing love when what they are really experiencing is faux love.

Spiritual unity is even trickier. It is essential that a husband and wife have spiritual unity. This unity is first based on the fact that they are both members of God's family and therefore indwelt by the same Spirit. But this unity is more than that; it is unity of biblical worldview, of theological persuasion, and of Christian experience. It is very power-ful when you are around someone who shares deeply held theological beliefs with you. It is very powerful when you are with someone who seeks in every way to look at life through the lens of Scripture. It is very powerful to be with someone as God is making his Word understand-able and relevant to you both. It is very powerful to be in services of worship where you are led to celebrate God's life-changing grace. These things create a connection and a unity that is like no other. To share the same values and to prize the same experiences is a sweet thing. To be connected to someone who takes his or her faith as seriously as you do is comforting and attractive. To be able to fellowship in the stunning wisdom of the Word of God together is an experience that must not be taken for granted.

All these things are good things, but they are things that you could probably experience with many believers. You can share a platform of spiritual values with someone you don't actually love in the full sense of what love is and does. This will trouble some of you, but it must be said: the powerful attraction of spiritual zeal and unity may not be love; it may actually be self-love in the mask of true love.

I can't number how many women I have counseled who married men because they were attracted to their "spirituality," their biblical literacy and their theological knowledge, only to sadly come to realize that the men didn't love them. Their future husbands were attracted to them because they shared a platform of spiritual unity that may make building a relationship a lot less work than it otherwise would be. And in almost every situation, the men were drawn by the way the women looked up to them as a theological mentor. But when the women demonstrated that they are sinners and not always willing students and the men showed that they love the theology of the women more than they do the women, the house of cards came crashing down.

Culture is a huge issue in marriage. You always drag your familial and cultural influences into the development of a relationship and ultimately into your marriage. God has crafted locations, situations, and relationships for you that have formed your cultural instincts and tastes. You have certain likes and dislikes (food, clothing, entertainment, etc.). There are experiences in life that have formed your sense of what is important and what is not, what is enjoyable and what is not, what is beautiful and what is not. You come to every relationship you have with certain assumptions about what is proper and to be expected. You have a certain definition of father, brother, sister, friend, worker, neighbor, boss, etc. Your wardrobe and your decorating both reflect enculturation.

We carry with us differing definitions of what is polite and what is not, what is tasteful and what is not, what is expensive and what is not, what is casual and what is dressy, what should be public and what should be private, and the list could go on and on. So you bring to your potential partner a whole set of assumptions and unspoken rules. Even though you may not be conscious of it, these exist in every area of your life. They become one of the lenses through which you look to evaluate the people in your life, so it is very compelling when you are in a relationship with someone and you share the same assumptions, expectations, and unspoken rules. It is hard not to be drawn to that person, and it is tempting to mistake your cultural unity and the attraction it creates as love.

Once again, the powerful attraction of cultural continuity may feel like love, but it may actually be self-love masquerading as love. Perhaps you are drawn to your spouse not because you love her, but because you love yourself, and you are stunned by how much she agrees with you. She is attractive to you because she thinks you are right about life as much as you think you are, and you find this to be a very attractive thing. Perhaps you don't actually love him. Perhaps what you love is the similarity of your cultural assumptions. This too will almost always be challenged in marriage as you come to realize that you are not clones of one another and you are faced with the reality that there are many places where you disagree and look at life differently. Again, what looks like love may be just another compelling form of faux love.

A Love Story

It had all come crashing down, and Chris and Sarah didn't know why. It began with Sarah complaining about Chris's silence and distance. Things had changed. Chris would come home from work and go to his office. Sure, he would say hello but not much else, and he would quickly retire to his nightly retreat. They had simply stopped talking except for the necessary conversations about plans, bills, and schedules. Sarah went to Chris more than once to talk to him about his withdrawal, but he would always assure her that he loved her and that everything was all right.

Chris was tired of being controlled, but every time he tried to talk with Sarah about it she would get emotional and shut down the conversation. It wasn't that Sarah was mean; it was just that she had to be in charge of everything. Chris felt that he was being smothered, but he told himself he would deal with it, that he loved Sarah too much to mess up their marriage.

Little irritations quickly began to morph into big arguments. Today's incident became the occasion for dredging up last week's or last month's hurt. Hurt and bitterness caused simple conversations to be nasty and complicated. Both Sarah and Chris carried anger and defensiveness into each conversation. Each argument went over the same ground. Sarah would accuse Chris of being cold, uncaring, and distant, and Chris would tell Sarah that she was the most domineering person he had ever known. Each was good at self-defense while repeating the same lengthy list of accusations against the other. And together they had become exhausted and discouraged with it all. For Chris that meant even more withdrawal, and for Sarah it meant that she was on Chris even more, telling him again and again that something had to change. Chris's withdrawal activated Sarah, and her activism drove Chris into hiding.

No, neither one of them had been unfaithful, and their arguments had never become physically violent, but they both wondered if they had made a huge mistake. Chris sat one Tuesday night at his desk in his office and realized that he had been staring at his flickering laptop for a long time. When he came to and realized what he had been thinking about, his thoughts scared him. For the first time, he had been fantasizing about what life would be like without Sarah. It sobered him that thoughts of being single would be so comfortable and attractive, but they were. No, he wasn't going to leave Sarah and file for divorce, but he did feel smothered, and he didn't know how in the world he was going to find what he needed to go on.

Sarah had hit a similar moment, but it was when she was with one of her friends. Jenny had asked Sarah if she could break away for lunch, and since it was such a nice day they decided get a sandwich and sit in the park. When Jenny asked Sarah how she was doing, it all came blurting out. Sarah talked of Chris's distance and of her discouragement. She told Jenny she just didn't think she could go on. She talked of how she dreaded the moment Chris would come through the door each night because it would mean either painful silence or another one of those horrible arguments. She said she tried to "make nice" but it never worked. Jenny looked into the face of a despondent and exhausted woman and looked for the right thing to say.

No one who knew Sarah and Chris had a clue. People in their small group noticed that they weren't as affectionate as they had once been, but they also weren't newlyweds anymore. They never fought in public and always managed to treat one another with polite respect when others were around. They stayed faithful to their church, and Chris continued to teach the Sunday school class he had taught for years. Sarah continued to go to the nursing home every other week. She loved her time with the old folks, and they loved her guitar and sweet voice. Sarah and Chris managed to cooperate with one another during the holidays when extended family was around, and they worked to limit their skirmishes in front of the children. From a distance their marriage looked much better than it was. The public smiles did not remove the private pain.

As I listened to their story, I knew I was going to have to say something to Chris and Sarah that would be hard to hear. They were going to have to face the fact that they were now harvesting seeds that they had planted. Let me explain.

Sarah met Chris during her last year of college. She remembers the moment very well. She was leafing through her mail in front of the bank of mailboxes near her dorm. He walked up to talk to the person next to her. It was an embarrassing but fateful moment. Sarah was so distracted by Chris that she dropped most of her mail at his feet. They both spontaneously bent down to pick up the mess and bumped heads. Then, laughing at what happened, they said hello and began to talk. Sarah said she was taken by what a beautiful human being Chris was. He was tall and handsome and didn't seem to take himself too seriously. They decided to get together later that week for coffee. Sarah was blown away when, in that first conversation over coffee, she realized that Chris was a Christian and, like her, had been raised in the Midwest. He was talkative, and she was the type who loved to listen. He was athletic, and she loved the outdoors. He loved good food, and she loved to cook. He loved movies, and so did she. He was from a small town, and so was she. He liked coffee—what else could she ask for?

It seemed so perfect. Their times together were comfortable and easy. This was the man Sarah had been searching for. Chris fit her life like a glove. He was physically attractive, fun to be with, spiritually in tune, and seemed like a guy who was going somewhere. Sarah couldn't be with Chris enough, and it wasn't long before she was making mental plans for their future. She knew Chris was the one, and she was going to make sure she would not lose him.

Chris liked the fact that Sarah and he had similar backgrounds. He felt she would have a natural sense of "where he was coming from." He liked the fact that Sarah was decisive. This was a woman who knew what she wanted. He liked the fact that there weren't many surprises with Sarah. She said what she thought and what she wanted. With a common background, shared interests, and that all-important spiritual connection, it seemed that Sarah really could be the one. Chris was in no hurry, but he really did like Sarah, and she seemed ready to make a lifelong commitment any time.

So six months later, on a cold winter afternoon, Chris popped the question. Sarah was in a daze with joy and managed to say yes about thirty-four times before Chris gave her the kiss of her life. Immediately Sarah began to make plans. She knew just what their wedding should be like and just the kind of house they would need to live in. She told Chris that he needed to find a job in a small town so that they could experience together the life they had both enjoyed growing up. Chris thought it was funny that Sarah was so focused and driven, and he teased her about planning their entire life in about three days.

They married the day after graduation, moved to small-town Ohio, and began their life together. Children and promotions came quickly, but their relationship quit being comfortable. Chris worked long, hard hours and spent most of his evenings and weekends exhausted. He didn't have much free time, but he loved hunting, fishing, and golfing with his friends. He also loved blogging and keeping up every day with the blogs that he had become hooked on. Chris wasn't very domestic. It wasn't that he refused to help. No, what began to bother Sarah was that he never volunteered to help.

Sarah loved her three children, but it was hard work. She felt that she had less and less time with her friends and that Chris and she had little time together. She also resented the fact that Chris seemed to think that the entire house was her job. She always had a list of projects for him to complete, but he took his good time getting around to them. Sarah felt that she had a house guest instead of a husband, and Chris felt that he had a home superintendent instead of a wife. Chris was growing tired of Sarah's demands, and Sarah was done with feeling that she lived alone.

Both Sarah and Chris couldn't help wondering what had happened. It all seemed so easy and so perfect. It had seemed as though their dreams were coming true. How did they end up in such a discouraging mess? There is but one answer to this question. It is hard to accept but vital to face. Sarah and Chris had a major love drought in their marriage because very early in their relationship they had confused faux love with true love.

It was devastatingly hard for Sarah to admit it, but she finally did: she had married Chris not because she loved him but because she loved herself. Physical attraction, emotional connection, and cultural and spiritual unity were what drew her in. She was drawn to Chris because he was everything she had ever wanted for her life. Her attraction to him was powerful and compelling. He could not have fit more perfectly into Sarah's dream for her life. Sarah's attraction to Chris was all about what Sarah wanted for Sarah. What masqueraded as love wasn't love.

It was also hard for Chris to admit that he had been drawn to Sarah because she made things so easy. She seemed to like Chris for who he was, and she made all the plans for him. Chris was able to coast his way into a great relationship; he thought he had hit the jackpot! But he didn't get married because he loved Sarah in the true sense of what that means. No, Chris loved what Sarah did for him and his life. Faux love wore the mask of true love, and Chris had been completely fooled.

The lack of unity, the constant misunderstandings, the distance and separation between them, the lack of physical intimacy, and the catalog of regular conflicts were screaming loud and clear that what was missing in Chris and Sarah's marriage was love—real, other-centered, self-sacrificing love.

Things began to go wrong when their relationship quit being self-satisfying and the need for other-serving became dominant. When the hard work, which faithful love requires, began, Chris and Sarah got discouraged and began pointing fingers of blame. The sad reality that they had to face and confess was that their relationship had not been built on a foundation of love. It had been built on the weakest and most impermanent of relational foundations—self-focus and self-love.

They had never really considered the hardship of a flawed person living with a flawed person. They had never considered the daily and costly sacrifices that are necessary to make a long-term marriage work. They didn't think about what they were being called to give to one another. No, what occupied their minds was what they were being given by the other. So their marriage was doomed to fail, because there is no such thing as a good marriage that is not fueled by love, and there is no such thing as love that does not require personal sacrifice. Selfish ambitions and unrealistic expectations had set them up for the discouraging moment that they were now in.

But this sad moment was a moment of wonderful, God-given, grace-infused opportunity. It was God, in love, who had brought Sarah and Chris to the end of themselves. It was God who had provided resources of help for them. God knew that until they gave up on the old way, the new way would not be attractive to them. Theirs was not a story of hopelessness and abandonment, but of persevering and transforming grace. It is an understatement to say it was a moving moment when Sarah looked at Chris and confessed that she had never loved him in the full sense of what that meant. And it was equally beautiful to hear Chris confess the same.

I was greatly privileged to witness this couple begin to love one another for the very first time, and in so doing to set their marriage on a new and better course.

What about you? Could there be a love drought in your marriage? Could it be that what you have called love is not really love? Could it be that God is bringing you to the end of yourselves so that you will look at yourselves with new eyes and seek the help that only he can give? Could it be that a brand-new commitment in love is what is needed for you to experience a brand-new beginning for your marriage?

If you are God's children, then like Chris and Sarah you are not alone, and this means there is hope no matter how big the love drought is in your marriage.

COMMITMENT 1:	We will give ourselves to a regular lifestyle of confession and forgiveness.
COMMITMENT 2:	We will make growth and change our daily agenda.
COMMITMENT 3:	We will work together to build a sturdy bond of trust.
COMMITMENT 4:	**We will commit to building a relationship of love.**
COMMITMENT 5:	We will deal with our differences with appreciation and grace.
COMMITMENT 6:	We will work to protect our marriage.

12

Ready, Willing, and Waiting

Ted thought he was ready, willing, and waiting to love Katie, and because of this he was excited to get married. People around them told them not to rush, that there was wisdom in waiting, but Ted didn't want to wait, and neither did Katie. They were both convinced they were ready. Ted was persuaded that there was no way he could love Katie more than he already did. He was convinced that there was nothing he would not be willing to do for her. And anyway, he told himself, Katie was easy to love.

Ted told himself that he was ready, willing, and waiting, but he really wasn't. As he looked forward to marriage he thought of it as an extended date. I am afraid that many people do. He had found Katie easy to be with on the many evenings they had spent together. He had found going to church and spending Sunday together to be comfortably enjoyable. The Christmas vacations Katie and he had spent together and the week they had spent at the shore with her family had left little behind but a pile of fond memories.

Sure, Ted knew Katie wasn't perfect. She was a bit of a perfectionist, and there were times she could be pretty stubborn. And he knew that he wasn't always the most patient guy on the block. But he loved Katie so much, and they had managed to get along pretty well so far, so he didn't think that being married would be that much of a struggle.

Ted told himself that he was ready, willing, and waiting to love his future wife forever, but he wasn't. It wasn't long after their wedding that he began to be driven crazy by Katie's tendency to follow behind him and clean up after him as he went. He struggled with her digging in and refusing to admit that she was wrong, even when it was clear that she was. He struggled with the reality that he had no independence left. He resented having to discuss everything with Katie. He felt that he had fallen in love with his girlfriend and ended up marrying his mother.

Ted loved being around Katie, but he felt smothered. When they were dating, their relationship didn't seem like work. Sure, there were times when they did or said dumb things and would have to work through their hurt and seek one another's forgiveness, but those times were rare. Ted began to feel that his marriage was more work than love, more struggle than companionship, and more something to face than something to enjoy.

A breakthrough came one morning, when in a burst of frustration Ted said, "If this is love, then I don't have any idea of what love is." Katie was devastated. She had never questioned Ted's love and had minimized the evidence she had encountered of his struggle. She too had told herself that they would be all right because they really did love one another. The problem was that neither Ted nor Katie knew what love is and what love does. They confused the enjoyment of shared experiences as love. They had confused physical attraction and romantic affection with love. They had confused brief moments of patience with love's long-term commitment to sacrifice. They thought it would be easy because they were in love and failed to understand that love wouldn't protect them from disappointment and struggles but would provide what they needed in the middle of it.

What was devastating to Katie was really a bright moment of turning for Ted. He was right. He didn't know what love is, and he was tired and needy—just the things he needed to be. Ted needed help, but he had to come to the place where he admitted that he needed help. He was about to reach out for help and find out what love is and what love does, and it would change him and his marriage forever.

What in the World Is Love Anyway?

Ted learned quickly that you don't get your best definition from a Web article on love. You don't get it from Wikipedia or from Dictionary.com. You don't get your best definition of love from Webster or Shakespeare.

The reality is that love is not best defined by a set of abstract concepts. Love is best defined by an event. Let me explain.

There are few discussions in Scripture of what love is that are more helpful and more practical than the words found in 1 John 4:

> Beloved, let us love one another, for love is from God, and whoever loves has been born of God and knows God. Anyone who does not love does not know God, because God is love. In this the love of God was made manifest among us, that God sent his only Son into the world, so that we might live through him. In this is love, not that we have loved God, but that he loved us and sent his Son to be the propitiation for our sins. Beloved, if God so loved us, we also ought to love one another. No one has ever seen God; if we love one another, God abides in us and his love is perfected in us. . . .
>
> God is love, and whoever abides in love abides in God, and God abides in him. By this is love perfected with us, so that we may have confidence for the day of judgment, because as he is so also are we in this world. There is no fear in love, but perfect love casts out fear. For fear has to do with punishment, and whoever fears has not been perfected in love. We love because he first loved us. If anyone says, "I love God," and hates his brother, he is a liar; for he who does not love his brother whom he has seen cannot love God whom he has not seen. And this commandment we have from him: whoever loves God must also love his brother. (1 John 4:7–12, 16b–21)

This passage tells us where we get our best definition of love. You get your best definition of love from an event, the most important event in human history. You get your best definition of love from the cross of the Lord Jesus Christ. Christ's sacrifice of love is the ultimate definition of what love is and what love does. In this passage John is calling us to *cruciform* love, that is, love that shapes itself to the cross of the Lord Jesus Christ (*cruci* = "cross" and *form* = "in the shape of").

Look at the words of verses 10 and 11: "In this is love, not that we have loved God but that he loved us and sent his Son to be the propitiation for our sins. Beloved, if God so loved us, we also ought to love one another." When it comes to love, the cross of Jesus Christ is our ultimate example. John says it clearly: if Jesus loved us in this way, in the same way we ought to love one another.

So what does *cruciform* love look like? Let me give you a definition and then unpack it. *Love is willing self-sacrifice for the good of another that does not require reciprocation or that the person being loved is deserving.*

Love is **willing**. Jesus said, "No one takes [my life] from me, but I lay it down of my own accord" (John 10:18). The decisions, words, and actions of love always grow in the soil of a willing heart. You cannot force a person to love. If you are forcing someone to love, by the very nature of the act you are demonstrating that this person doesn't in fact love.

Love is willing **self-sacrifice**. There is no such thing as love without sacrifice. Love calls you beyond the borders of your own wants, needs, and feelings. Love calls you to be willing to invest time, energy, money, resources, personal ability, and gifts for the good of another. Love calls you to lay down your life in ways that are concrete and specific. Love calls you to serve, to wait, to give, to suffer, to forgive, and to do all these things again and again.

Love calls you to be silent when you want to speak, and to speak when you would like to be silent. Love calls you to act when you would really like to wait, and to wait when you would really like to act. Love calls you to stop when you really want to continue, and it calls you to continue when you feel like stopping. Love requires you to lead when you really would like to follow, and to follow when you really want to lead. Love again and again calls you away from your instincts and your comfort. Love always requires personal sacrifice. Love calls you to give up your life.

Love is willing self-sacrifice **for the good of another**. Love always has the good of another in view. Love is motivated by the interests and needs of others. Love is excited at the prospect of alleviating burdens and meeting needs. Love feels poor when the loved one is poor. Love suffers when the loved one suffers. Love wants the best for the loved one and works to deliver it.

Love is willing self-sacrifice for the good of another **that does not require reciprocation**. The Bible says that Jesus died for us while we were still sinners. If he had waited until we were able to reciprocate, there would be no hope for us. Love isn't a "you scratch my back and

I'll scratch yours" bargain. Love isn't about placing people in our debt and waiting for them to pay off their debts. Love isn't a negotiation for mutual good. Real love does not demand reciprocation, because real love isn't motivated by the return on the investment. No, real love is motivated by the good that will result in the life of the person being loved.

Love is willing self-sacrifice for the good of another that does not require reciprocation or that the person being loved **is deserving**. Christ was willing to go to the cross and carry our sin precisely because there was nothing that we could ever do to earn, achieve, or deserve the love of God. If you are interested only in loving people who are deserving, the reality is that you are not motivated by love for them but by love for yourself. Love does its best work when the other person is undeserving. It is in these moments that love is most needed. It is in these moments that love is protective and preventative. It stays the course while refusing to quit or to get down and get dirty and give way to things that are anything but love.

There is never a day in your marriage when you aren't called to be willing. There is never a day in your marriage when some personal sacrifice is not needed. There is never a day when you are free from the need to consider the good of your husband or wife. There is never a day when you aren't called to do what is not reciprocated and to offer what has not been deserved. There is never a day when your marriage can coast along without being infused by this kind of love.

Now, maybe you're thinking, "Paul, where in the world do I get this kind of love?" John answers the question for us. "We love because he first loved us" (1 John 4:19). These words carry a rich content of many things, but one of the things surely meant by these words is that true love doesn't best grow out of the soil of duty. No, true love grows out of the nutrient soil of gratitude.

Imagine me plopping down on the couch next to my wife and with a stern, unexcited, sadly flat, and monotone voice saying to her, "Luella, I have come to the understanding that it is my responsibility to love you. So I am going to do my duty. I am going to love you because that is what I am supposed to do." Do you think Luella would throw her arms around me and say, "Thank you, thank you for loving me so!" No, she would be heartbroken because she would instinctively know that what I have expressed is not love.

Love is not born through begrudgingly succumbing to duty. No, love is born out of remembering and celebrating. When I remember the lavish, faithful, patient, forgiving, and empowering love that has been poured on me—that I could never have earned and will never be able to fully reciprocate—I will want to give that love away to someone else. When I wake up in the morning and—although my bills are not all paid, and my house needs work, and my children are a bit of a mess, and my husband or wife is less than perfect—I am filled with gratefulness that love has been poured down on me that has changed me and my life forever, then I am motivated to look for opportunities to be a tool of that kind of love in the life of the person whom God has given me as my lifelong companion.

Perhaps one of the most unrecognized sins in marriage is the sin of forgetfulness. When we forget how we have been loved, it becomes even easier to be comfortable with a failure to love others. No one loves better than the person who knows that he desperately needs it himself.

John says one more thing that is very powerful while being ground-level practical, as well: "If anyone says, 'I love God,' and hates his brother, he is a liar; for he who does not love his brother whom he has seen cannot love God whom he has not seen" (v. 20). John is saying that if you want to know the true character and quality of your love for God, examine the quality of your relationship with the person near to you. Your love for your husband or wife is a very accurate barometer of your true love for God.

But these words mean something more. These words call us to face the fact that we must fix our marriages vertically before we ever fix them horizontally. Why? Consider my own marriage. My core problem is not that I don't love Luella enough. No, my problem is that I don't love God enough, and because I don't love God enough, I don't love Luella as I should.

When I fail to love God as I should, I insert myself into his position, desiring to be sovereign over my little kingdom of one and demanding that those around me do my bidding. If I am not loving God as my king, I will set up my own kingdom and live for myself.

I would ask you, right here in this place in the book, "Is your marriage fueled, moved, and motivated by real God-worshiping, other-focused, self-giving, willing love? Have you made and are you living out this commitment? Where do you need to seek forgiveness and commit yourself to a new and better way?" Perhaps what comes next will help you to answer.

Marital Love in Action

Even with all my zeal to carefully define *cruciform* love in the context of a marriage, you may still be fuzzy as to what this kind of love looks like at ground level. Here are some concrete descriptions of how real, Christlike love thinks and acts. As you read, I invite you to use these words as a mirror to look into and examine the quality of your love for your husband or wife.

Love is being willing to have your life complicated by the needs and struggles of your husband or wife without impatience or anger. This should bring two things to mind. First, you should be reminded of Jesus, who was willing to face all the complications of life in this fallen world in order to meet our greatest need, new life. You should also be confronted with the fact that you don't like your life to be complicated. You don't want your plans interrupted, and you don't enjoy having to deal with problems you have not anticipated. One of the great challenges of real love is the willingness to abandon your demand for a comfortable and predictable life, and one of the most important calls of love is to find greater joy in meeting the need of another than in getting your own way.

Love is actively fighting the temptation to be critical and judgmental toward your spouse, while looking for ways to encourage and praise. It is so easy to be picky and irritable. It is often easy to be better at catching your spouse doing what is wrong than it is to recognize the many places where they do what is right. When you forget who you are, failing to recognize your own weaknesses and failures, it is much easier to be critical of your spouse. Critical responses to others are always rooted in self-righteousness. It is when we are affirming our need of grace and celebrating the grace we have been given that we delight in giving grace to the person we live with.

Love is the daily commitment to resist the needless moments of

191

conflict that come from pointing out and responding to minor offenses. You are a flawed person living with a flawed person, and if the paradigm of your relationship is to jump on every failure or offense, no matter how small, there will be no end to the hurt, conflict, and disappointment in your marriage. Love is sympathetic. Love is understanding. Love is patient. Love is kind. Love doesn't delight in evil but rejoices in the truth. You have married a person in process. That means, by God's grace, that your spouse is better than she was yesterday, but not what she will be tomorrow. Your husband or wife will fail in little ways every day, so it is important to recognize what is important and needs to be lovingly addressed and what is insignificant and needs to be lovingly overlooked. And in both instances it is important to give grace.

Love is being lovingly honest and humbly approachable in times of misunderstanding, and being more committed to unity and love than you are to winning, accusing, or being right. It doesn't matter how unified you have become and how comfortable with and knowledgeable about one another; you will still face situations of misunderstanding. One of the benefits of marriage is that we don't look at life the same way as our husband or wife does; but that can create misunderstanding in the marriage. It is also true that we don't always communicate as clearly as we think we do. We also don't always hear well. There are times when our mind is so engaged in thinking about how to communicate our perspective that we are not actually hearing what our spouse is saying. Along with these things, you and I are quite prone to changing our minds. We learn, grow, and reconsider, but we often don't communicate those changes as they happen along the way. So, the unity of a marriage is not the result of absence of misunderstanding, but rather the unity of a marriage is formed as you work through inevitable misunderstandings with patience, kindness, and grace.

Love is a daily commitment to admit your sin, weakness, and failure and to resist the temptation to offer an excuse or shift the blame. It is so tempting to believe you are more righteous than you actually are. It is so tempting to erect excuses and defenses for the wrong you have done. It is so easy to point out the sin of your husband or wife while being blind to your own. Self-righteousness is a daily spiritual war that all of us must face and be willing to fight. It is only when we are doing this that we will be owning and saying no to patterns of thought, desire, word, and action that get in the way of what God has called us to, and so fall below the level of the love that is the daily calling and protection of a marriage.

Love means being willing, when confronted by your spouse, to examine your heart rather than rising to your defense or shifting the focus. As long as there is sin remaining in us, we all carry around inside ourselves that inner lawyer, ready at any moment of challenge, rebuke, or confrontation to rise to our own defense and present arguments in support of what we have done. Love means being willing to fight with these defensive instincts of your heart. It means refusing to be closed and defensive. It means being unwilling to turn the tables and work to convince your spouse that you are not the only sinner in the room. Love means admitting that you need your spouse to help you see yourself with accuracy. Love means being willing to own your wrongs, to examine them in the light of God's Word, and to confess them to God and to your husband or wife.

Love is a daily commitment to grow in love so that the love you offer to your husband or wife is increasingly selfless, mature, and patient. Love means not living with your feelings of "arrival." Love is not lazy and self-assured. Love means accepting the reality that God is still calling you to grow and change. To love another person means you are willing to admit that there are places where your love needs to grow and mature. When you love your husband or wife, you will be committed to personal honesty and personal growth so that you can increasingly love your spouse in a way that is more consistent and more mature. Love doesn't coast but always carries a personal-growth agenda.

Love is being unwilling to do what is wrong when you have been wronged but to look for concrete and specific ways to overcome evil with good. You see it in the behavior of little children; you see it in the anger of the elderly and in everyone in between. It is very tempting for all of us to hurt another when we have been hurt. It is tempting to speak unkindly when we have been spoken to harshly. It is very tempting to act in anger when we have been the object of the anger of another. It is very tempting to treat our husband or wife with disrespect when we feel we have been disrespected. It is not naturally our response to look to do good when we have been wronged. It is not natural to look for ways

193

to love a person who has hurt us. It is natural for sinners to push back when they have been shoved. So, if we are ever to concretely overcome evil with good, we need the intervention and strengthening of God's grace, and we must admit that we find it hard to do good in the face of wrong, not because of what is inside the person we live with, but because of what is inside us.

Love is being a good student of your spouse, looking for his physical, emotional, and spiritual needs so that in some way you can remove the burden, support him as he carries it, or encourage him along the way. Love is not only reactive; it is willingly self-starting and active. It is good when your husband or wife communicates a need and you willingly respond, but real love is more active and aggressive than this. It finds joy in studying her—her opportunities, responsibilities, temptations, gifts, weaknesses, strengths, family, friends, schedule, etc.—so that it may anticipate her needs and move quickly to meet those needs or support her in the middle of them in whatever way is possible. Love doesn't wait around to be told what is needed and what to do. Love never sees her needs as an interruption. Love is burdened when she is burdened and finds joy in her relief. If you really love your husband or wife you will be willing to increase your load in order to lighten his or hers.

Love means being willing to invest the time necessary to discuss, examine, and understand the problems that you face as a couple, staying on task until the problem is removed or you have agreed upon a strategy of response. You live in a broken world; problems will come, and they won't always go away with the passing of time. You will face relational problems, personal problems that impact your relationship, and problems that come from outside your marriage. As much as you would like to, you will never exercise the kind of control over people, locations, and situations that would be necessary to keep your marriage problem-free. In fact, these problems are often a good thing, in that God uses them to take you beyond your own strength and wisdom to learn what it really means to live together in dependency on him. A good marriage is the result of two people who have learned together to be active problem-solvers and have learned to celebrate the growth and change that results.

Love is always being willing to ask for forgiveness and always being committed to grant forgiveness when it is requested. You are not yet perfect and neither is your husband or wife, so forgiveness is an essential calling. You will say some wrong at some time. There will be a moment when you desire what is wrong. You will act, react, or respond in a way that is wrong. You will be selfish, unloving, unkind, irritable, or impatient at some time. There is probably never a day when we don't sin against one another in some way. So, it is vital to recognize that your spouse has to live with a person like you—still struggling with temptation and sin and still failing in some way. And you should find joy in relieving the burden of living with you by seeking your spouse's forgiveness whenever he or she has been impacted by your failure. It is also important that you are ready and willing to forgive your spouse, as well. You can't be in a marriage without being sinned against in some way. So, you must say no to keeping a record of wrongs; you must say no to vengeance of any kind; you must say no to bitterness; and you must always be willing to grant forgiveness whenever there has been an offense and your spouse is seeking to make things right by asking for your forgiveness.

Love is recognizing the high value of trust in a marriage and being faithful to your promises and true to your word. We have already examined the importance of trust to a healthy marriage, so not much needs to be said here. But it is worth connecting love and trust in this way: love loves, trusts, and works in whatever way possible to strengthen it. Because you love your spouse, you want her to know that she can depend on you. You want her to be free of the need of following you around and checking up on you. You want her to rest assured that whatever you promise, to the best of your ability you will do, and whatever you say to her will be reliable and true. Love also means living with your spouse in such a way that he never has to wonder who you are with or what you are doing when you are apart. Love means your spouse can rest, knowing that there are no secrets in your life or subtexts in your words about which he needs to be concerned.

Love is speaking kindly and gently, even in moments of disagreement, refusing to attack your spouse's character or assault his or her intelligence. My brother, Tedd, says that the old saying, "Sticks and stones may hurt my bones, but names will never hurt me," could not be further from the truth. Long after physical bruises have healed, the wounds of words still live in the heart. I have seen the peace and hope of a marriage destroyed by horrible words that should have never been spoken, but they are difficult to remove from the memory once they are said. When you are hurt or engaged in a high-stakes disagreement, it is very important to edit your words, not giving yourself permission to go on the verbal attack. If you want to have a marriage of unity, under-standing, and love you cannot allow yourself to say whatever you think or go wherever your emotions are leading you. Love says no again and again, not to your husband or wife but to yourself, resisting the tempta-tion to get your way by using words as weapons of warfare rather than as tools of love.

Love is being unwilling to flatter, lie, manipulate, or deceive in any way in order to co-opt your spouse into giving you what you want or doing something your way. It is an act of love toward your spouse to keep yourself aware of the war that still rages in your heart between the kingdom of self and the kingdom of God. It is a commitment of humble love to daily acknowledge your struggle with the selfishness of sin. It is your calling to resist the temptation to use whatever tools are at your disposal to get your husband or wife to submit to the agenda and rules of your little kingdom of one. Love serves and gives. Love is not complaining or demanding. Love is being willing to sacrifice what you want in order to give your spouse what he or she needs. Love is never deceitful or manipulative in the pursuit of self-interest, because true love is other-centered and other-motivated.

Love is being unwilling to ask your spouse to be the source of your identity, meaning and purpose, or inner sense of well-being, while refus-ing to be the source of his or hers. If you really do love your spouse, you won't try to turn him or her into your personal messiah, and you won't want the power and buzz of being your spouse's messiah. Your husband or wife is not capable of carrying your hopes or happiness. Your spouse cannot be the reason you get up in the morning or the thing that keeps you going during the day. To ask your spouse to do this is not only an act of spiritual selfishness, but it also places on him a burden he cannot bear. If you do this, he will fail and then have to deal with the conse-quences of his failure in your disappointment and the negative impact all this has on your marriage. Love means you never ask your spouse to do for you what only God can do. Love never demands from your spouse spiritually what God has already given you in Christ. Love seeks vertical fulfillment so it can horizontally serve.

Love is the willingness to have less free time, less sleep, and a busier schedule in order to be faithful to what God has called you to be and to do as a husband or a wife. Marital love means you are willing to give up your individual control over your time, plans, and schedule in order to build real and lasting friendship, intimacy, and communion with the person you have committed your life to. You cannot think, choose, or decide as one and at the same time be committed to the unity and love of your marriage. Love is willing to give up your right to control your time, energy, and resources. Love is willing to add more duties to your living and more complication to your schedule. Love is willing to get up early and stay up late. And love is willing to do all these things because of the joy of serving your spouse and helping her experience what God says is best.

Love is a commitment to say no to selfish instincts and to do everything that is within your ability to promote real unity, functional understanding, and active love in your marriage. There is probably no more important commitment of love than the commitment to say no. Are you confused? Let me explain. If you are ever going to say yes to the moment-by-moment call to make personal sacrifices for the good of your husband or wife, you must first say no to yourself. Remember that the DNA of sin is selfishness. So as long as sin remains inside you, there will be a constant temptation to live, act, react, and respond to your spouse in a way that is self-focused and self-centered. If you are ever going to live a lifestyle of real love, you must first fight this battle of the heart. Like any other war, this battle can only be fought in the concrete, that is, in moments of specific temptation that greet you in specific locations and situations.

Perhaps you are tempted to start your day so consumed with your own desires and duties that you take little time to notice or respond to the needs of your husband or wife. Or maybe your struggle is with self-ishness in your use of your free time. Maybe you are tempted to be self-ish in your use of money. Or perhaps you struggle with selfishness when it comes to participating in the normal chores of the home. Or maybe, at the end of a long day, you just want to be left alone. The point is that if you are ever going to love your husband or wife, there are specific temptations to which you must say no.

Love is staying faithful to your commitment to treat your spouse with appreciation, respect, and grace, even in moments when he or she doesn't seem to deserve it or is unwilling to reciprocate. No one reading this book has been or ever will be married to a perfect person. Marriage means that the sin, weakness, and failure of your husband or wife will be your firsthand, daily experience. It means loving your spouse when she is having a bad day or struggling with particular disappointment. Marriage means loving your spouse when he is irritable and impatient. It means loving your spouse when she has hurt you in some way. Marriage means loving your spouse when he is demanding and critical. It means continuing to love even when your spouse refuses to participate, cooperate, serve, give, or help. It means persevering through hard times and difficult days. It means refusing to use words as weapons or let the sun go down on your anger, even when your husband or wife is doing both.

Love is never letting the failure of your spouse become a reason for changing the rules of the game. True love is respectful. True love looks for ways to express appreciation. True love finds joy in giving grace. True love wants to build and encourage. And true love does these things no matter what.

Love is the willingness to make regular and costly sacrifices for the sake of your marriage without asking anything in return or using your sacrifices to place your spouse in your debt. There are moments when love is fairly easy. On that romantic weekend when you are alone together and away from the normal responsibilities and pressures of everyday life, it is easy to love. When your husband or wife has anticipated a need and served you in some way, it is easy to love. When you have been given a special gift, it is easy to love. When your spouse has communicated how much she respects and appreciates you, it is easy to love.

But real love doesn't live only in these grand, affectionate moments. No, real love lives at street level. It lives when no violin is playing or bird is singing. It lives when life is busy, boring, or hard. Real love doesn't demand that life is easy or exciting. Real love loves as much in the dark of the night as it does in the warmth of the sun. Real love loves when love isn't much fun and isn't very fulfilling. Real love doesn't quit when things are hard and doesn't check out in the face of disappointment. So there is no such thing as real love that does not require real, willing, and daily sacrifices. There is no way to escape it—real love is costly. Real love calls each of us to be willing to suffer. It calls us to sacrifices of time, energy, and money. It calls us to be willing at times to be silent and at other times to have the courage to speak. It calls us at times to refuse to fight and at other times to fight for what is right. It calls us at times to act decisively and at other times to be willing to wait. It calls us to lead the way and at other times to be willing to follow. It calls us to follow a plan and at other times to be willing to give up our plans. Love doesn't run in the face of sacrifice.

Love is being unwilling to make any personal decision or choice that would harm your marriage, hurt your husband or wife, or weaken the bond of trust between you. Love means giving up your autonomy. It means no longer living as if your life belongs to you. It is no longer treating your life as an investment you can individually make. It is approaching every desire, choice, decision, word, or action in the context of what is best for your husband or wife and best for your relationship to them. Love is surrendering my independence for the greater calling and greater joy of union and communion with you. Love is refusing to view myself as being separate from you. Love is understanding that now that we are together in a lifelong relationship, everything I do is an act of relationship; whether constructive or destructive. Love is understanding that in marriage it is impossible to act independently. In some way all of my choices, decisions, and actions will affect you.

So love means living relationally; that is, always choosing and acting with your marriage in view. It means never choosing what would seem to be good for you but would harm the relationship in some way. It means never indulging an emotion or desire that would end up hurting your husband or wife. It means never making a choice or acting in a way that would weaken the trust that is so important to your marriage.

Love is refusing to be self-focused or demanding but instead look-

ing for specific ways to serve, support, and encourage, even when you are busy or tired. One of the things that harms marriage is entitlement. Sinners have great skill at turning blessings into needs. It is very easy for us to reason that we are deserving of something and therefore it is right for us to be demanding of it. It is very easy for us to load into our personal "need" category things that are not needs, and because we have, to be expectant and demanding. Here's how it works: If I am convinced that something is a need, and you say you love me, it seems right to expect that you will meet this need. It seems right then to watch to see if you are committed to meeting it and to be demanding if you haven't, because, after all, it is a need! Calling something a need that is not actually a need is one of the ways we tend to excuse self-focus and the demands that accompany it.

The biblical model of love provides rescue from this temptation. In Matthew 6:25–32, Jesus reminds us that we have a heavenly Father who knows precisely what we need. He is never confused by the question of what constitutes a need and what does not. It is best to let him define our needs. And he has promised that he will supply for us everything we need.

How can you know this for sure? Well, the cross of Jesus Christ is your guarantee. Paul says this in Romans 8:32: "He who did not spare his own Son but gave him up for us all, how will he not also with him graciously give us all things?" If God went to the extent of sacrificing his Son so that we might have relationship with him, would it make any sense whatsoever for him to abandon us after we do? Paul says, "Absolutely not!" So you do not have to live fretfully, making sure that all your needs are met. You can humbly admit that you are often confused about what your real needs are, and you can rest assured that your true needs will be met by a loving heavenly Father, who paid a huge price so that you might be the object of his eternal favor. The cross of sacrifice on that ancient hill outside the city is your written guarantee.

Because you are loved in this way, you are free to take your eyes off yourself and to love your spouse. And you do not have to look over your shoulder to see if God is still there and still active, and you do not have to worry in your heart. You can know for sure that if he gave you his Son, there is no way he will abandon you in your time of need.

Love is daily admitting to yourself, your spouse, and God that you are not able to love this way without God's protecting, providing, forgiving, rescuing, and delivering grace. After reading this chapter, there are two things you should be left with. First, you should be confronted with the fact that love is fundamentally deeper and more active than some warm, romantic feeling of affection toward someone to whom you are attracted. It is not some generalized response of happiness when you are with this particular person. No, *love is a specific commitment of the heart to a specific person that causes you to give yourself to a specific lifestyle of care that requires you to be willing to make sacrifices that have that person's good in view.* Love is never general, and it never remains in the realm of feelings. Love desires, love thinks, love chooses, love decides, love acts, and love speaks in an ongoing, day-by-day commitment to the welfare of another. Real love is concrete, specific, and active.

But there is an even more powerful reality that should hit you after reading this chapter. This realization should give you pause and then spur you to action: it is impossible for any of us to love as has been described. The bar is simply too high. The requirements are simply too great. None of us has what it takes to reach this standard. This description of love in action has left me humbled and grieved. It has faced me once again with my tendency to name as love things that are not love. It has forced me to admit how self-focused and self-absorbed I actually am. It has reminded me that when it comes to love, I am not an expert. No, I am poor, weak, and needy. But I am not alone and because of this, the realization of failure should not defeat or paralyze you or me. No, it is meant to drive you to seek help. I am not talking about reading a good marriage book, attending a good marriage class, or getting good marriage counseling. All these can do is describe what is best. They do not have the power to help you to desire and do what is best. They can inform you as to what love is, but they can never transform you into a person who loves. But isn't that what all of us need?

You see, God's call to love confronts us with our weakness and inability. It makes us face how cold and fickle our hearts actually are. It helps us to see how weak our resolve is. It calls us to humbly admit how unwilling and impatient we are. Being faced with our weakness is one of God's goals for marriage. This comprehensive, lifelong relationship is a tool in the hands of God to expose our delusions of wisdom, righteousness, and strength and to mobilize us to seek help. And there is help, wonderful and sufficient help, for all who seek it.

As John begins that long discussion of love that we have already considered in this passage, he says these words: "God sent his only Son into the world, so that we might live through him" (1 John 4:9). John says that the purpose for Jesus' coming to earth, suffering and dying, and rising from the dead is that through him we might have what we need to be able to live the life to which he has called us. And the life to which he has called us is fundamentally, comprehensively, and perseveringly a life of love. John is saying that Jesus died not only so that we would have forgiveness for not loving as we should, but also so that we would have the desire, wisdom, and power to love as we should.

Jesus shed his blood for the conversation that started out right but has now become angry and tense. Jesus died for the daily pressure of living with someone who is very different from you. Jesus died so that you would win your struggle with forgiveness and be able to resist the seductive call of bitterness and vengeance. Jesus died so that you would have what it takes to make the decision to get out of bed and do what you promised even though you are weary and discouraged. Jesus suffered so that you could face hurt and mistreatment with wisdom and grace. Jesus died so that you would resist the temptation to give in, give up, run away, or quit. Jesus shed his blood so that you would have the power to edit your words and say what is wholesome even when you have been spoken to in ways that are unkind. Jesus shed his blood so that in specific moments you would have the power to say no to irritation and impatience and respond in kindness and self-control. Jesus died so that in the face of the death of your dreams you would take up the better dream of what he has called you to. Jesus suffered so that you would have the wisdom you need to deal with things you did not expect and don't fully understand. Jesus shed his blood so that you would have the power to grow and change.

Jesus suffered in love so that in your struggle to love you would never, ever be alone. As you give yourself to love, he showers you with his love, so that you would never be without what you need to love. He was willing to make the ultimate sacrifice of love because he knew that that was the only way that you would ever get what it takes to love as you have been called to love. Jesus knew that your struggle to love is so deep that a certain system of wisdom or a certain set of provisions wouldn't be enough. He knew the only thing that would help you would be if he gave you himself. So that is exactly what he did. He gave himself so that right here, right now, you would have the resources you need to live a concrete and continuing life of love.

So don't let regret paralyze you. Don't be overwhelmed by love's call. Don't be discouraged by the size or number of the things you are facing. Don't let the failures of the past rob you of hope for the future. No, left to yourself you don't have what it takes, but he is with you, in you, and for you. Walk forward in hope and courage, and commit yourself to real, active, and specific cruciform love, knowing that his grace really does have the power to make you ready, willing, and waiting.

Teach me to feel another's woe, to hide the fault I see, that mercy I show to others, that mercy show to me.

ALEXANDER POPE

The more we love any that are not as we are, the less we love as men and the more as God.

JOHN SALTMARSH

COMMITMENT 1: We will give ourselves to a regular lifestyle of confession and forgiveness.

COMMITMENT 2: We will make growth and change our daily agenda.

COMMITMENT 3: We will work together to build a sturdy bond of trust.

COMMITMENT 4: We will commit to building a relationship of love.

COMMITMENT 5: We will deal with our differences with appreciation and grace.

COMMITMENT 6: We will work to protect our marriage.

13

Amazing Grace

You didn't do it, and the sooner you understand that, the better it will be for you and your marriage. You couldn't have done it. You're simply not that powerful and not that wise. You and I like to think that it was all our initiative, but it wasn't. When you face the fact that your marital story is all about the wisdom and will of Another, your understanding of marriage completely changes forever.

I was raised in the white-bread normalcy of Toledo, Ohio. My dad worked at a sporting goods store, and my mother was an IBM key-punch operator. Everything about my family was Midwest American normal. The big event of my childhood was when we moved to the suburbs, to the little town of Maumee. Life in Ohio was an endlessly repeated routine. It would have made sense that I graduate from high school, go to college, at some point marry an Ohio girl, and settle in to repeat the routine for another generation. But the one who is the Author of my story had another plan.

There was a little girl named Luella who was born in Placettas, Cuba. Luella was the daughter of Canadian missionary parents. From the vantage point of an Ohio boy, her life was anything but normal. She lived a life in which she was surrounded by a big extended "family" as part of her everyday experience. Ministry was the thing that took her family to Cuba and shaped the way they lived. She lived in a land of white-sand beaches, palm trees, and avocados. Her favorite snack was Cuban crackers with queso blanco and guava paste. Throughout most of my childhood I never saw the ocean. I certainly did not know that there was such a thing as a guava or an avocado! The closest I came to a beach was the shores of Lake Erie.

The revolution of Che Guevara and Fidel Castro took Luella's family to Hartsville, South Carolina, still far from Toledo in distance and culture. Her father pastored a small church, and her mother worked as a seamstress. Hartsville was a quaint and quiet Southern town of ten thousand people. It really was the deep and sleepy South.

My parents had discovered a little Christian college in Columbia, South Carolina, that gave a good biblical education, and they really wanted me to go there for at least a couple years before I went anywhere else. I wasn't excited about that. I was a bit concerned about the traditional conservatism of the South, but I applied and was accepted.

I went to college with a closed mind and an apprehensive heart. I was not interested in putting down any roots or in making any long-term relationships, including with any of the female students I would find there. I expected all the women to look as if they had just stepped off an Amish farm or, on the other hand, that they all would be fresh from the bush of Africa or the jungles of South America and know little of American culture. I was interested in the Beatles, Bob Dylan, and the Vietnam War. I wasn't really interested in meeting someone who had plans to return to the wilderness!

My first week in college was hard. I hated everything about the environment I was in. In fact, I didn't unpack my things that whole first week because I was convinced there was no way that I would stay. I had been forced to cut my hair, even though I had already cut off several inches; it was an indignity I would not forgive! However, I made it through the orientation week and decided to stay.

Luella had enrolled in the same college (just sixty miles from her home) the year before. Her first year was one of constant personal struggle, but she decided to return. The very first lunch that returning students ate at the cafeteria on the first day after orientation week, I stood behind Luella in the cafeteria line. I was immediately smitten. She didn't look as though she had Amish parents or had just arrived from the jungle. She was stylish and beautiful, and I couldn't take my eyes off her. As I mentioned earlier, it was love at first sight for me. For Luella, it was first sight!

I decided that I would find out about her, and within a month we had had our first date. Luella was not interested in a long-term relationship and told me not to ask her out again. But I did and she accepted.

I determined that I would continue to ask as long as she continued to accept and, as they say, the rest is history.

My life has been changed and enhanced by Luella in a thousand ways. There is no way that I would be who I am, doing what I am doing, without her. I cannot imagine what my journey would have been like without her. She is my hero and my dearest friend. There is no one on earth I would rather spend time with. There is no voice in my life more influential than hers. I am deeply blessed to be married to someone like her, and I know I could have never found her on my own.

The story of my marriage really does illustrate a powerful theological point. You and I are not the authors of our own story. Think with me for a moment. Let your mind expand and your heart reflect in wonder. Think of all the locations, situations, and relationships—individual, cultural, national, and international—that you would have to have absolute control over to guarantee that this little girl from Cuba and this little boy from Ohio would meet at any time and in any way. Consider the mathematical possibility. Consider how little of these situations, locations, and relationships Luella and I had any involvement in, let alone any control over. Consider how neither of us had any idea whatsoever that the other existed or that our stories were marching toward that fateful moment of intersection. Consider how neither one of us was insightful enough to find one another or to understand how our lives would mold together. And consider how we could not have written the story of our relationship since that first day of meeting.

Now, you know that our story is not unique. You know that your life has not worked according to your plan. Last month didn't work according to your plan. Last week didn't work according to your plan. Some of you are a bit ruffled as you read this today because you are being confronted with the reality that yesterday didn't work according to your plan. Ten years ago you couldn't have written yourself into the situation in which you are now living. Luella and I are living in a loft in Chinatown, Philadelphia. There is no way that I could have ever known that this was the direction my story was taking.

You don't need to read a mystery novel; your life is a mystery that only makes sense to you after the fact. When it comes to marriage, you didn't do it, and the sooner you come to understand what this means, the better. Yes, you made decisions along the way, and the decisions were very important and left a trail of consequences. But there is something even more foundational going on, and when you understand it, you will have a new understanding of the struggle of marriage and what to do about it.

The Artist of Your Marriage

No one plans to struggle in marriage, but we all do. People don't think that differences between them and their spouse will in some way and at some time bring them to the end of themselves, but such differences always do. You have to ask, "What is all this about?" This is where it is vital to understand that the biblical story is the only story that can make sense out of the story of your life and your marriage.

The biblical story begins with the Creator. John 1:3 says, "All things were made through him, and without him was not any thing made that was made." The physical world and all that is in it is a 24/7, surround-sound, Technicolor display of the creative artistry of God. If you stop, look, and listen for a moment, it will blow you away.

I was in three cities last week: Denver, Philadelphia, and Phoenix. I was in the locations of three mountain ranges, but they couldn't have been more different from one another. You would think that you could use the word *mountain*, and everyone reading it would immediately know what you were describing, but this simply isn't the case. The vastness of God's creative design prevents it from being that simple. I was amazed as we drove through the sheer, rock-faced splendor of the majestic Rockies at the intimidating glory of these mountains. I listened to the rapids of the mountain river as it coursed its way down through the canyon; it sounded like a spontaneous ovation for the beauty that was visible everywhere. I said to myself as we drove on, "Now these are mountains!" You see, I am used to the Pocono Mountains near Philadelphia, where I live. When measured against the Rockies, the Poconos aren't really mountains. I have reasoned that the Poconos are just God's speed bumps to slow you down before you hit the ocean at the Jersey Shore.

At the end of the week I was in the Catalina Mountains in the Phoenix area. These are bleak, sharp-edged desert mountains, their angles only softened by the angular cacti that march, with hands raised, toward their barren peaks. Each range came out of the mind of God. Each was constructed by his finger, and each is a sign that points to his glory. I could say more about how different the vegetation is in each location, how each is inhabited by different creatures, and how each has weather that is unique to its setting, but you get the point.

What does this have to do with your marriage? You will only ever begin to understand the struggles you face as a couple in forming a marriage of real and functional unity, and how to forge a lifestyle of real respect and appreciation between you, when you begin to look at your marriage through the lens of Genesis 1. The real and significant differences between you began in the mind of the Creator. Everything that makes up your wife—what she looks like, her innate gifts, and her particular personality—came out of the mind of an incredibly creative designer. Everything that makes up your husband—what he looks like, his innate gifts, and his particular personality—came out of the mind of an incredibly creative designer. He was not locked into one model of what a human being is. There is no end to the gradations of differences that he can form into the hardwiring of a human being. There seems to be no end to the endless variety of body design. There seems to be no end to the range of human personality. There seems to be no end to the catalog of built-in human gifts and abilities.

Think about it: some people are mechanical, some analytical, some conceptual, some mathematical, some organizational, some artistic, and some relational. Some people are outgoing and extroverted, some are quiet and introverted, and some are middle-of-the-road *verts*! Yet even inside each of these categories there are vast differences. Consider hair color (bottled color excluded) and hair texture and the endless variety of combinations. Look around at the size and shape of people's jaws, noses, foreheads, ears, chins, lips, teeth, and cheeks and consider the endless variety of the architecture of human faces. Then combine that with all the variables of body shape with size of limbs and torso and with weight and girth. You will never find two human beings who look completely alike. Not even identical twins are completely identical.

When you start with Genesis 1, you are confronted with the fact that it is virtually impossible for you to marry someone who is like you.

Because you were not formed by some evolutionary factory that manu-factured you by a strict set of scientific formulas but by the hand of an infinite divine artist, you are unique. There is no one quite like you. You will never marry your clone, and in marriage you will never be able to turn your husband or wife into your clone.

Here's where all this leads: unity in marriage is not the result of sameness. You will never ever be exactly the same as your spouse. God has designed that you will be married to someone different from you. Unity is, rather, the result of what husband and wife do in the face of the inevitable differences that exist in the lives of every married couple. So, what are you to do with the differences between you and your spouse, which constantly confront you in your marriage? Let me suggest some things.

Celebrate your Creator. Dealing with your differences in a way that builds a sturdy bond of unity between you begins here. The more you look at your spouse and see the imprint of God's fingers and are amazed, the more you will be able to resist the temptation to try to remake him or her in your own image. The more you esteem what God has created, the less you will want to remake it. The more you see divine beauty and divine glory in the differences between you, the less you will be irritated by them. Here is the bottom line: the more you look at your husband or wife and honor God as creator, the more you will tend to esteem and appreciate the person who you live with, who is so incredibly different from you.

Refuse to see the differences as right or wrong. When we talk about what the Creator has hardwired into your husband or wife, we are not talking about things that are morally right or morally wrong. For example, Luella is not a time-oriented person. By nature, she is much more attuned to the task she is doing or the person she is with. She approaches life with a thoughtful slowness. She is seldom in a rush or distracted by the next thing on her schedule. I am her complete opposite. I am very project-oriented. I try to get as many things done in a day as I possibly can. I am very time-oriented, and I am always thinking about what I need to do next.

This difference between us in time orientation is not a matter of maturity or morality. I am not a better person than Luella because I tend to be more oriented to time and punctuality, and Luella is not more righteous than me because she is better able to attend to the task of the moment. We have been put together by an amazing Creator. We are both people but are very different at the same time.

When you begin to think and act as though your hardwiring makes you better, more mature, or more righteous than your spouse, you will act and respond in ways that are dismissive and disrespectful. And when you respond this way, you not only do not build the unity of your marriage, but you also create pockets of needless and debilitating conflict.

Determine to respond to your differences with appreciation and respect. This will take a change in orientation, attitude, and action for many of us. We are used to being impatient and irritated in the face of differences. We are used to subtly disrespecting those differences. And we are used to doing what is necessary to get our own way. Here's what you need to face: those responses are more about your relationship with God than they are about your relationship with your husband or wife. It is not your husband or wife's choices that you are rejecting, but God's. Luella didn't decide to be methodical any more than she decided her height. It is God who formed your spouse with his or her natural gifts and personality, and after he did, he stood back and declared your spouse "good." It is hurtful to your spouse when you disrespect her for things she did not choose or reject her for things she cannot change. Every difference is an opportunity to celebrate God's creative artistry and a chance to communicate specific respect and appreciation for who God has formed your spouse to be.

Learn where your differences create difficulty and call yourself to unification work. There is no doubt about it: the things that I now celebrate, I once struggled with greatly. I did think that when it comes to time, I was right and Luella was wrong. I did think that I was a better creator than the Creator, so I worked, to no avail, to re-create Luella in my image. To my regret, I said and did things that were dismissive and disrespectful. Early in our marriage, I had no sense of how much I needed Luella in my life.

What I failed to do was examine our differences with a commitment to do anything within my power, as I dealt with them, to grow and deepen our unity. No, what I did caused disharmony and disunity. I was convinced that unless Luella and I were the same, we would never be unified. Because of this, I did not work to build a solid unity around our differences. Luella is better at a house-painting project than I am because she doesn't mind taking her time. I am better at laying the schedule for a vacation because I am more realistic about time. We have learned to capitalize on each other's unique God-designed strengths, and this protects both of us from our natural weaknesses. We have learned that the greatest mutual benefit has come from our places of biggest struggle. And we continue to work at not fighting over what God means for us to benefit from.

Admit where these differences challenge you to grow. What I struggled with was the fact that these differences were calling me to grow and change. I needed to be more patient. I needed to be more appreciative and respectful. I needed to be kinder and more encouraging in those moments when we were discussing our differences. I needed to be more humble and approachable. I needed to have my selfishness and self-righteousness exposed. I was so busy looking at Luella with a critical eye that I had little time or interest in looking with an examining eye at myself. I was angry that she just didn't get it, and I responded in anger again and again. I didn't get what God was doing. He was using his Creator hardwiring to expose character deficiencies. Our differences not only reflected his glory; they were for our good, and when I got that, I began to change (character) and quit trying to change things in Luella (hardwiring) that will simply never change. This sets up what we must look at next.

Planned Struggle

The struggle over differences is not some cosmic accident; no, it is a plan. You see, the same God whose creative artistry created the hardwired differences you and your spouse experience daily brought you together for his plan and purpose. Recognizing his sovereignty is key to understanding your marriage struggle and what to do about it.

We began this chapter with recognizing that each of our marriage stories has been authored by Another. We now want to reflect on his reason for doing what he has done in each of our marriages. Let me give you the steps of the biblical plan that you need to understand if you are ever going to deal, in an attitude of humility and grace, with the differences that you have with your spouse.

1) *God is in absolute control of the details of our lives.* I have written many times that I find Acts 17:24–27 to be one of the most helpful and encouraging discussions in the New Testament of God's rulership over our lives:

> The God who made the world and everything in it, being Lord of heaven and earth, does not live in temples made by man, nor is he served by human hands, as though he needed anything, since he himself gives to all mankind life and breath and everything. And he made from one man every nation of mankind to live on all the face of the earth, having determined allotted periods and the boundaries of their dwelling place, that they should seek God, in the hope that they might feel their way toward him and find him. Yet he is actually not far from each one of us.

Here is Paul's basic view of God's involvement in the details of his life: "Having determined allotted periods and the boundaries of their dwelling place . . . " (v. 26b). What does Paul mean by these words? Well, let me paraphrase. God determines the precise place where each of us will live ("boundaries of their dwelling place") and the exact length of our lives ("having determined allotted periods"). It is God who determines the precise details of location, situations, and relationship in which each of us lives. This means not only that God is in control of where you end up and who you finally live with, but also that, in order to do this, he has been in control of everything that brought you to where you are. This means that God has been in control of all the experiential, cultural, and familial influences that shaped how you desire, think, act, and respond. So, God is in control not only of the locations in which you live, but also of the influences that have shaped you as a person. He has not only written the story of you and your spouse and determined that your stories would intersect, but he has controlled all the things that have made you different from one another.

As you struggle, you must not view your marriage as bad luck, or poor planning, or as a mess that you made for yourself. No, God is right smack-dab in the middle of your struggle. He is not surprised by what you are facing today. He is up to something.

2) *He has a purpose for the situations and locations in which he places us.* What is the question that every believer somehow, someway, asks at some time? Here it is: "Why would a God of love and wisdom purposely plan for us to struggle?" This is a question that must be answered if we are ever going to understand our marriage and how to respond to it in a way that promotes unity, love, and understanding.

To answer this question, we have to step back and look at the big picture. In the here and now, God's focused zeal is redemption. What does that mean? Well, if you are God's child, the power of sin has been broken in your life (see Rom. 6:1–14). But you still have a deep problem. The presence of sin still remains. God is unwilling to rest, unwilling to leave you to yourself, until every microbe of sin has been eradicated from every cell of your heart. So this is the thing that he is working on in the here and now. He is working to rescue you from you, to deliver you from sin, and to form the character of Jesus in you.

So, this means that marriage, the world's most long-term and comprehensive relationship, is taking place in the middle of sanctification, the world's most important unfinished process. Why would God do this? Wouldn't it be easier to completely change us than to have us marry? Hasn't he gotten the proverbial cart before the proverbial horse? Well, the reason this doesn't seem to make sense to us is that our purpose for marriage tends to be different from the Lord's. We're just not on God's agenda page. Our desire is that our marriages would be the location of our comfort, ease, and enjoyment; we often have desires no bigger than this. But God's purpose is that each of our marriages would be a tool for something that is way more miraculous and glorious than our tiny, little, self-focused definition of happiness. He has designed marriage to be one of his most effective and efficient tools of personal holiness. He has designed your marriage to change you.

Your differences and the difficulties that they place you in are not a sign that God has forgotten you or has been unfaithful to you. Your difficulties with your differences are not an interruption of his plan; they are part of his plan. Getting this is basic to responding to those difficulties in a new and better way.

3) *Marriage is one of God's primary tools of personal change and growth.* I don't know about you, for sure, but I would imagine you are like me. I have struggled with Luella's and my differences and resisted change for two reasons. First, I don't want to deal with the hassle. I want my life to be easy and predictable. I want things to go as I have planned. I want Luella to say, "Yes dear, that is a wonderful idea," or, "I agree with you completely." I don't want to have to deal with an alternative perspective or plan. I want to be sovereign over my world and have it operate in a way that meets the demands of my personal definition of happiness. But that is not all; I tend to think that I don't need to change. Here's what I am saying: I am persuaded that beneath our struggle with the differences we have with one another is a desire for self-sovereignty and the delusion of self-righteousness. We want to be more in control than we will ever be, and we think we are more righteous than we actually are.

When we resist change and complain about the daily difficulty of marital differences, we are not first moaning and groaning about the person we live with. No, we are struggling with who God is and who God says we are. The horizontal struggles are the fruit of vertical struggles between us and our Lord. God, in the zeal of his love, is employing our marriages to deliver to us things of eternal value; our struggle is to value these gifts of transforming grace as much as he does.

4) *Three main tools of difference are used to reveal and change our hearts.* There are three primary tools of difference that God uses in marriage to reveal our hearts. The first tool we have already examined. It is the difference in personal hardwiring that the Creator has formed in each of us. Second is the difference in viewpoints, instincts, and tastes that have been formed in us through the experiential, cultural, and relational influences that we have lived in and which have formed the way we see the world and respond to it. And, finally, there are the differences in personal sin and weakness and in our growth in grace. We are not all in the same place on our journey to Christlike maturity.

It is so important to remember that these three things are not to be viewed as the potholes to be avoided on the road to a good marriage but as effective instruments of change in the hands of a loving, wise, and faithful Redeemer. He is worth trusting, even in those moments when it is hard for us to trust one another, because, no matter what the motives of our spouse might be, our Savior is up to something good.

5) *Change begins when we see these differences as grace rather than obstructions of grace.* I really do think that there are moments in our marriages when we are crying out for grace, not recognizing that we are getting it. We are not getting the grace of relief or the grace of release, because that is not the grace that we really need. No, what we are getting is something we desperately need, the uncomfortable grace of personal growth and change. With the love of a Father, your Lord is prying open your hands so that you will let go of things that have come to rule your heart but will never satisfy you. With the insight of a seasoned teacher, he is driving you to question your own wisdom so that you will find your understanding and rest in his. With the skill of the world's best counselor, God is showing you the delusions of your control so that you will take comfort in his rule. With the gentleness of a faithful friend he is facing you toward the inadequacies of your own righteousness so that you find your hope in his.

When you are tired and uncomfortable because you have been called to live with someone who is not like you, what you tell yourself about what you are going through is very important. It is in this moment that you must preach to yourself the theology of uncomfortable grace (See Romans 5; James 1; and 1 Peter 1), because when you do, you begin to be less resistant and more appreciative, and you are on your way to forging a marriage of unity, understanding, and love. Remember, genuine appreciation for your spouse begins with practical, day-by-day worship of God.

6) *God is with you in your struggle.* I really do love the way Paul talks about God's rule over the practical details of our daily lives. He says, ". . . that they should seek God, in the hope that they might feel their way toward him and find him. Yet he is actually not far from each one of us" (Acts 17:27). Paul is arguing that God's absolute rule over the intimate details of our lives doesn't make him distant and unapproachable, like some great chess player in the sky. Paul is actually presenting the opposite here. God is in the middle of the details of your marriage, and because he is, he is near. This means that at any time you can reach out for his help. You are never alone in your struggle. Not only has God

determined the situations and relationships in which you will live, but he is with you in them. He will never abandon you in disgust. He will never take a break to rest. He will never get tired and give up. He is near you and for you and will not quit until what he has begun is complete.

Dealing with Difference: A Beginning

So, what are you to do when you are hit with how different you are from your husband or wife? I will suggest a few things here and then complete the discussion in the next chapter. Don't run away in fear. You haven't made a horrible mistake. No one has ever married someone who is completely like them. What you are dealing with is part of the plan. Don't try to comfort yourself by denying the differences that are actually there. I have counseled many engaged couples in a state of deep denial. They were convinced that they could never disagree with one another. I knew my job was to awaken them out of their denial. Don't resist the other person and fight for your way as if your way is the only way. Remember, when you resist, you are not first resisting your husband or wife; you are resisting God. He calls you to work for unity even though you are different because he knows that this work will not only change your marriage, but it will also change you, and that is exactly what God is after. Don't allow yourself to be dragged into needless debates and petty battles. Work on differences that make a difference. The pattern on the couch is probably not worth fighting about, but the church you are going to involve yourselves in is. The differences that you have between one another will be used by God to help you get your priorities straight and to practically remember what is important and what is not.

It really is a gorgeous plan; in your marriage God will take you where you never thought you would go in order to give you what you could not achieve on your own. He is working on something that is very good—lasting personal change—and he is with you during the process, giving you what you need, to be what you have been designed to be, and to do what you have been called to do. Now, that is a reason to be encouraged, even on the days that are difficult.

COMMITMENT 1:   We will give ourselves to a regular lifestyle of confession and forgiveness.

COMMITMENT 2:   We will make growth and change our daily agenda.

COMMITMENT 3:   We will work together to build a sturdy bond of trust.

COMMITMENT 4:   We will commit to building a relationship of love.

COMMITMENT 5:   We will deal with our differences with appreciation and grace.

COMMITMENT 6:   We will work to protect our marriage.

14

Before Dark

John and Jackie got into a pattern; they didn't know how harmful it would prove to be. Jackie was quiet and thoughtful, the type who would rather curl up with a good book than go out for the evening. Jackie's father was a history professor at a major university, and her mother stayed at home and concentrated on the children. There was an attractive regularity to Jackie's home growing up. Holidays were always spent the same way, and every summer the family would spend a week at the same lake house. Jackie went to school with the same group of friends from kindergarten to high school graduation and went off with many of them to the local university where her father taught. Nothing much changed in Jackie's life, and she liked it that way.

John was raised in big cities. His father was a very powerful lawyer who had worked his way up the food chain to big-time success. John had lived in Los Angeles, Dallas, and finally New York City. John was a big-city boy. He loved the sights, sounds, and chaos of the city. John wasn't afraid of change; in fact, he liked it. He loved a new location with all its new challenges, and he was not afraid to do something he had never done before. So this is how John arrived at a major university in a relatively small town. He had never lived in a small town, and he liked the fact that the university was the center of what was happening there. By the time he graduated from high school, John was ready for something new, and he determined to stick around until it wasn't new anymore.

Jackie's family was quiet and careful. There wasn't much ruckus in their house, even when they were celebrating something. The TV was used primarily for news, and the music that was played around the house was usually classical. Jackie's parents were careful financially, as well, the result of raising four children on a professor's salary. They lived in the same house for thirty-five years, building one addition about ten years after they purchased the house. They never bought a new car, and they furnished their house very modestly.

John's family lived in a succession of bigger and bigger houses. It wasn't long in John's father's career before money was no longer an object. John's family bought and did expensive things. John was given a car on his sixteenth birthday and took a European road trip the summer after graduating from high school. John's family had taken vacations around the world and seemed determined not to take a vacation to the same place twice. They were a family who liked action and excitement. In the evenings their television was always on and music always seemed to be playing.

John and Jackie met during the second semester of their second year. They were across from one another in Starbucks near the Student Union. Jackie was taken by John's infectious laugh. Before long they were talking, and before the conversation was over they had agreed to get together later that evening for coffee. It wasn't love at first sight, but it was close.

John loved how grounded Jackie seemed. He had never met a girl her age who was so mature. Jackie projected a quiet confidence. She didn't need excitement or drama in her life. She seemed to know who she was and where she was going. She was a font of information about the town and the university; it made John feel that he was always getting the insider's tour. And to top it off, Jackie was a very committed believer.

Jackie loved how John seemed to want to live life to the fullest. It was exciting that somehow John got her to do things she had never done. She loved John's laugh and the fact that he made her laugh more than she ever had in her life. It was a fun and new experience to be with someone who didn't need to pinch his pennies. Jackie couldn't believe it when they began to talk about their faith that very first evening. She really did think she had hit the college-boyfriend jackpot.

Graduation was followed quickly by a beautiful wedding in the church where Jackie had grown up. John was accepted into law school in a big city, so off they went to start their life together. But Jackie and John got into a pattern, and they didn't know how harmful it would be. There were two aspects to this pattern. First, John and Jackie hadn't taken time to think about how different they were in personality, lifestyle, and Christian maturity. It was almost as if they didn't want anything to mess up the joy they were experiencing in their relationship with one another. Yet once they got married, things immediately got sticky. It didn't take long for John's spontaneity and impulsiveness to drive Jackie a bit crazy. No two days ever seemed the same. Nights always seemed to be filled with some kind of activity. It seemed that she was on a ride that she could not get off. And if Jackie attempted to question or debate John's plan, John would pout.

John began to think that if he saw Jackie with another book in her hand, he would lose it. It bothered him that she was so slow and methodical. It irritated him that she took so long to make even the most minor decision. He couldn't handle watching her labor over what outfit to wear to wherever they were going. He was sick of her saying she just wanted to stay home. He had quickly grown tired of her constantly telling him that he was spending too much money. And he simply did not want to be told again how noisy he was.

Jackie and John were tired of how both of them held forth their respective families as a better example of how to live. But Jackie and John had never examined how different they were from one another and how these differences would tempt them to criticism, anger, and bitterness.

But there was a second part to their pattern: they never talked about their moments of tension and disagreement, and they seldom asked for forgiveness for wrong attitudes, words, and actions in those moments of argument or debate. Night after night they would go to bed tense or angry. Morning after morning they would wake up silent, discouraged, or a bit bitter. Day after day they would rehearse the events of the previous evening in their heads. There were many suppers where they would eat quietly, the silence broken only by the percussion of their utensils on the plate.

John began to enjoy being away from home more than being at home, although he didn't know it at first. He would make any excuse he could to extend his day. Jackie began to wonder if she had made a mistake, although she wasn't aware that she was having this conversation with herself. The fact was that two very different people had gotten married, and these differences created almost daily difficulties, but they were working harder to deny their difficulties than to deal with them, and they were paying the price. They were both discouraged and increasingly bitter, and it didn't seem to be getting any better.

Jackie and John weren't in trouble because of their differences. No, they were in trouble because of the way they were dealing with their differences. They had established patterns of denial, wrong communication, anger, and unforgiveness—all without decisive moments of resolution. They were sucking the life out of their marriage, and they didn't even know it.

Dealing with Reality

So, what should you do as you are confronted with daily differences between you and your spouse when it comes to the way that you think about and respond to the issues and situations of daily life? Let me suggest steps of a productive pattern that will work to strengthen the unity, understanding, and love of your marriage as it again and again calls you to reconcile with one another.

1) *Face reality.* It never works to deny, reject, or avoid reality. You simply cannot deal with reality in a way that leads to change by refusing to face it. Yet, I am afraid that this is exactly what many, many couples are attempting to do. They work to convince themselves that things are not as bad as they seem, that things will work out, or that they just need to give things a little more time. Perhaps they are afraid that in attempting to deal with things, they will just make things worse. But inaction is seldom an effective course of action leading to change. Reality is something you should always face. The truth is something you should not be afraid of.

Here is where Scripture provides the exact model that we need. I am daily appreciative for the way the Bible deals with reality. Scripture is on one hand brutally honest. The level of honesty in the Bible never fails to stun me. The blood and guts of a broken world filled with flawed people is on every page of the Bible. There are stories in the Bible that force you to deal with how dark and dangerous things can get in this fallen world. There are passages that require you to accept things about yourself that you would be tempted to deny. On the other hand, the Bible is the most hopeful and encouraging book you could ever read. Scripture's offer of life, real and eternal life, is on every page in some way. The whole story of the Bible marches to a glorious end where sin and death will die and things will be right forever.

Why do we have both these themes in the Bible? Because God is inviting us to understand that when we place our trust in him, we don't have to sacrifice either honesty or hope. The honesty of the Bible is not softened by its hope, and the hope of the Bible is not negated by its honesty. Because of who God is and because of the grace he has given us in Jesus Christ, we can face reality unafraid. We can look difficulty in the face and not panic. You can face your differences with honesty and hope even on days when those differences seem huge and unity seems distant.

2) *Deal honestly with your anger.* As with reality, it never works to deny your anger. You know how it works. You know your wife is angry because there is more pot and pan percussion than normal as she is preparing dinner. So you go into the kitchen and ask her what is wrong. She replies rather sharply, "Nothing's wrong!" You respond, "Honey, I think you're angry about something." So she replies, "I'm not angry. It makes me so mad when you accuse me of being angry! I'm just trying to get dinner on the table. It would be helpful if you would leave me alone and let me do what I need to do." You say, "I think we need to talk." And she replies, as she turns her back on you, "You don't want to talk to me right now!"

One of the most important steps in dealing with your differences is to admit to, and own, the things that are going on in your heart. You need to admit and confess when you have been irritated, impatient, or angry, and you need to own the wrong things you have done or said in those moments. I was always amazed when I would counsel couples who had struggled with their differences for years that they would begin to admit and confess their anger for the very first time in my office.

If you are going to deal with your anger, then you must be willing to overlook minor differences. You cannot live with another person and make every difference equally important and equally an issue between you. Some differences are not important at all. It is not important that you and your husband or wife don't always like to eat the same thing or appreciate the same kind of movie. It is not important that one of you is neater than the other. There is plenty of room for these kinds of differences to live in a good marriage. When dealing with your differences, you must prioritize the places where there should be some kind of functional unity in order to cooperate. For example, it is probably not workable or healthy for you to attend different churches. It wouldn't work to have different approaches to parenting. You have to reach agreement on how you are going to approach your financial decisions and your daily use of money. These you cannot and should not overlook, but there are many places in your marriage where you should allow your differences room to breathe.

There is one final thing that is essential to commit yourself to do. Deal with your anger before it gets dark and you go to sleep. The failure to do this was a fatal error for John and Jackie. It allowed both their anger and their hopelessness to grow. Paul gives wonderfully practical counsel: "Be angry and do not sin; do not let the sun go down on your anger, and give no opportunity to the devil" (Eph. 4:26–27). Each of his three directives here is helpful.

First, in a commitment to keep short accounts and deal with things humbly and quickly, don't be angry and don't give way to sin. There are many things loaded into these words, but here is one commitment you must have. When you are angry, resist going where your anger is leading you. In Jesus, you do have the power to say no to the desire to indulge your anger by saying and doing things that you shouldn't. When you do this, you are complicating your own trouble, layering more hurt on the hurt that is already there.

Next, in marriage it is vital to refuse to let the sun go down while you are still angry. I cannot tell you what a protection this biblical directive was and is to Luella and me. We determined from day one that we would not go to sleep angry. Sometimes that meant we would be lying in bed, propping our eyes open, waiting for the other person to ask for forgiveness first! But we were protected by keeping short accounts, and bad moments were not allowed to grow.

Paul adds one more thing. When you have done sinful things in the heat of anger and have refused to deal with what you have done before you go to bed, you give the Devil an opportunity to do his nasty work of deceit and division. It is amazing how, if you give hurt and anger time, they will grow even though nothing further has happened! So keeping short accounts by dealing with your anger humbly and quickly is a great protection for you and your marriage.

3) *Communicate in ways that are wholesome.* What we have done with our understanding of wholesome talk is sad. We have reduced wholesome communication to vocabulary; that is, wholesome talk is understood as little more than refusing to speak a certain set of words. The biblical definition of wholesome communication focuses not so much on our vocabulary but on the intentions of our heart. Let's consider the words of Paul again: "Let no corrupting [unwholesome] talk come out of your mouths, but only such as is good for building up, as fits the occasion, that it may give grace to those who hear" (Eph. 4:29). The addition of the word *unwholesome* is mine. Every one of our marriages would benefit from a daily commitment to speak to one another in this way.

When you are dealing with your differences and the hurt and anger that has resulted, it is essential that you commit yourself to communicate with your spouse in a way that lives up to the biblical standard of wholesome communication. It is possible to never raise your voice, never use a curse word, and never call the other an unkind name, yet still to be proud, unkind, and unwilling to change, more worried about what you want than what the other needs. Wholesome communication is other-focused and other-directed. You say what you are saying in a way that considers your spouse, and you speak in a way that is helpful to him or her.

What does this look like practically? Paul tells us. It means you want to speak to your spouse in a way that builds him up. You want to leave your spouse hopeful, encouraged, and feeling loved. You don't want to leave him discouraged and hopeless. You don't want to communicate to him in a way that stimulates him to be angry or bitter. You don't want to say anything that would tempt him to doubt God, his presence, and his help. It means that you will want to speak to your spouse in a way that fits the moment. If you are in a public setting or if you are with a group of people, it is not wholesome to engage your spouse in a conversation about your differences, nor is it loving to force your spouse to talk to you about how he has once again irritated you when he is exhausted or distraught. When you are not conscious of your surroundings and talk to your spouse in a way that is insensitive or embarrassing, you are talking to him that way not because you are considering him, but because you are considering yourself. You are indulging your anger and are unwilling to wait until you are in a moment that will be more helpful for your spouse and more productive for your relationship.

The last thing Paul says is his ultimate definition of wholesome communication. It is talk that gives grace to the one hearing. Wholesome talk gifts a person with the grace of love, the grace of hope, the grace of comfort, the grace of forgiveness, the grace of wisdom, the grace of peace, the grace of patience, and the grace of faithfulness. When you speak with this kind of grace, you become a tool of transforming grace from a wise, loving, and powerful redeemer, who is at work in this moment of struggle to change you and your spouse and your marriage. He has an amazing ability to turn bad things into beautiful things. Think of the cross; the worst thing that ever happened became the best thing that ever happened. When you function as a tool of grace, God is able to do in you, through you, and for you things you would never, ever be able to accomplish on your own.

You see, the hope of your marriage is not your ability to win an argument or to forge some sticky compromise. The hope of your marriage is not convincing your husband or wife that your way is the right and only way. The hope of your marriage is not your ability to swallow your anger and edit your words. The hope of your marriage is not acting as if things are okay when they are not. The hope of your marriage is not following demands with threats until the other succumbs to your power. No, the hope of your marriage is not to be found in your husband or wife. It is found in one place and one place alone—the amazing grace of an ever-present and ever-faithful Lord. He alone is able to take you where you need to go in order to experience what he designed your marriage to be.

The problem you really need help with is not so much that you are different, but how the sin inside you causes you to deal with your differences in a way that deepens your trouble rather than solving it. This is why God's grace is the real hope of your marriage. His grace gives you everything you need to say no to sin and do what is wholesome, even in moments when you are angry or discouraged.

4) *Run to your resources.* As you're dealing with your differences, it is important to remember that your marriage was never meant to exist in isolation. To be healthy, your marriage needs to be connected to a larger community that offers you resources that you could not offer to one another if left to yourselves. The community of help that God has designed for you is the church. Right near you in the body of Christ are couples who have been through what you are now going through. Luella and I wonder where we would be in our marriage if we had not benefited from the wisdom of brothers and sisters who honestly shared their struggles with us and graciously shared what God had taught them.

There is also the teaching and preaching ministry of the church. It is amazing to me as I preach how many people come up to me, e-mail me, or text me and let me know that what I said on Sunday was exactly what they needed to hear. I've had many husbands or wives ask me after a sermon whether I had talked to their spouse, or if I had a secret camera placed in their house! God will apply his Word to your situation with a specificity that no preacher in his best application moment would be able to.

Then there are the sacraments of the church that so powerfully remind you of who you are as a child of God and the amazing gifts that are yours because of the broken body and shed blood of the Lord Jesus Christ. Along with this there is the encouraging and strengthening fellowship of a small group and the insight and hope that can be gained from solid Christian books. You are not alone. God is not unkind and unfaithful so as to leave you without the resources to do what he has called you to do.

5) *Resist the lies of the enemy.* He will whisper two deadly lies into your ears. The first lie is, "It's not your fault." Here he is working to convince you that you are okay, that you have no need to grow and change. He will work to convince you that your big problems are outside you and not inside you. And if he successfully convinces you of this, then you quit being excited about the help that God has offered you, because you don't think you need it. If he can convince each of you that the other is the problem, then you can spend all your time pointing the finger and

assessing blame, and in your standoff you grow more self-righteous, and the condition of your marriage worsens.

But there is a second lie. The enemy of your soul and your marriage will whisper this in your ear as well: "You don't have enough." He will work to convince you that you simply do not have what you need to face the realities of your differences with hope and courage. He will tempt you to give in and give up. He will tempt you to run and hide. He will tempt you to give way to things that you have the power to resist. He will work to make you feel poor and weak. And if he can get you to minimize your sin and doubt God's provision, he's got you.

Dealing with your differences is never just about communication, negotiation, and compromise. It is spiritual war. You are still a sinner, and so is your spouse. You are both capable of desiring, thinking, speaking, and acting in ways that are not only fundamentally wrong but are destructive to the unity, understanding, and love of your marriage. It is never just the two of you. You live in a world where evil still exists. You and I cannot live in our world with a lazy, comfort-oriented, peace-time mentality. The war still rages. We must be wise and alert, good soldiers in the war that is being fought for control of our hearts.

6) *Create something new.* Marriage was never intended to be a lifelong series of his-way/her-way skirmishes. Your home, your lifestyle, and your schedule shouldn't reflect the vision, tastes, desires, decisions, or instincts of one of you. No, God has intended your lives to become so fundamentally intertwined, so beautifully woven together in every way, and so much a reflection of a daily commitment to cooperation, that the only term that could be used for your union is "one flesh." You have celebrated your created differences and how the influences throughout your life have shaped each of you, but you have also caught the vision of how God has chosen you to be melded together in marriage in a way that makes each of you better-rounded in experience and perspective and more mature in character. In other words, by God's grace you have made use of your differences to become better people, better able to be what God created you to be and do what he created you to do.

As I sat with John and Jackie and listened to the story of the hurt and disappointment of their marital struggle, I was impressed at how skillful they had been at living separately together. They had not become "one flesh" in any way. They had become increasingly irritated by their differences and increasingly distraught with the fact that they had gotten to a place where it was practically impossible to do anything together without a major debate that would quickly descend into a debilitating argument. Hurtful things were said and done, leaving each of them determined never to go through that again. So, rather than following the pattern we have been considering of growing in appreciation and unity, they dealt with their differences by living separate lives, and they worked to win the day and control the outcome when it was necessary to do something together. Night after night they would go to bed discouraged or angry. And the more this happened, the more they separately wondered if they had made a terrible mistake.

Yet, the more I got to know John and Jackie, the more I could see God's wisdom in bringing them together. John really did need to become a more reasoned and measured man. He did need to see the value of thoughtful planning. He did need to grow in his commitment to examine his thoughts and edit his words. He had so much to learn from Jackie if he would stop feeling threatened and celebrate the wonder of God's bringing her into his life.

Jackie needed to be yanked out of her comfort zone. She carried with her a package of unused gifts because she always seemed to opt for what was familiar and comfortable. She seemed unable to be spontaneous and got way too uptight when she was required to deal with something that she had not anticipated or that had not been part of her plan. Jackie was more motivated by fear than she knew. It was impossible to get to know her and not be impressed with the wisdom of God in causing her story to become intertwined with John's. In a real way, John was the perfect man for Jackie, and it was good that he was with her. No, I don't mean that he was perfect. John was far from perfect, but he brought a set of innate gifts and experiences that were the perfect balance for Jackie. She really did have so much to learn and to gain from John.

Here's what I am saying. John was strong where Jackie was weak, and Jackie was strong where John was weak. It is amazing to stand back and consider the wisdom of God in bringing them together. Yet, rather than capitalizing on one another's strengths and growing as a result, they played to one another's weaknesses. In so doing, instead of growing in character and unity they participated in a silent conspiracy in a marriage of distrust, fear, disunity, hurt, anger, and disappointment. They thought their marriage was impossible. The real truth was that they had taken a relationship of beautiful possibility and made it impossible by a stubborn unwillingness to listen, give, serve, and learn.

I would sit with Jackie and John and think to myself, "This marriage could be a thing of beauty, but look at what it's become." However, there is one thing John and Jackie did that was right: in their hurt and disappointment they ran to their resources. They were not alone. Jackie had developed a relationship with an older woman at the church who had been married for over thirty years. Fear and shame had kept Jackie from being honest with her older friend about what was going on in her marriage, but she got desperate enough that her desperation became stronger than her fear, and she reached out for help. It was through the counsel of this older woman that John and Jackie ended up with me. It took a while, but these two desperate people became celebrants and began a life that was truly lived together.

7) *Humbly admit your ongoing struggle.* The good news of the grace of the Lord Jesus Christ is that you have all the help you will ever need to face whatever is written into your life by the one who is writing your story. But you must humbly face the fact that until you are in his final kingdom, where sin, suffering, and death are no more, you will need his rescue, forgiveness, empowerment, and deliverance moment by moment every day. You will never become a grace graduate! This means that there will never be a point in your marriage where you can just lay back, chill out, and coast. As long as sin still lives inside you, with its self-focused, antisocial instincts, you need to live with open eyes, listening ears, and an approachable heart.

None of us is yet all that grace is able to cause us to be. None of our marriages is all that God has designed each of them to be. No one reading this can say, "Our marriage is perfect and without need of growth in any way." We all must confess that every day we struggle with sin. Every day we say and do what is wrong. Every day we desire things we should not have and think things we should not think. Every day we fall once again into living for ourselves rather than for God and others. We don't celebrate who God has made our husbands and wives to be in the way that we should. We do get irritated and impatient because we want our spouse to be our clone, and we don't really want to have to deal with the difficulty of molding our lives together into one. We love our comfort more than we love one another. We want to have our own way rather than going God's way. We want things done our way rather than having to consider another way or being required to admit that there is a way that may be better than ours. We don't want to admit that there are ways in which our husbands or wives are stronger or more mature than we are. We don't want to admit that not everything can be reduced to a moral right or wrong. We don't like having to live with differences.

We each have to humbly admit that the struggle still goes on, but we do not have to give way to fatalism or cynicism, because grace guarantees that we are not alone. Grace has bound Jesus to us and us to him forever. Grace is working to pry each of us out of our tiny little kingdom of one to live together in the lushness of God's big kingdom of love.

Your King and Savior is at work, even when you have given up. He loves you even when you don't have sense enough to love one another or to love him in return. He is working outside you to produce in you a sense of need, and working inside you to give you what you need. You never arrive at a location where he is not present. You never live in a relationship without him being there as well. You never face a disappointment, temptation, responsibility, obligation, opportunity, or calling without the resources of his grace. In your darkest moment, his grace lights your way. In your deepest disappointment, his love gives you hope. When you are weak and exhausted, his strength gives you reason to go on. When you are confused and don't know what to do, his wisdom gives you direction. In the moments when you feel wounded and alone, he comforts you with loving and healing hands. When you have lost your way, he seeks you and finds you and brings you back.

Your hope of a long-term, loving marriage is found in one place—God's love for you. Admit that you need it and then give yourself to celebrating that this God of love has brought you and your spouse together for his glory and your good. And remember, he will not call you to a task without giving you, in his grace, what you need to do it.

What counts in making a happy marriage is not so much how compatible you are, but how you deal with incompatibility.

LEO TOLSTOY

Love doesn't commit suicide. We have to kill it. Though, it often simply dies of our neglect.

DIANE SOLLEE

COMMITMENT 1: We will give ourselves to a regular lifestyle of confession and forgiveness.

COMMITMENT 2: We will make growth and change our daily agenda.

COMMITMENT 3: We will work together to build a sturdy bond of trust.

COMMITMENT 4: We will commit to building a relationship of love.

COMMITMENT 5: We will deal with our differences with appreciation and grace.

COMMITMENT 6: We will work to protect our marriage.

15

Eyes Wide Open

Beth wanted out, and Eric had little motivation to convince her to stay. I had seen it before, so I wasn't shocked, but it was sad nonetheless. Beth and Eric had known each other for thirty years and had been married for twenty-five. Just two months short of their twenty-fifth anniversary they were in my office to talk about dissolving their marriage. Beth had already designed her escape plan, and Eric had already decided not to fight. I wasn't too clear on why they wanted to see me.

Yes, I had seen it before, but I was reminded once again of the very first time. It had been a couple named John and Judy. They had been married for thirty years, but they both desperately wanted out. I had been immediately confronted with the irrationality of it all. You would think that if a couple could make it for thirty years, they could make it forever. You would think that in thirty years, they would have learned what it takes to live together. You would think that after thirty years, they would have benefited from all the wisdom that they had gained from difficulty and failure. You would think that if they had lived that long with one another, they would have been determined to die together, but that is simply not always the case. Beth and Eric reminded me of John and Judy.

Beth's tears flowed easily, and Eric seldom looked up. With slumped shoulders and few words, Eric was about to let his marriage go. And with an almost delusional hope in a renewed future, all Beth could think about was life beyond Eric. What they said wasn't at all unfamiliar. They both wondered where the love had gone. They had a detailed litany of the wrongs the other had done. They both came armed with arguments for why it was impossible for their marriage to continue. But it hit me that their analysis of their marriage was marked more by accusation than regret. It was this that caught my attention. Somewhere they had quit living as one and begun living separately together. Let me explain.

There is a sometimes subtle, but always dramatic, difference between standing as one to fight together the things that threaten your marriage and standing separately and keeping a record of the things the other does that make marriage difficult for you. The first is an act of relational commitment; the second is a posture of self-preservation and survival. The first strengthens a marriage; the second weakens it. The first draws you closer together as you learn to protect yourself from your weaknesses; the second tears you apart as weaknesses morph into accusations and judgments. The first makes you growingly aware and merciful in the face of struggle; the second causes you to be increasingly impatient with, and intolerant of, your spouse's struggle. The first leads you to seek God together; the second causes you to seek escape separately. The first leads you to hope; the second reinforces your despair. The first convinces you that you must and you will; the second convinces you that you can't and you won't. The first builds your resolve to stay; the second gives you reason for going. The first refuses to consider options; the second thinks that options are the only hope. The first accepts that staying means sacrifice; the second has had enough of sacrifice. The first knows love means work; the second is done with the work of love.

Clearly Beth and Eric were no longer standing together and defending their marriage against threat. Clearly they stood separately in a daily state of finger-pointing acrimony. It was this that gave me hope. You see, it was not that their marriage hadn't worked. It wasn't that it had been a cosmic mistake so that the only sensible course of action was escape. It wasn't that God's structures, principles, and promises had failed. No, Eric and Beth had quit being married. What I mean is that they had quit doing the things that make up the content of this book, and when they quit, it didn't take long for their marriage to be in trouble.

Now, get prepared because I am about to surprise you: I think they quit doing the good things that make a marriage sturdy and beautiful not because they had a bad marriage but because they had a good marriage. At some point they quit watching and praying. At some point they began to lie back and enjoy the ride. They took good as an invitation to quit working, and now they were paying the price. This was not a marriage without hope; this was a marriage without work, and this side of heaven, walking away from the work never works.

Lifetime Warranty

Grace gives your marriage a lifetime warranty. What this means is that God will give you everything you need to be what you are supposed to be and do what he has called you to do in your marriage. But you must do it. His grace enables, reconciles, restores, and repairs. His grace teaches you and changes you. His grace gives you what you need to ask forgiveness and to forgive. His grace empowers you to overlook minor offenses and target what is truly important. His grace helps you see yourself with greater and greater accuracy and respond to what you see with greater and greater wisdom. His grace gives you strength to continue when you feel like quitting. His grace gives you the power to resist temptation and to turn and do what is right. His grace rescues you from your obsession with self-love and welcomes you to the joyous work of loving another. His grace enables you to be good and angry at the same time. When grace works a commitment to God's kingdom and righteousness in your heart, you will be angry at what sin does to you, to those you love, and to the situations in which you live, and that anger will motivate you to be a tool of change. His grace causes you to be committed to giving grace. His grace is a marriage warranty, because it gives you what you need, but what you get is grace in motion.

You see, Eric and Beth were not in trouble because God's plan for marriage was infected by inherent defects or because his grace had practical gaps. No, they were in trouble because they got lazy and quit doing the things that would deliver to them the grace they had been given. It is here that I think Old Testament biblical accounts can help us. Consider Israel encamped on the shore of the Red Sea. It was a scary and discouraging situation. In such moments you have only two choices. You can look around and say to yourself, "This is nuts! There is no way out, so the best thing to do is cut and run." Or you can remember God's promise that he would deliver that enemy into your hands, and you can wait for his instruction. You will not experience the grace of redemption from the bondage of Egypt and from the threat of the enemy if you cut and run. You will only experience this grace if you do what God has called you to do and walk across the Red Sea between those gurgling walls of water, no matter how crazy and terrifying that may seem.

Or consider Jericho. How in the world is this ragtag group of recently freed slaves going to defeat this walled city? Now, again, you can respond based on the seeming impossibility of the task and give up the hope of ever living together in the Promised Land, or you can remember the promises of God and do what he calls you to do. This incident is especially helpful, because the walls didn't come down after the first day's parade. They didn't come down after the second or third day either. You can see some of the Israelites either doubting this is ever going to work or wondering how many processionals it will take before it does. There is perseverance called for here. On the seventh day, at the sound of the trumpets, the walls crumbled.

From ground level, God's call to Israel is humiliatingly irrational. No one would march around a walled city in close proximity to its weaponry and expect to live, let alone defeat them! But maybe that is the point. God uses occasions of trouble to deepen our trust in him and our willingness to do what he says, no matter how much it goes against our natural instincts. In order for Israel to receive the grace of the defeat of their enemy, they had to be willing to take the walk until the walls came down.

Yes, the Red Sea was an obstacle, a huge and discouraging one. And, yes, Jericho was an obstacle, one that seemingly could not be overcome. But they were both much more than this. They were both part of God's plan. If you examine the first few verses of Exodus 14, you will realize that Israel didn't end up in front of the Red Sea because Moses had a defective internal GPS. No, God commanded Moses to guide Israel there because God knew exactly what was going to happen and what he would do. He was going to use this scary occasion to reveal his glory to Israel so that they would know that he was with them and would exercise his power on their behalf. And he was going to use this situation to let Egypt know once and for all who is Lord.

God was also not surprised that fortified Jericho was in the way of Israel's possession of the land of promise. In fact, it was his plan that Israel participate in the clearing of the land of promise. In so doing, Israel was to become strong in faith and in worship of the Lord. In the same way, God is never surprised at the obstacles you encounter as you live with your husband or wife. He planned for you to be married to a flawed person and for you to live in a fallen world together. He intended marital hardship to drive you to his grace and, as it does, to cause you to grow and mature together. He also ordained these changes in you, and your marriage, to be a process and not an event. He is with you and gives you what you need, but you must get up and follow him across the sea into battle.

Where Things Often Go Wrong

The sad thing about the broken state of Eric and Beth's marriage was how quietly it went bad. It was going bad and they didn't even notice it. They didn't see that they were coasting, and that this side of heaven you can't be a sinner living with a sinner and coast. You have to get up every morning and reconcile once again to one another and to God. You have to accept the call to work every day to make your marriage what it was intended to be. You have to humbly admit that you are a person who is still in need of change and growth. You have to be willing to be confronted and to examine your choices, desires, thoughts, words, and behavior. You have to live with your eyes and heart open. You have to be a good student, studying your spouse and learning how to love him or her in fresh new ways. You have to locate the potholes in your marriage that have the potential of bumping your marriage out of line. You have to be willing to go through tough and sometimes tense moments of honesty to get things on the table that need to be examined and discussed. You have to be willing to get up early or stay up late because there are things you need to finish between you. You have to be willing to open up your marriage to God and others, getting the help you need for the things you are facing. You have to remind yourself daily of the amazing resources of grace that you have been given, and celebrate. You have to resist giving way to cynicism and discouragement. You have to battle giving way to anger or fear. You have to fight the "what ifs" and the "if onlys." You really do have to believe that God will always supply what is needed at the moment it is needed. You have to pay attention to your marriage and remember him. You have to watch and pray.

Your marriage may be good. It may even be great. You may have grown together in appreciation, respect, unity, understanding, and love. You may have learned where problems typically exist for you as a couple, and you may have learned how to solve them together. You may have identified places where you and your marriage need to mature. You may have created a lifestyle of honest communication and efficient problem solving. You may have forged a solid and enjoyable friendship between you. You may be able to look back and be thankful because you recognize what you once were compared to what you are now.

But there is one thing that you need to accept: your marriage may be great, but it is not safe. No marriage this side of eternity is totally problem protected. No marriage is all that it could be. This side of heaven daily temptations are constant threats to you and your marriage. This side of heaven the spiritual war goes on. This side of heaven good marriages are good marriages because the people in those marriages are committed to doing daily the things that keep their marriages good. Things go wrong when couples think they have reached the point when they can retire from their marital work and chill out, lie back, and slide. Perhaps the greatest danger to a good marriage is a good marriage, because when things are good, we are tempted to give way to feelings of arrival and forsake the attitudes and disciplines that have, by God's grace, made our marriage what it has become.

What It Looks Like to Coast

So maybe you're thinking, "Paul, I get the point; we cannot allow ourselves to coast, and we need to keep watching our marriage, but I'm not sure I know what coasting looks like." Well, let me give you six characteristics of a coasting couple.

1) *Visual Lethargy*

In some way, at some time, we all quit looking. Some place in all of our lives we live with lazy eyes. Let me give you a couple of illustrations. The first time you drove to work, you were wide-eyed and attentive because you didn't know where you were going. You marked down particular landmarks in your mental notebook so that you would remember your journey a second time. For the first few weeks you watched your surroundings closely as you drove, making sure that you identified your markers and made all of your turns. But after a while it didn't seem so necessary to pay such careful attention. After a while you quit looking. Someone new rides with you and says, "Hey, when did that gas station close?" And you say, "I don't know, I didn't notice that it was closed." You didn't notice because at some point you quit looking. At some point you began to be preoccupied and easily distracted. Your drives to work were occupied with coffee and a scone, messing with the radio, and texting while driving. There are now times when you get to work and don't remember stopping at lights or making those important turns. You don't remember because you have quit looking. You are suffering from visual lethargy.

Luella and I have recently moved. From our previous location, we had to take a beautiful, tree-lined winding road along a river to get to Center City Philadelphia. Recently, we were in our old neighborhood and had to drive that road again. We both remarked how beautiful the drive was. As we were talking, I was thinking about how many times I drove that road and did not see its beauty.

To use another illustration, maybe you're at an art fair and you have no intention of making a purchase. You are just there because it's something fun to do. But as you're strolling from booth to booth, a painting reaches out and grabs you. You say to your spouse, "Come here for a minute; you have got to see this." After what seems to be an interminable negotiation, you are putting the painting in the car. You know exactly where you are going to hang it, and for the first few days you pause and look and smile when you are in the room where the painting is. You can't believe that you own it. You are impressed with how it changes the atmosphere of the entire room. You are very grateful that it is yours. You reason that it needs proper light, so you have some track lighting installed. You notice that the pillows on the leather chair clash with the color themes of the painting, so you buy new pillows. When you have guests, you proudly show them the painting, and you share with them the story behind it.

But there comes a point where you are no longer aware of your prized purchase. There comes a time when you don't smile anymore when you walk by it. There comes a time when a visitor is sitting in the room with you and says, "I love that painting," and you say, "We got it a few years ago at a fair someplace," and you go on with the conversation. You are no longer excited, because you no longer see. You are living with lazy eyes. It takes an outsider to get you to focus for a moment on what once captured your attention. You are suffering from visual lethargy, and you probably don't know it.

Such is the state of many married couples. Beth and Eric had their eyes wide open during courtship. They listened to and watched one another carefully. Beth hung on Eric's every word, and Eric watched all Beth's reactions. They were always on the lookout for problems that might arise between them, and they were quick to solve what needed to be solved. There wasn't much about their relationship that they took for granted, and they didn't mind being good students in the laboratory room of the school of love.

The early days of their marriage were much the same. Beth couldn't believe that she had actually been blessed to marry a man like Eric, and Eric knew that in marrying Beth, he had married way above his pay grade. They worked at their marriage, both being afraid to mess up the good thing that they had been given. But at some point, as the years rolled on, their eyes got lazy and their schedules got busy. At some point they began to feel that they were okay, and they began to coast. At some point they quit noticing the blessings. At some point they quit being thankful and watchful. And when they quit, they began to let things creep into their marriage that they would not have tolerated before. Because they quit paying attention, they quit noticing things that needed attention, and because they quit noticing, they quit working on the things that needed work. Lazy eyes were a major part of what led their marriage to disaster. *Where is there evidence in your marriage that you have been living with lazy eyes?*

2) Habit Inconsistency

There is no doubt about it—a marriage of unity, understanding, and love is the result of good attitudes, which result in the instituting of good habits. There are many examples of the importance of good habits in your life if you just look around.

When you purchase a new car, you are very aware that it is new, and you are very committed to keeping it that way. You don't think that your new automobile will keep itself washed on the outside, clean on the inside, and mechanically maintained. You accept the reality that, if your car is going to remain clean and in good working order, you have to approach it with the work ethic of good habits. You don't mind doing these things because you like your car, you are pleased that it belongs to you, and it is a source of pride for you to keep it well maintained. The weekly washing and vacuuming, the warranty inspections, and the regular oil changes aren't hassles for you; no, they are things you want to do because you appreciate your new car. You even buy special gadgets, cleansers, and deodorizers to keep things fresh and clean. And when you are driving you listen for sounds that may indicate that something is not right with your car.

The problem is that at some point your car is not new anymore. It doesn't smell new since you spilt coffee on the way to work. When you drive it, it makes sounds that it didn't make when it was new. And besides, you seem to have gotten a whole lot busier since you bought the car, and finding time to keep it clean and the oil changed is not as easy as it once was. At some point it doesn't bother you that there are a week's worth of empty Starbucks cups on the back floor of your car, and you don't really mind that it's not so clean. You have begun to let go of the good habits of auto maintenance, and you probably haven't noticed, but your car begins to pay the price. One morning, quite unexpectedly, you go to start your car, the oil light comes on, and the car won't start. You are surprised because you didn't know that anything was wrong, for months ago you simply quit paying attention, and you forsook the habits that would have kept your car in good repair.

Beth and Eric started their life together committed to good habits. They committed to humble approachability, wholesome communication, rapid problem solving, quick conflict resolution, spiritual communion, and patterns of forgiveness and to communicate thankfulness and to build trust. These commitments resulted in a marriage that was godly, enjoyable, and fulfilling, and they both grew in the process. But they began to feel all too satisfied and all too comfortable, and they began to let their good habits slide.

They began to allow themselves to go to bed in the middle of a conflict. Sure, they would say that they would discuss it in the morning, but they seldom did. They began to allow themselves to step away from habits of wholesome communication and say things they would not have allowed themselves to say earlier. There were times when they failed to seek or grant forgiveness, telling themselves that it was a little thing and wouldn't make any difference. They became more and more inconsistent in doing the good things that make a marriage loving, peaceful, and sturdy. The more they became inconsistent, the more their marriage suffered until they reached the point where it seemed to them that they had an insurmountable set of problems, and they were overwhelmed at the thought of continuing. *Are there good habits that were once a regular part of your life together that you have now forsaken?*

3) Laziness

I drove by it almost every day for years, and I couldn't believe what I was seeing. It didn't happen overnight, but it happened nonetheless, and it was sad to see. It was a beautiful house with a complicated, cross-shaped roof. It was beautiful the way the gables all came together in the center. I thought about what a source of pride it must have given the builder when the house was completed and he was able to stand back and take a look. It was the nicest house on the block.

But there was a problem. The house was inhabited by lazy people. You could tell that by the lawn, which was closer to needing to be bailed than mowed, and by the bushes that had grown widely in every direction. One morning as I drove by, I noticed a small tarp over one part of the roof. Now, a tarp only means one thing: the roof is leaking and needs repair. A tarp nailed down to a leaky roof is not a repair. No, it is what you do as an emergency measure until you can get the roof properly repaired. But the tarp stayed there and was soon accompanied by another tarp. It was not long before the entire roof had been tarped, but no repairs seemed to be in sight. Some of the tarps had been on the roof so long that they had frayed and torn and now flapped in the breeze.

There was no way that the patchwork of tarps created the kind of moisture barrier that a properly shingled roof would. So under those lazy tarps, the structure of the house was absorbing moisture and slowly deteriorating. I remember the day I saw workers removing the tarps, but over the next few days, I realized they were removing more. They removed the roofing, the sheathing, and the gable structures themselves. Lazy neglect had rendered the roof irreparable, and if the family was going to continue to live there, major structural repair would have to be done. Laziness is destructive to anything that needs to be maintained.

Yet, there are many lazy marriages out there. Well, to be more accurate, the marriages aren't lazy; it's the people in them that are. They want good marriages, but they just don't want to do the daily work necessary to keep them healthy.

Beth and Eric got tired of the hard work. They somehow fantasized that their marriage would remain good, long after they had quit working on it. In their laziness, Beth and Eric became quite skilled at throwing tarps over the roof leaks. When offended they would say, "It's okay," when it really wasn't okay. In their laziness they would try to squeeze a big conversation into a little moment. In their laziness they sheltered themselves from one another by busyness and entertainment. But the leaks in their marriage got bigger. It wasn't long before the structures that were holding them together became weak and rotten. Laziness was part of what had rendered their marriage virtually unlivable. *Where is laziness damaging the health and beauty of your marriage?*

4) Impatience

I would like to say that I am patient, but I am not. I would like to say that I am always willing to wait, but I am not. I would like to say that I have learned the value of waiting, but I am still learning. I would like to be able to confess that I have seen the value of approaching my marriage with a process mentality, but I don't always appreciate the process. There are times when I would like instant marriage—you know, just add water and stir. But when I resist the processes that make a marriage beautiful and demand things in an instant, I am not resisting marriage or resisting my wife; no, I am resisting God.

It is God who designed change to be a process and not an event. It is God who chose to put flawed people together in the intensity and close proximity of the intimacy of marriage. It is God who designed marriage to expose your heart, to take you beyond the borders of your own strength and wisdom, and to mature and grow you as you quit relying on yourself and begin to seek the help that only God can give. It is God who created marriage as a workroom to form you into a person who loves as you have been loved and finds joy in giving the same kind of grace that you have been given. It is God who knew that the messiness of marriage would be productive in advancing the work that he began in us when he adopted us as his children.

Every marriage between the fall and eternity is in the middle of a lifelong process of change. Your marriage may be better than it once was, but it is not yet all that it could be. In marriage you are meant to grow together in an increasingly maturing love and to grow personally in your love and service of the Lord.

You see, patience in marriage is vital, because the goal of marriage is greater than marriage. The goal of marriage, from God's perspective, is not that you would reach some mutually agreed-upon plateau of romantic and interpersonal happiness. No, God's goals are much wider and more beautiful than that. God's goal is that your marriage would be a major tool in his wise and loving hands to rescue you from claustro-phobic self-worship and form you into a person who lives for nothing smaller than his kingdom, his righteousness, and his glory. God's goal is to transform you at the causal core of your personhood—your heart. He is working so that everything you think, desire, say, and do is done in loyal and joyful service to him. God's goal is not to deliver to you your well-thought-through dream of personal happiness. No, his goal is nothing less than holiness; or as Peter says, that you may become "partakers of the divine nature" (2 Pet. 1:4).

Eric and Beth began to grow impatient. Beth would say, "Eric, how many times do I have to tell you . . . ?" Eric would complain, "She does the same thing over and over again even though she knows it drives me crazy." They both began to see opportunities to grow as obstacles in the way of the good life, and they worked harder at moving the obstacles than they did at growing. In their demandingness and impatience, rather than learning from their problems and progressively learning how to solve or avoid them, they repeated them over and over again. Again and again they settled for instantaneous solutions that did not get at the heart of the matter. They wanted more in an instant, but what they got was less. *Are there places where you are demanding in an instant what will only be formed in a process?*

5) Responding in Discouragement

There is an insightful little directive in Psalm 37:8: "Do not be afraid; it will only lead to evil" (my translation). There is a point in the lives of many couples when they quit responding in faith, hope, and love and begin to respond to one another in discouragement and fear. Their practical, everyday responses are formed more by what they are afraid of than by what they hope for. They are more driven by discouragement at what is than they are by faith in what could be. They respond more out of hurt than love.

Now, let's be honest. Marriage is often discouraging. We have already concluded that all of us have been disappointed in our marriages in some way. We have all had to deal with the undesirable and the unexpected. We have all sinned against one another, and we have all been sinned against. All of us look back with remorse and regret because our marriages have not been all that we hoped they would be. It is true that the person whom you love the most has the ability to hurt you the most. In some way, we all get our dreams dashed and our expectations thwarted.

So we will struggle at moments with disappointment, and we will wonder if things will ever get better, and the fear of things staying the same will grip us. The problem is that you tend not to make your best decisions when you are discouraged, and you usually live to regret the decisions you make out of fear. It is in moments in our marriages when we are revealed as the sinners we actually are that fighting discouragement with hope and battling doubt with faith is so important.

Where do you get this hope and faith? Well, you don't get it from your husband or wife. No, you get it from the third person in your marriage, the person we are tempted to forget. You get hope when there seems to be no reason for hope from Immanuel. Your Savior shed his blood and died for you; does it make any sense that he would abandon you in your hour of need? You see, hope is not to be found in your spouse or in your circumstances. No, hope is found in one place and one place alone—in Jesus your savior, your brother, and your friend. He loves you, and he will never turn a deaf ear to your cries.

So you have to fight the instinct to respond in discouragement and remember who you are and who God is and act in hope, even when hope is hard to see. *Where are you tempted to respond in discouragement and fear?*

6) Dining with the Enemy

Earlier in this book we looked at Ephesians 4 and Paul's directive not to let the sun go down on your anger nor give the Devil an opportunity. But this is what many couples end up doing. They not only give the Devil an opportunity, but they end up inviting him for dinner! How? By thinking that they have arrived and by letting go of the good habits that made their marriage a relationship of unity, understanding, and love. When you quit paying attention, let go of good habits, allow yourself to be lazy and impatient, and respond in discouragement, you are inviting the Devil into your marriage to do his nasty work of deceit, division, and destruction.

Remember, marriage is spiritual warfare. There really is good and evil. There really is someone who is the enemy of your soul, the enemy of everything good, true, wise, and beautiful. There really is someone who does not want to see you grow and change. There is someone who fights against the unity, understanding, and love of your marriage. Living blindly and naïvely gives him an opportunity to destroy the good things that God has created in you and in your marriage.

So we must remain alert. We must commit ourselves to being watchful. We must resist growing tired and becoming lazy. We must refuse to give way to cynicism and discouragement. We must not demand in an instant what will only come as the result of a process. We must not do these things, because when we do we are dining with the Devil, and that never leads to anything good. *Are there places right here, right now, in your marriage where you are giving the Devil an opportunity?*

Restoring Grace

Yes, it was true, Beth and Eric were a bit of a mess, and so was their marriage, but they did the right thing. They stepped out of their secret world of discouragement and acrimony and sought help. It was hard for them to admit how bad things had become. It was hard to own how petty and divisive they had both been. It embarrassed them to admit to things they had said and done. But they were tired and afraid and grabbed hold of hope anywhere help could be found. I was glad to help, because I had a sense of what was going on.

Beth and Eric had done one disastrous thing in their marriage, and it had created a mess. They had given in to the delusion that they had arrived, and so they quit paying attention. Good habits waned and bad ones took over. Laziness replaced the daily work of love, so things got progressively worse. But God met them at their moment of need and enabled them, by his grace, to get back up and to do the good things that have to be done for a marriage ever to be what God designed it to be.

There were many places where forgiveness needed to be sought and given. There were many habits that needed to be replaced with the old habits of attentive love. There were clear places where each was being called to wait, and there was grace for the waiting. There were many topics they needed to discuss with a commitment to humble listening and wholesome speaking.

But they did listen, and wait, and forgive, and God began to restore the unity, understanding, and love that seemed beyond repair. They learned the importance of being committed to *watch and pray* no matter how good things were and to *respond in hope* no matter how bad things seemed, and they learned that they were never alone.

COMMITMENT 1:   We will give ourselves to a regular
                lifestyle of confession and forgiveness.

COMMITMENT 2:   We will make growth and change our
                daily agenda.

COMMITMENT 3:   We will work together to build a sturdy
                bond of trust.

COMMITMENT 4:   We will commit to building a relationship
                of love.

COMMITMENT 5:   We will deal with our differences with
                appreciation and grace.

COMMITMENT 6:   We will work to protect our marriage.

16

On Your Knees

It's the thing that many couples miss. It is so simple, so biblically logi-cal, but it seems to slip through the cracks in the lives of many couples. If it is true that all the horizontal skirmishes a husband and wife have are rooted in a deeper war for the heart, and if it is true that a marriage must be fixed vertically before it is ever fixed horizontally, then the place where you win the war for marriage is on your knees. Perhaps there is no more important command for marriage in all the Bible than the simple words of Paul in 1 Thessalonians 5:16–18: "Rejoice always, pray without ceasing, give thanks in all circumstances; for this is the will of God in Christ Jesus for you."

If marriage is a flawed person living with a flawed person in a fallen world, and if the war for control of our hearts still rages, then we can-not and must not quit seeking God's help for our marriage. This side of heaven there is nothing more important for our marriage than to *pray without ceasing*. There is never a moment in our marriage when we are not in need of the rescuing, enabling, delivering grace of the Redeemer. There is never a moment when we do not need his wisdom, strength, and forgiveness. There is never a time when we have grown up enough that we no longer need his mercy. This side of heaven we will never graduate from the school of grace.

Every day we face things that we had not anticipated we would face. Every day, temptations, sometimes subtle and sometimes powerful, greet us. Every day we sin against our spouses and are sinned against by them in some way. Every day the fallen world, in all its brokenness, presses in on us and makes life more difficult and complicated than it was originally designed to be. Every day we are greeted with the seductive voice of the kingdom of self, wooing us to live for nothing bigger than our wants, our needs, and our feelings.

Every day we are called to fight what is wrong and give ourselves to what is right. Every day we are called to humbly examine ourselves and to commit ourselves to change. Every day there are things in our marriage that need to be uprooted, and every day there are new and better things that need to be planted. Every day there is some issue for which we need the insight of biblical wisdom. Every day we must surrender what we want to the better agenda of what God has commanded. Every day we must fight to be good stewards of the blessings we have been given. Every day we must identify the places where we must say no and the places where we must say yes.

Every day we are called to love each other in ways that are practical and specific. Every day we must live with open eyes and an open heart. Every day we must fight the things that distract us from loving, serving, and nurturing one another. Every day we need to act in sacrificial love toward one another, even though we are busy or tired. Every day we must work to protect the unity, understanding, and love of our marriage. Every day in some way we are called to love when the other person doesn't deserve it. Every day we are called to give to our husband or wife the same grace that God has given us. Every day we must be motivated not only by our own interests but also by the interests of our spouse. Every day we are called to have a myriad of conversations in a way that gives grace and builds up the other person. Every day we must resist keeping a record of wrongs and instead genuinely forgive. Every day we need to look for ways to communicate encouragement, appreciation, and respect. Every day we are called to lay something down in order to capture an opportunity to love.

What Marriage Is Meant to Do

Now, let's be honest. You and I are not up to the task. Consider the call of this book. Consider the paragraphs above. Could you honestly look at yourself in the mirror of God's Word and say, "I do all these things well"? As I have written this book, I have been convicted once again about the many places I fall short. I have been convicted about the places where my words and actions are more formed by the kingdom of self than by the kingdom of God. I have been convicted of my impatience, that desire for marriage to be instantly easier than it now is. I have been convicted that I don't always speak in a way that is gracious. There are times when winning a discussion (read: argument) is more important to me than the unity of my marriage. I am convicted of ways in which I am still demanding and self-centered. I have been convicted that in my heart the war still goes on.

No, I know I can't stand up and say, "I do all these things well." In fact when I consider God's call for marriage, I think, "The bar is too high; I'll never reach it!" But hear what I am about to say next: this is exactly what marriage is meant to do. It is meant to be a tool in God's hands to expose your heart and to drive you to the end of yourself. Marriage is meant to expose your self-focus and self-reliance. It is meant to convince you that you are needier than you thought you were and to encourage you that God's grace has more power to transform than you thought it did. Marriage is meant to teach you how to give, love, serve, forgive, support, encourage, and wait.

Think of it this way: although you are to be married for life, your marriage is not a destination. Your marriage is not an end in itself. No, the radical thing that the Bible teaches about all that is going on is that no experience or relationship in the here and now is an end in itself. Everything we are going through now is a God-designed and God-controlled means to an end. Your marriage is not a destination; no, it is a toll of preparation for a final destination. You will never understand your marriage struggles and your personal needs in the midst of them until you understand this. So God is not only working to form your marriage into what he designed it to be; no, more foundationally he is working to reform you into what you were created to be. It is only as we grow and change that our marriages can thrive.

So, feeling weak and unable is a good thing. The thing that keeps each of us from growing is not our assessment of weakness. The grace of God is greater than any weakness we may experience. No, the thing that keeps us from growing is our delusion of strength. When we think we are righteous and strong, we do not seek the help that God so tenderly and faithfully offers. Our marriage is not damaged by cries of weakness but by pronouncements of strength. Our marriage is harmed by our reliance on our own wisdom, righteousness, and strength. In the biblical model, weakness is the portal to strength. It is when I admit that I am weak that I seek the help of a God of incalculable power, who is near me and willingly meets me in my time of need.

The Transforming Power of Prayer

Here is where prayer is so important and so powerful. Prayer makes no sense unless two things are true. First, our lives do not belong to us. Since we have been created by God, everything we are, everything we have, and every situation and relationship in which we live belongs to him. Because we are his creatures, our number-one calling in every area of life is to worship him. Everything we do and say in every situation and relationship of our lives must be done in recognition of his existence and for the purpose of his glory. We were created for his pleasure, and we are called to live in constant worship of him. So, everything in our lives has verticality to it. Everything we do must be done in recognition of God's presence and his rightful ownership of our lives. We must live in our marriage in a way that is distinctively and comprehensively Godward, even in the most mundane moments of life.

There is a second thing that must be true for prayer to make any sense. It is that sin makes us comprehensively needy. Every area of our personhood has been in some way damaged by sin. We don't desire what we should. We don't think as we should. We don't speak as we should. We don't act as we should. We need help. We need rescue. We need wisdom. We need forgiveness. We need strength.

So, here is what prayer does for you and your marriage. In a way that is powerfully protective and relationally transforming, each time you pray, you are reminded of the *context* of your marriage. The context of your marriage is not a situation or a location. The context of your marriage is a person. The context of your marriage is *God*. He is above, around, below, and in you. He created everything that makes up your existence. He controls every situation and relationship you are in. It is his power that keeps you and your world together. He has written the story of your life and your marriage. His plan, purpose, and will are meant to be the reason for all you do in your marriage. He alone offers the help that reaches to the deepest areas of your personal and relational need.

He is the rightful owner of you, your life, and your marriage. He is the conceiver and creator of your marriage, and because he is, he is best able to diagnose what is broken and to cure what needs to be fixed. He is the only reliable one who can define what is right or wrong, good or bad, true or false, and wise or foolish. He is not only near you, but because of the cross of Jesus Christ, he is now living inside you by his Spirit. He is your life and the hope of your marriage. He is your counselor, protector, advocate, teacher, guide, and friend. He surrounds you with his love and bathes you in his grace. It really is that "in him we live and move and have our being" (Acts 17:28). God is the context of your marriage.

But prayer does something else; it reminds us of the *reality* of our marriage. The reality of our marriage is a constant, moment-by-moment dance of sin and grace. Every day, sin rears its ugly head, and every day, grace gives us what we need to deal with sin. In the same way that we cannot understand marriage without understanding God's existence, his ownership, and his power, we cannot understand what we experience in marriage and how to deal with it unless we understand sin and grace. Sin is the reason for all the struggles of marriage, and grace is the only reliable hope of being able to deal with them.

Because of the fact that sin still remains in you and in your world, you need to be reconciled to God every day, and every day you need to be reconciled to one another. Every day you do something that offends God in some way, and every day you do something that offends one another. As we have observed before, these dynamics of sin, struggle, and rescue take place in the smallest and most mundane moments of daily life, moments so normal and in all ways so unremarkable that they pass by without getting our attention. We get used to the daily pace of our lives, we get used to our daily schedule, and we get used to our daily relationships and responsibilities. At some point we quit observing and we quit examining, and we settle into the routine, day piling upon day, month piling upon month, year piling upon year.

This is why couples look back during one of those moments that God sends to get their attention once again, and they ask, "What happened to us? How in the world did we end up here?" It feels to them that they have driven into some kind of marital fog. It feels that what was once bright and sunny has suddenly gone dark. But nothing has been sudden. The changes of their marriage have taken place in progressive, little steps. In those unremarkable moments that occur in every marriage, wrong thoughts, desires, words, and actions changed the character and direction of their marriage; they took place in little moments, and no one was paying attention.

We all do it. It's not that we suddenly quit loving one another. No, that's not what typically happens. Marriages don't typically change with an explosion. Marriages typically change by the process of erosion. Even where marital explosions take place, they usually take place at the end of a long process of erosion. The movement of a marriage from an active commitment to an active lifestyle of unity, understanding, and love rarely takes place in one step. Rather, this movement takes place in ten thousand little steps. The problem is that as these changes are taking place we tend to be asleep at the wheel. What we once committed to value and protect has progressively become the thing we take for granted. What we were once deeply appreciative of, we have become used to having over the long haul. The person that was so much the focus of our affection and attention has morphed into little more than the person that we live with—you know, a part of our environment and daily schedule. I can't tell you how many wives have said to me, "When he is at home, he acts as though I'm not even there."

What does this have to do with prayer? Well, prayer not only attaches you to the wonderful resources of a God of grace, who is present, powerfully near, and willing, but prayer reminds you of what you are (needy) and what God is (gracious). Prayer awakens you from your sleep and calls you to pay attention again. Prayer is about affirming weaknesses and blessings. Prayer is about getting your identity and God's glory right. Prayer confronts you with what is and preaches to you about what is important. Prayer is a very important part of a lifestyle of paying attention.

When Did We Quit Noticing?

Bryan and Martina were so excited that they were actually getting married. Neither had had much of a social life in college. Bryan had told himself that he had given up on the "relationship thing," and Martina had been afraid to let a relationship with a man go beyond the casual.

They were both well into their careers when they met. Bryan was on a sales call to Martina's firm. Martina was the person responsible for potentially purchasing what Bryan was attempting to sell. On his third visit to discuss with Martina her company's product needs, Bryan became aware that he liked being with Martina.

On the next visit, while mumbling embarrassed apologies for stepping over workplace boundaries, Bryan asked Martina if she would have coffee with him sometime. To his surprise, she said yes. Bryan had been thinking about this for awhile. This was not going to be a boring latte-at-Starbucks mini-date. No, Bryan had decided to take her to the cool, local coffee place with the unmatched furniture, the offbeat lamps, and those killer caramel brownies. Martina was mad at herself for agreeing to get together so easily, but after their date she couldn't believe what a good time they had had, and she couldn't wait for Bryan to ask her out again.

Well, Martina hadn't had to wait. To her shock, Bryan called her as she was putting the key in her condo door, and their next date was on. They were both aware, as their relationship progressed, that they had pretty much given up on love. They were both deeply appreciative of the fact that God had written their stories together, they were very thankful for one another, and they were very committed to building and protecting the relationship that they both treasured.

Their wedding day was a blur of activity and emotion. Both Bryan and Martina were emotional all day long because they could not believe that it was actually happening. They could not believe they had found each other. They could not believe they had fallen in love. They could not believe they were actually getting married. They could not believe they would be spending their lives together. They were both filled with a sense of privilege.

Few couples go into marriage with the level of intentionality that Bryan and Martina did. They were not about to mess this thing up. They knew that if they were going to have a marriage that was mature and sturdy enough to last, no matter what, they had to commit to the lifestyle of relational work that makes every good marriage a good marriage. It wasn't a burden to them. With joy they determined to pay attention and to deal with the stuff that would get in the way of what their marriage was and could potentially be. And they had done it. In the early years, the attentiveness and the intentionality helped them form, by God's grace, a marriage that really was a place of unity, love, and understanding.

But, in a subtle process of change, two things happened. They got comfortable and they got busy. Bryan got so used to loving Martina that he quit being as conscious of his love and expressing it so often to her. Martina got so used to being appreciative of Bryan that she quit looking for those moments to express her thankfulness. Over time they went from attention and action to assumption and passivity. But Martina and Bryan were pretty much blind to the changes, because something else had taken place: they had become very busy.

Together Bryan and Martina got tired of condo life, so they purchased a single-family home of their own. The problem was that they could only afford a fixer-upper. If their new home was ever going to be comfortable and livable, it was going to demand lots of work, and since it was an old home, it would always need lots of care and maintenance. Along with this, Bryan and Martina were the parents of twin English bulldogs and three beautiful, little girls. And there was something else: through a series of promotions Bryan was now the regional director of his division at his company. His work days were very demanding, and he had to travel more than he had anticipated when he took the position. He came home exhausted every evening and wanted little more than some downtime.

Martina was thankful for Bryan, but between household chores (which Bryan seemed oblivious to) and the care for and activities of the girls and the dogs, there just didn't seem to be enough time in the day for her to do all of that and also pay much attention to Bryan. No, they hadn't stopped loving one another, but they had quit paying much attention, and they surely had forsaken their commitment to do daily what was necessary to build and protect their marriage. Their marriage had become a relationship of inattention, distance, and distraction. When this happens in any marriage, sin, with all its self-orientation, irritation, and impatience is given room for expression and growth. And this is exactly what happened to Bryan and Martina.

Little disagreements and unsolved conflicts grew into major battles.

Service morphed into impatient selfishness. Appreciation devolved into irritation. A willingness to serve and wait disintegrated into impatient demands. Forgiveness gave way to criticism and judgment. Peace gave way to anger and tension. Bryan and Martina had quit paying attention and had quit working on their relationship. What once was had not been enhanced and maintained. The commitments they had made had been progressively forsaken. Their marriage was like a garden without attention; the weeds had simply overwhelmed the flowers. Martina and Bryan needed help; their marriage needed prayer.

The Power and Protection of Marital Prayer

In our marriage, prayer pushes us in all the right directions. It reminds us of the kinds of things we have said are so important to a marriage of unity, understanding, and love. Daily prayer reinforces all the commitments we are tempted to forsake but that are vital to maintain. Prayer opens our eyes and our heart. Prayer is a necessary ingredient of a healthy marriage. On our knees is the best posture for our marriage.

Using the Lord's Prayer as a model, here are some things that prayer does in you and will do through you in the heart of your spouse.

"Our Father in heaven . . ." (Matt. 6:9). Prayer reminds you that in your marriage, you are never left alone to the resources of your own strength and wisdom. Bryan and Martina not only lost sight of one another and the commitments they had made to their marriage—daily, active love—but they forgot their Lord as well. Yes, they continued to go to church, and they wouldn't have thought of forsaking their faith, but in the hallways, bedrooms, and family rooms of everyday life, they had begun to feel that it was all up to them, all on their shoulders. Part of the slow devolution of their marriage was a view of the responsibilities, opportunities, struggles, and blessings of marriage that did not include God. Here is why this is so devastating to any marriage: when you forget God's presence, promises, and provisions, either you tend to get overwhelmed and give up, or you try to do God's job. Neither is a workable option.

Perhaps the most powerful way in which daily prayer for your marriage not only has the power to transform your marriage, but to transform you as well, is this: prayer reminds you that you are never alone. Prayer reminds you that you are never left to your own righteousness, wisdom, and strength. Prayer reminds you that each location or situation where your marriage exists is not only inhabited by God but, even more encouragingly, that each is ruled by him. The one who controls the situations in which your marriage lives is not only a God of awesome power but is the definition of everything wise, true, faithful, gracious, loving, forgiving, good, and kind.

But there is even more that the Lord's Prayer confronts you with. It is that this God who is powerful and near is your Father by grace. If you are God's child, there is never a moment when you are outside the circle of his fathering care. Like a father, he loves you and is committed to faithfully providing what is best for you. When you are facing those disappointing moments of marital struggle, when you're not sure what to think, let alone what to do, prayer can rescue you from hopelessness and alienation. Prayer encourages you to say, "I am not sure how we got here, and I am not sure what we are being called to do, but there is one thing I am sure of—I am never, ever alone because I have a Father in heaven who is always with me."

Acknowledging God will protect you from yourself. It will protect you from discouragement and fear and the passivity that always follows. It will protect you from the pride of self-reliance and self-sovereignty. If you are ever to have a marriage of unity, understanding, and love, you must begin with this humble admission: you have no ability whatsoever to produce the most important things that make a wonderful marriage. The changes of thought, desire, word, and action that re-create, rebuild, mature, and protect your marriage are always gifts of God's grace. As you choose to do things God's way, he progressively rescues you from your own self-interest and forms you into a person who really does find joy in loving another. It is only a God of love who will ever be able to change a fundamentally self-oriented, impatient, demanding human being into a person who not only desires to love but actually does it. There is a word for this in the Bible—*grace*.

Prayer reminds you that you have been graced with a Father's love and that love will not let you go until it has changed you in every way that is needed.

"Hallowed be your name. Your kingdom come, your will be done, on earth as it is in heaven" (Matt. 6:9–10). Prayer reminds you that

God's purpose for your marriage is always bigger than your marriage. You will never understand your marriage or be content in it until you understand that your marriage is part of something bigger that is meant to define and shape your marriage and how you respond to it. Remember one of the major themes of this book: marriages break down because people have no bigger vision for their lives then the establishment of their own little kingdoms. When there is no larger kingdom to unify a husband and wife, their marriage sadly becomes a war between the kingdom purposes of the wife and the kingdom purposes of the husband. Whether they know it or not, each will be working in the mundane moments of life to realize their dream for their life.

Bryan and Martina lost sight of a world bigger than their marriage and of a kingdom bigger than their individual kingdoms of one. Martina's kingdom dream had to do with the things she had always wanted to experience as a mom and the dreams she had always held for her children. All she wanted was for Bryan to participate in the delivery of her kingdom dreams, and if he did, she would feel loved and be happy. Increasingly, Bryan's kingdom dream was located outside their home. More and more he was taken by the dream of potential success and power that was available at work. Bryan wanted Martina to do everything she could to support his career dreams, no matter what it cost on the family front. The problem was that Martina and Bryan's kingdoms were in conflict. Martina's dream for her children demanded that Bryan not spend so much time and energy at work, and Bryan's career dreams demanded that Martina forsake her plans for him and the family.

Prayer reminds you that real life is found only ever when you forsake your little kingdom of one for the bigger and better call of the kingdom of God. Prayer reminds you that God gives you his grace, not so much for the purpose of making your kingdom work but to welcome you to a better kingdom. Every time you pray, you are acknowledging God's rule over you and your life. Prayer is an act of submitting your purposes to God's. Prayer is all about confessing the self-focus and self-sovereignty of sin. Prayer is a willing offering of your life and all it contains to the loving and wise authority of God. Prayer is an active part of what it means to live for a bigger kingdom than your own.

Real unity begins when a husband and wife quit trying to be sovereign over their lives. Real unity begins when a husband and wife quit try-ing to set the agenda for their marriage and begin, in practical everyday ways, to pursue God's agenda together. Real marital unity begins when a husband and wife quit being kings and begin to willingly and joyfully submit to the plans, purposes, and call of the same King. The more each one individually loves and serves the King of kings, the more they will be drawn together, sharing one dream and its practical implications for their everyday life together. Prayer reminds you of a King greater than you and a kingdom better than your own.

"*Give us this day our daily bread*" (Matt. 6:11). Prayer requires you to see yourself as needy. The prayer for something as normal as bread for the day makes no sense unless it pictures something true about you. We are needy and dependent. We were never hardwired for an independent, self-sufficient existence. Prayer makes no sense at all unless it is really true that you are dependent upon God for the basic necessities of life. Prayer always requires you to acknowledge personal inability, weakness, and need. Daily prayer acknowledges daily need. Daily prayer acknowledges God's call for you to be content with what he gives you today and to trust tomorrow into his hands. And if you are dependent on God for something as basic as bread, then there is a whole catalog of things necessary for your life that you are unable, in and of yourself, to provide.

I cannot and do not control all the things that need to be controlled in order to guarantee that I will have a job that can support my family. I do not rule all the circumstances that must be in place to ensure that my family has an adequate home to live in. I do not control all the things that will result in my family being healthy and safe. I do not determine all the things that must be in place for my children to have a good school to attend. I do not exercise authority over the things that will ensure that we have a solid church to attend. There are many important needs in my life that I do not have the power to independently meet.

But there is more. If your marriage is to be a place where real unity, understanding, and love shape the character of every day, then there are things that you and your husband or wife need to be and to do. But you can't become these things or do these things by yourself. You do not have the ability to turn yourself into a person who is loving, kind, patient, thankful, gentle, forgiving, faithful, and self-controlling. And you surely have no power whatsoever to ensure that your spouse will be that kind of person. These essential character qualities of a good marriage are only ever the fruit of the transforming work of the Spirit of God in your heart. They only come as he progressively delivers you from *you* and forms you into the likeness of Jesus.

Prayer yanks you out of your delusions of self-sufficiency and reminds you of how deeply needy you really are. Prayer reminds you that you will never be what you need to be and do what you are called to do without divine rescue and restoration. Prayer humbles you, and as it does, it makes you more patient and more understanding of your spouse. No one is more patient with the weaknesses and needs of another than the person who has admitted that he is also deeply needy.

Somewhere in the early days of good commitments, wise choices, and loving responses, Bryan and Martina quit seeing themselves as needy, and the result was devastating to their marriage. At some point they felt that they had figured it out. More and more it seemed to them that they had arrived. They didn't know it, but they were turning gifts of God's grace into an occasion for personal and marital pride. There were times when they would wonder together why certain couples they knew just didn't seem to be able to get their acts together. But this pride in their wisdom, ability, and strength was subtle and deceptive. It almost always is. No, they never announced, in some moment of theological change, "We don't need God anymore." And they didn't quit praying before a meal and at the end of the day, but their prayers were more a spiritual routine than an indicator of what they really believed about themselves and God. They never quit participating in the programs and ministries of their church, but there was a clear separation between the Sunday celebration of God's grace and the self-sufficiency of the rest of the week.

In fact, in a real way, Bryan and Martina quit praying, because they quit seeing themselves as needy. Sure, they would mumble well-rehearsed religious phrases with heads bowed and eyes closed. But these "prayers" were no more true prayers than the prayer of the Pharisee in the temple in Christ's illustration in Luke 18. Their prayers were devoid of a deep sense of personal need, and because they were, they were also devoid of heartfelt appreciation and celebration.

I wish I could say that I have never been in this position, but I have.

Much of the trouble that we experienced in the early years of our marriage was due to my pride and my impatience with Luella, who was "not as righteous and mature as me." My prayers were more an act of external religiosity than they were an honest expression of the cries of a needy heart.

Real prayer transforms you as it requires you to acknowledge how fundamentally needy you actually are.

"Forgive us our debts, as we also have forgiven our debtors" (Matt. 6:12). Prayer reminds you of God's daily call to give the same grace to your spouse as God has given to you. Prayer requires you to love others as you have been loved. Prayer makes no sense if it is not rooted in recognition that God has placed his love on you even though you could never have earned, achieved, or deserved it. Prayer makes sense only when it is rooted in the reality that you have been gifted every day with patient forgiveness and empowering grace. Prayer humbles you as it forces you to acknowledge that the most valuable thing in your existence, the love of God, is the thing that you had no capacity whatsoever to earn. And as prayer calls you to celebrate undeserved love, it requires you to commit yourself to love others in the same way. There is a direct connection between self-righteousness and an inability and unwillingness to love others.

It is a contradiction to seek God's help yet be unwilling to help your husband or wife. It is a contradiction to celebrate God's love yet refuse to love your spouse. It is a contradiction to be deeply aware of your moment-by-moment need of grace yet unwilling to give grace to the person you live with and say that you love. It is a contradiction to know that your only real hope in life is God's forgiveness yet refuse to forgive your husband or your wife. It is a contradiction to know that God will only listen to your requests because he is patient and kind and then turn and respond to your spouse in irritation and impatience.

It makes no sense to participate in an act that, by its very nature, recognizes that you have been blessed by divine love and grace yet to have no practical commitment to love and grace in your marriage. It makes no sense to celebrate God's forgiveness and then refuse to forgive your spouse in those moments when forgiveness, reconciliation, and restoration are so obviously and practically needed. As prayer calls you to celebrate vertical forgiveness, it requires you to offer horizontal forgiveness as well.

Prayer reminds you of God's call to love. It reminds you that you have been designed to live a lifestyle of willing self-sacrifice for the good of another. Prayer reminds you that successful living is all about loving God above all else and loving your neighbor as yourself. Prayer reminds you that your marriage is always about the daily dynamics of a sinner living with a sinner, and because it is, there is no more important commitment in all of marriage than the commitment to forgive. Prayer reminds you that in your marriage there is never a day when you aren't called to give one another grace that has not been deserved or earned.

Here is the thing that happened to Martina and Bryan and that happens to many of us as well. Pay attention to the cycle that I am about to describe. As Martina and Bryan lost sight of their daily need for forgiveness, they quit being so willing to forgive one another. As they quit forgiving one another and putting away their offenses, they began to keep a record of the other's wrongs. As they kept a daily record of wrongs, they were increasingly aware of how much their life was affected by the weakness and failure of the other. As they carried this awareness with them, they became increasingly irritated, impatient, and intolerant with one another. So, since they were not fighters, they dealt with their disappointment with one another by protecting themselves from one another with distance and busyness.

A mutual commitment to give grace daily is the only hope for a marriage of a sinner to a sinner, which is the only kind of marriage there is. Prayer reminds us of God's call to love and forgive, and it reminds us that this call is most needed when it is most undeserved.

"And lead us not into temptation, but deliver us from evil" (Matt. 6:13). Prayer reminds you that your biggest marital struggles exist inside, not outside, of you. Real prayer always leaves you humbled because real prayer requires you to admit who you really are. We would all like to think we are fundamentally good people whose biggest struggles in life exist outside, not inside, of us. But prayer confronts us with a humbling reality: we are only hooked by the evil outside of us because of the evil inside of us.

Prayer requires us to face the fact that no matter what we suffer in our marriage, the deepest, most abiding dilemma of our life exists inside, not outside, of us. Prayer requires us to face the dark and devastating reality of our sin and how it distorts what we think, desire, say, and do. Prayer requires us to acknowledge that we need rescue and protection because we carry around something inside ourselves that tempts us away from what is right toward what is wrong. Prayer humbles us as it welcomes us to admit that we carry around something inside that is self-focused and antisocial and therefore destructive to our relationships.

Prayer requires us to confess that the biggest problem in our marriage, the one thing we cannot escape by changes of situation and location, is ourselves! It is our sin that seduces, deceives, and entraps us again and again. It is our sin that causes us to want things we should not want, to think things we should not think, to say things we should not say, and to do things we should not do. Prayer calls us to quit blaming our husband or wife for our words and actions. Prayer welcomes us to accept responsibility for our behavior and, as we do, to receive forgiveness and help.

Prayer destroys the finger-pointing, it's-your-fault, blame game that paralyzes many marriages. When the husband is deeply persuaded that the hope of the marriage is to get the wife fixed, and the wife is deeply persuaded that the future of the marriage is to get the husband fixed, you can be sure that their marriage will not change. It is only when both confess that it is the sin inside them that leads them to do what is wrong in their marriage—not the failure of the other—that each hungers for growth and change and then reaches out for God's help.

The more Bryan and Martina pointed to one another as the cause of their attitudes and actions, the more their marriage got stuck and change seemed remote and impossible. Change in a marriage always begins with looking within, and that is exactly where prayer calls us to look. The celebration of a Savior, which lies at the heart of prayer, makes sense only when we acknowledge that we cannot escape from the sin inside us. When we acknowledge our sin, we quit blaming our spouse and begin getting serious about getting help. In marriage, prayer reminds you again and again that your biggest, most abiding problem is you.

"*For yours is the kingdom and the power and the glory forever. Amen.*" Prayer reminds you that the key to a marriage of unity, understanding, and love is rooted in an allegiance to God's kingdom and not your own. True, heartfelt prayer ends as it begins—with recognition of God's kingship and his glory. Prayer reminds you that life is not about you. Prayer reminds you that the center of your universe is a place reserved for God and God alone. Prayer reminds you that real peace, satisfaction, and contentment come when you live for a greater glory than your own. Prayer reminds you that the hope of marriage is not found in a husband and wife conspiring to build their own kingdom but in submitting together to the wisdom and rule of a better King. Prayer calls you away from the kingdom of self, which is so destructive to everything a marriage is intended to be, and welcomes you to the kingdom of God, where a God of love rules in love.

Still in the Battle, Still Recognizing Need

No matter how long you have been married, no matter how much you have learned, grown, and changed, you must stay in the battle (that war that rages in your heart between the kingdom of self and the kingdom of God), and you must continue to admit your need. Every day there is evidence that sin stills lives inside you, and as long as it does you must not let down your guard, you must not allow yourself to think that you have arrived, and you must not permit yourself to coast. The war will someday end and the fight will someday be over, because sin will someday be finally defeated, but today the sin still lives within you and the battle must still be fought.

But you don't fight alone. As you commit to watch and pray, God graces you with his forgiveness, protection, wisdom, and strength. He loves you with everlasting love. He never grows tired of you or weary with your struggles. He never throws your failures in your face or uses your sins against you. He shed the blood of his Son so that in your struggles, you would have the forgiveness and power you need.

When you pray for your marriage, you remind yourself that you are not alone. When you pray, you remind yourself that grace has invaded your marriage, and because it has, there is hope. There really is.

COMMITMENT 1: We will give ourselves to a regular lifestyle of confession and forgiveness.

COMMITMENT 2: We will make growth and change our daily agenda.

COMMITMENT 3: We will work together to build a sturdy bond of trust.

COMMITMENT 4: We will commit to building a relationship of love.

COMMITMENT 5: We will deal with our differences with appreciation and grace.

COMMITMENT 6: We will work to protect our marriage.

17

Worship, Work, and Grace

So what is it that produces a marriage of unity, understanding, and love? This kind of marriage is the result of a lifelong commitment to daily marital work and deep trust in God's transforming grace. What produces a commitment to work and a trust in grace? There is only one thing, and one thing alone, that can form in you this commitment to *toil* and *trust*. It is worship.

Think of the commitments that make for a wonderful, God-honoring marriage, the commitments that form the content of this book. What does it take to *deal honestly with your sin, weakness, and failure*? Toil and trust. What does it take to *make growth and change your daily agenda*? Toil and trust. What does it take to *build a strong foundation of trust*? Toil and trust. What does it take to *build a relationship of love*? Toil and trust. What does it take to *deal with your differences with appreciation and grace*? Toil and trust. And what does it take to *work to protect your marriage*? Toil and trust. It is a lifelong lifestyle of joyful marital work and living together as you really believe in God's grace, which really does give you everything you need to do the work he has called you to as husband and wife. But what propels you to give yourself to the daily labor of a good marriage and a practical belief that God will not call you to work that he does not enable you to do? Worship. This and this alone is the foundation of a marriage of unity, understanding, and love.

Luella and I will leave tomorrow to go away for the weekend to celebrate our anniversary. It may sound cheesy to some, but I am married to one of my heroes. Luella is my confidant, my adviser, my mentor, and my dearest friend. I am constantly amazed at her courage and perseverance. I marvel at her natural love for people and the many ways she instinctively ministers to others. I have a deep appreciation for how she lives each day with purpose and cares about what really matters. I have been struck again and again by how she never stops thinking and how she thinks by implication. I love how she loves the Lord and thinks about his will in everything she does. I am so grateful that I have lived with a person with such stability and maturity.

As much as I love, appreciate, and respect Luella, I do recognize that she is not perfect (although she is much closer than I am). Yes, she is a woman of character, but sin still lives inside her as it does in me. The battle still rages for control of our hearts in those small moments where every marriage lives. We long for our life together to be loving, peaceful, unified, and productive. Our number-one desire is that God would look into our marriage and be pleased. But we don't always live with him in view. There are times we want our own way. There are times when we step outside his boundaries. There are times when we let the differences between us that God has created become the occasion for conflicts. There are times when we still find it difficult to listen, forgive, serve, or give. There are times when self-focus still gets in the way of love. There are times when we fail to overlook a minor offense or turn a little thing into a big thing. There are times when we allow ourselves to be too busy, and our relationship suffers.

We have a wonderful relationship. It is a long-term friendship and a long-term romance. I can honestly say I love Luella more, as I head out on this anniversary weekend, than I ever have. But we cannot, and we must not, quit working on our relationship. We cannot act as if we have arrived. We cannot rest on our laurels and coast our way through our marriage. We cannot retire from the good things we have been called to do as a husband and a wife. Sin still lives inside us with all its self-focused, antisocial instincts. We have to keep watching, examining, listening, thinking, confessing, forgiving, and persevering. We still have to work to keep God in constant view. We still have to have conversations we wish weren't necessary. We still have to say, "I am sorry," and "I forgive you." We still have to hold tightly to our commitment to do what is right no matter what. We still have to remind ourselves of grace, give each other grace, and rest in grace.

We have a wonderful marriage, but there is still work to be done every day. And as we do this work, we still have to remind ourselves of God's presence, promises, and provisions. He is in us, he is with us, and he is for us, but his work in our hearts is not yet complete. Until it is, each day of our marriage must be a day of willing toil and trust, and we will live that way only if each day is also a day of worship. Worship really is the foundation of a marriage that is not only good, but good for the long run. Good marriages are built vertically before they are built horizontally. Troubled marriages are repaired vertically before they are ever repaired horizontally.

When it comes to marriage struggles, worship is the problem and worship is the cure. Let me remind you again what this means. It is only when God is in his rightful place that other things will be in their rightful place. It is only when I love God above all else that I will love Luella as I love myself. If love for God is not the practical driving force of my life, love of self will be. If God's kingdom is not my reason for doing what I'm doing in my marriage, my kingdom will be. If I am not resting in God's control, I will look to take control. If I don't think that I am dependent on his grace, I probably won't give Luella grace. If I forget the call of his will, my responses will be directed by what I want, how I want it, where I want it, and when I want it.

This tendency in all of us to worship ourselves, which is the antisocial impulse that is so destructive to marriage, is only ever defeated when it is replaced by willing, active, and consistent worship of God. I will repeat my confession: my problem has never been that I have not loved Luella enough; no, my problem has always been that I have not loved God enough, and because I have not loved God enough, I have not loved Luella as I should.

This is the bottom line: the war for our marriages is a war of worship. The fundamental problem of every marriage is misplaced worship. The cure for every marriage is renewed worship of God. Does it sound too simple? Well, it is and it isn't. Although this principle is true of every marriage, the war and the cure look different for every couple, because the way the war plays out and the way the cure heals is different for each of us. It is different for each couple due to how God has hardwired us, who he placed us near, and where he has chosen for us to live. Yet, despite our differences, we all suffer from the same problem, and we all look to the same cure.

Perhaps you're thinking, "Paul, this doesn't sound very romantic." My intention here is not to disrespect romance. I love romance. On the vast continuum of what defines maleness, I am way over on the romantic end. I do think intimacy and romance are important ingredients in a healthy marriage, but as this book has argued, a good marriage doesn't grow out of the soil of romance. No, the soil in which a good marriage grows is the soil of worship, and the fruit that a good marriage produces is the fruit of sweet, long-term, and mutually satisfying romance. Worship really is the soil of a wonderful marriage. Permit me to explain one final time.

Your Marriage and Worship

When I got married, there was no real or necessary connection in my mind between worship and marriage. I thought that those two words, *worship* and *marriage*, existed in two separate domains of my life. But they don't. I now understand that our lives aren't divided neatly into spiritual and secular or vertical and horizontal. They aren't divided into neat categories, like "things that have to do with worshiping God," and "things that have to do with everything else."

Because God not only lays claim to the formal religious dimension of your life but to everything else as well, your relationship with God will shape your relationship with everything else, including your marriage. Life and worship are never separate. Whether you recognize it or not, you worship your way through every day. The question is, "What is it that you are worshiping?" Let me make concrete connections for you between vertical worship (love for God) and horizontal love (love for your spouse) as a way of summarizing the content of this book and to give you one more tool for assessing your thoughts, desires, and response in your marriage.

When your life is shaped by the worship of God, you live with his plans and purposes in view. When you live with God in view, your fundamental perspective on marriage changes. Rather than approaching marriage with your self-oriented marriage dream, you will instead ask, "What has God designed my marriage to be and to do?" This shift in perspective will radically alter the way you relate to your husband or wife. Now, rather than working to get your spouse to participate in, or even to deliver, your dream and judging him accordingly, you now want to humbly work with him to build a marriage that is a practical, everyday-life expression of God's will. Rather than seeking to make sure that your will is done in your marriage and working to get your spouse to serve your plan, you now find joy in God's will.

Let me put this in the terms we have been using in this book. I am convinced that many marriages, between people who name themselves as believers, have almost nothing to do with God at all, and this is where the trouble actually begins. Perhaps the couple has had a little premarital counseling, and perhaps they recited Christian vows before their pastor and the people of their church, but the Christian part of the marriage often ends there. If you take time to do a little examination, you will soon discover that it is not a joyful, disciplined, and daily pursuit of the kingdom of God that shapes the marriage. No, these are two people, who, although they probably don't know it, are in full pursuit of their own little kingdoms of one, and there is evidence already that these kingdoms are beginning to collide. If you marry propelled by the dreams of the kingdom of self, you will say that you love the other person, but what you will actually be doing is working to manipulate that person somehow or some way into the service of your kingdom. If you are able to do this, and they acquiesce, you will be happy and glad that you are married. If they resist, you will be disappointed and dissatisfied and wonder if you made a terrible mistake.

Worshiping God in your marriage blows this away. When together you are worshiping God and seeking his kingdom, you quit trying to make sure that your kingdom comes and your will is done. You quit manipulating, demanding, and working to co-opt your spouse into the service of your kingdom. You quit examining your spouse and your marriage through the lens of your wants, needs, and feelings. When you worship God, demand gives way to service, entitlement gives way to gratitude, and dissatisfaction gives way to joy, because selfishness has given way to a daily love for God and your spouse. Worship radically changes your expectations of and the way you relate to your spouse.

I am very aware that my anger in the early days of my marriage was rooted in worship. Anger wasn't the core of my problems. No, it was a symptom of a greater problem. I wanted to be sovereign over my life and my marriage, and I was angry that Luella always seemed to be in my way. I had a plan for my life and for hers, and I just wanted her to get on my train and ride. I was a pastor and counselor, yet I was blind to the fact that God's kingdom had little to do with what went on inside the door of my own home. Luella was hurt and confused because she would do what seemed to be best, but I would be upset because what she thought was best did not agree with what I had determined was best. No, I wasn't a man of abusive and malevolent intentions. If you had asked me, I would have told you that I adored Luella, but I had functionally replaced God in my marriage, and because I had, we were heading for disaster.

You see, the hope for our marriage was not to be found in my attending some anger management classes. I didn't need anger management so much as I needed worship realignment. It was only when God was in his rightful place that things began to change at street level in the Tripp marriage. As I said before, my problem wasn't that I didn't love Luella enough. No, my problem was that I didn't love God enough, and because I didn't love God enough, I didn't love Luella as I should.

If you are not worshiping God in your marriage, somehow, someway you will insert yourself into his position. You will work to be Lord over your marriage. You will work to make sure your kingdom comes and your will is done, and you will evaluate and respond to your spouse depending on her willingness to serve your kingdom purposes. Only the functional worship of God is sturdy enough to break your allegiance to self and turn you into a person who really does find joy in loving another. Whose will sets the agenda for your marriage?

When your life is shaped by the worship of God, you live thankfully. When you really do begin to examine yourself in the mirror of God's Word and see how undeserving you are, you are hit with how great, patient, kind, gentle, and forgiving God's love is. In your heart of hearts you know that you have no right to expect or demand good things in your life and in your marriage. You know that you cannot stand before God and say, "Because of who I am and because of what I have done, I deserve a marriage of unity, understanding, and love." When you examine yourself in light of God's character and his Word, it is hard to hold onto the belief that you are righteous and deserving. When you stand in the shadow of God's glory, you are filled with a sense of how weak, failing, undeserving, and unworthy you really are.

Here is the point: it is only worship of God that can destroy your worship of yourself. It is only when you are worshiping God that you are able to look at yourself with humility and accuracy, and it is only when you look at yourself accurately that you quit being demanding and start being truly thankful. When you are at the center of your world, you are still being deceived by the delusion of your own righteousness and worthiness. It seems right to expect and demand good things, because you are convinced you deserve them.

Worship of God puts us in our place. It teaches us that every good thing in our lives is an undeserved gift from the hand of one who is the definition of love and grace. Worship turns demanding husbands and wives into thankful husbands and wives. Worship turns entitled spouses into grateful spouses. Worship turns disappointed husbands and wives into joyful celebrants.

So, because you are beginning to live thankfully, your vertical thankfulness produces horizontal appreciation. Instead of being demanding and dissatisfied, you look for any opportunity that comes your way to express appreciation. Instead of being critical and judgmental, you are impressed with the fact that you don't deserve any of the good things that you have experienced in your marriage. These have come your way not because you are good but because God is, and he blesses you with his gracious love, even on the days when you have done little to deserve it. Worshiping God for his goodness, grace, and love is the soil in which thankfulness and appreciation for your spouse will grow. Would your husband or wife describe you as consistently thankful and relationally appreciative?

When your life is shaped by the worship of God, you don't shrink your world down to the size of your wants, needs, and feelings. Marriages in conflict tend to be shrunken marriages. What does this mean? It means that they are tense and disappointing, because even though the husband and wife do not know it, they have shrunk the hopes and dreams for their marriage to the size of their individual wants, needs, and feelings. The wife looks at their relationship through the lens of her little kingdom of one, with its self-focused catalog of wants, needs, and feeling, while the husband does the same. They are in conflict because their kingdoms are constantly colliding.

Marriages like this will not become places of peace by giving the husband or wife conflict resolution skills. No, they need change at a deeper level than that. In the early days of my marriage when I struggled so with anger, that anger was actually the symptom of a deeper problem. I knew exactly what I wanted my marriage to be. I knew exactly how I wanted Luella to think, act, and respond. I knew exactly what would make me satisfied and content. I had shrunk my hopes and dreams for my marriage to the small size of my own wants, needs, and feelings.

Now, you may have looked at me and thought, "This man needs anger management classes." But that is not what I needed. I didn't so much need anger management as I needed worship realignment. When it came to the day-by-day realities of my marriage, God was out of the picture. Sure, I was a believer, but I was in hot pursuit of my own kingdom, and I was judging my wife based on her willingness to participate in my kingdom purposes. In my frustration I failed to recognize that my problem was me. I failed to recognize that God didn't pour his love on me in order to make my little kingdom work but to welcome me to a much bigger and better kingdom.

It is only when a husband and wife are in love with the same King and live in practical pursuit of the same kingdom that they have any hope of functional unity, understanding, and love. My anger revealed that my problem wasn't, first, that I didn't love Luella enough. No, my problem was that I didn't love God in such a way that would constantly keep his presence and the call of his kingdom in view. So, I inserted myself into the center of the world and made it all about what I wanted, what I felt, and what I thought I needed, and in so doing, I threw any hope of real unity out the window.

Thankfully, God rescued me from me, and Luella and I began to care more about the will of the King than we did about building our own little self-focused kingdoms. Are there places in your marriage where your actions, reactions, and responses are still shaped by little more than what you want, feel, and tell yourself you need?

When your life is shaped by the worship of God, you don't try to do his job. There are many exhausted, frustrated, and discouraged husbands and wives out there, because they are trying to do God's job. You see, it doesn't take too long in marriage to be confronted with the reality that you have married a less than perfect person. It doesn't take very long to realize that you have married a person in need of growth and change. It is what you do with this realization that is so important.

There are husbands and wives who take it upon themselves to do God's job and try to turn their spouse into the person he or she needs to be. Now, of course, they don't know that this is what they are doing, but they do it nonetheless. They begin to buy into the delusion that by the tone and volume of their voice, the power of their arguments, the infliction of guilt, the threat of what may happen, or some other human tool, they will be able to change the person they married. But the opposite is actually true. You and I have no ability whatsoever to change our spouse. And when we try, we tend to permit ourselves to be judgmental, critical, and condemning. We tend to focus on the negative instead of the positive. We tend to be more skilled at uncovering what is wrong than we are at encouraging what is right. As we do all this, we get more and more frustrated and discouraged, and the person we are working on feels disrespected and unloved, and the changes that take place are more negative than they are of positive personal growth.

When you live in your marriage with a constant God-awareness, you tend to be more willing and able to accept your limits. You are comforted by the knowledge that not only is he present with you and your spouse, but he is also more committed to changing you both in the places where that is needed than you will ever be. He never grows tired, he never feels like giving up, and he will never turn his back on you. You can rest, even when change is clearly needed, because you know that you are not alone. God is with you, and he is willing and able to do the things in your marriage that you are unable to do yourselves. Are there places in the life of your husband or wife where you are still attempting to do God's job?

When your life is shaped by the worship of God, you want to give to others the same grace you have received. The more you live aware of God's power, wisdom, holiness, faithfulness, and love, the more you will live humbly aware of how deeply needy you really are. It is when you are living in the light of God's glory that you get the most accurate sense of who you are, and an accurate sense of self will always lead you to affirm how desperate your need of grace really is. This accurate sense of self then spills over to the way you view your life and the way you view others. Rather than looking at the good things in your life and saying, "Look what I have achieved for myself," you look at these good things and say, "Look at the many evidences in my life of the fact that God has been with me and has blessed me with his grace." Looking at life this way changes the way you look at others. When you affirm how you have been the daily recipient of God's patience, kindness, forgiveness, and love, there will tend to be a natural tenderness and patience in your responses to your husband or wife.

When you forget who you are, when you forget your need of grace, it is very easy to be critical, condemning, harsh, and judgmental with your spouse. It is easy to allow yourself to be too quick to speak critically and too ready to give room to the self-righteous, I-am-better-than-you anger that is so destructive to a marriage. Many couples, in forgetting who God is and therefore forgetting who they are, which results in criticism and unforgiveness, begin to keep a record of wrongs against one another. Although they probably don't know it, this record of wrongs gets dragged into the next moment, and it colors the way they see and hear one another. It becomes increasingly hard for them to look at one another with appreciation and respect. More and more their view of their marriage is: "Look what I have had to deal with because I am married to you." Anger becomes more of a theme in their marriage than forgiveness, and criticism more frequent than appreciation.

The best defense against all this is to keep God in your eyes at all times. It is when we are looking at ourselves in the light of God's glory that we see, with accuracy, how needy we are, and we will look for ways to give our husband or wife the same grace that we so desperately need. People who love best are those deeply appreciative of the way they have been loved. People who forgive most faithfully and willingly are those who know they are in desperate need of daily forgiveness. The most patient are those who recognize that every day they are blessed with God's patience and kindness. When you are actively worshiping God for his grace, it makes it hard for you not to give grace to your husband or wife. Does an accurate sense of your own need encourage you to respond with grace to the needs, weaknesses, and failures of your husband or wife?

When your life is shaped by the worship of God, people and things are in their right place. Human beings always look to something to give them identity, meaning and purpose, and an inner sense of well-being. We were created to get these things vertically, in relationship to and in the worship of God. But when we forget who we are as creatures and children of God, we shop for identity somewhere else. I have written before that identity amnesia always leads to identity replacement. Here's what this means: what we were designed to get vertically from a God who never changes or fails, we try to get horizontally from people, places, and things.

Maybe you're thinking, "Paul, I get what you're saying, but I'm not sure what it has to do with marriage." Let me recall some examples. John doesn't know it, but his work has become the place where he gets his identity. It is the place where he feels alive, successful, and complete. The position, power, success, and respect he has achieved at work are what give him that inner sense of "all is well" that gets him up in the morning. So John is spending more and more time at work, looking to achieve more of that success that gives him his sense of self. Because of this, John is spending less and less time with his wife. In fact, when John drives away from his job and toward his home, he is driving away from what is important to him and gives him value. This means that when he enters his house each night, he doesn't enter excited to be there and engaged in what goes on. No, John punches out from life as he drives home, and all he wants to do there is chill out and rest up for his next day at work.

John doesn't know it, but work has become his replacement messiah, and because it has, it has sucked the life out of his enthusiasm for and commitment to his marriage. His wife has come to understand that she lives outside the circle of what gives John value. Their marriage is more characterized by distance and distraction than by unity, under-standing, and love.

Mary is not aware that it happened, but somewhere along the way she began to attach her identity and sense of well-being to the beauty of her home. In ways that shape her relationship to Bill, her husband, and to her three children, Mary has turned her home into a museum to her domestic dexterity. She cannot stand to have the house messy, disor-dered, or unclean in any way. She has a specific set of rules for how the people she lives with are to behave in every room. Bill and the children are constantly walking on eggshells and getting themselves into trouble because they have somehow, someway broken one of Mary's domestic commandments. What Mary actually wants is for her home to look like no one lives in it.

Mary does not know it, and would probably be offended to hear me say it, but she really does love the order and beauty of her home more than she loves Bill. No longer is he the active object of her affection; no, Bill has been reduced to either a tool of domestic order or an obstacle in the way of it. In ways she is not aware of, Mary personalizes all the stains, dusts, and messiness. Bill has heard her say again and again, "If you really loved and respected me, you would help me keep some order around here."

Mary is seeking to get identity from where it was never meant to be found, and it is damaging her marriage. Bill doesn't like to be home, because he feels that he is always in trouble, and Bill doesn't enjoy being with Mary, because she is constantly critical and dissatisfied.

John and Mary are identity amnesiacs, and their search for identity is sucking the life out of their marriages. It will be only when John and Mary are worshiping God for his presence, power, and daily provision that their hearts will rest and they will be free from looking for identity and rest elsewhere and able to give themselves to love as they have been loved. Does inner rest and peace of heart free you to give yourself to your marriage in daily acts of love and service?

When your life is shaped by the worship of God, you celebrate his work in your spouse. When you look at your husband or wife, are you a celebrant or a critic? Now, I don't mean that, in blind love, you should swindle yourself into thinking you have married a perfect person, because you haven't. There is a way in which it is very important that you be aware of the places where your spouse needs to change and grow, because God has called you to be one of his tools of personal transformation in the life of your husband or wife. But having said all that, the fact is that you should not be able to look at your spouse without seeing God's hand. He has been and is there as creator and savior.

Worshiping God as creator in your marriage means that when you look at your husband or wife, when you consider your spouse's personality and gifts, and when you think about how differently he or she is hardwired from you, you will celebrate the glory of God as creator, expressed in who he designed your spouse to be. This should cause you to celebrate your spouse and the way in which your perspective has been broadened and your life enhanced by the marriage, and it will protect you from ever wanting to clone your spouse into your image.

Worshiping God as Savior means that you will look for and affirm the good things that he enables your husband or wife to be and do. It also means that you will not seek to be a better messiah than the Messiah, trying to do what he alone can do—change a person from the inside out. Do you celebrate God's work in your spouse by communicating appreciation and respect?

When your life is shaped by the worship of God, you don't live in fear. When you worship God, you are aware of his presence, power, and promises. Because God is in your thoughts, you will tend to remember that you are never alone. As you remember that you are not alone, you will not panic when you face things in your marriage that are bigger than the size of your character, maturity, wisdom, and strength. You will know that the potential for your marriage to become what God designed it to be is not carried by you and your spouse. No, God is with you, in you, and for you. He will give you the grace to do what he calls you to do.

Sometimes he will give you the grace of courage, when otherwise you would have been afraid. Sometimes he will give you the grace of wisdom, when otherwise you wouldn't have known what to do. Sometimes he will give you the grace of patience, when otherwise you would find it very hard to wait. Sometimes he will give you the grace of forgiveness, when otherwise you would have been bitter and despondent. Sometimes he will give you the grace of strength, when otherwise you wouldn't have the power to carry on. Sometimes he will give you the grace of hope, when otherwise discouragement would have paralyzed you. Worship reminds you of God's presence, and as it does, you are protected from giving way to fear.

Why was David able to walk into that valley to face the mighty warrior Goliath? How did Gideon get the courage to lead three hundred men against a great army? What made Samuel able to speak so strongly and clearly and with such courage? What gave Shadrach, Meshach, and Abednego the ability to say no to the king, even if it meant being thrown into a furnace of fire? Why was Peter able to stand before the religious leaders of his day and refuse to be silenced? The answer to these questions is the same. They were all able to do what they did because they recognized they were not alone; they were deeply aware that God was with them, so they measured their potential accordingly. It was not "little them" against a huge obstacle. No, it was a huge God against a puny problem. Worship of God in your marriage will always protect you against fear and mobilize you to do things that, in fear, you would have shied away from. Does the knowledge that God is with you give you courage in places where fear would otherwise set the agenda?

Worship and Work

You may already have anticipated what I am going to say next. Worship is much, much more than a set of feelings and a theological outline. Worship is a lifestyle. It is a way of thinking about and responding to everything that is in your life. Worship is believing that God exists, that he is with you in your marriage, and that what he calls you to do is worth doing. Worship and work go hand-in-hand. If you believe that God is wise and true, then you will take seriously what he says, and you will willingly do the things he says are good and right to do. You will not do them once, but you will do them again and again, day after day. Because you trust God, you are willing to give yourself to the toil of a good marriage. A marriage of unity, understanding, and love takes a daily commitment to work.

Perhaps one of the principal sins of a bad marriage is the sin of laziness. Being committed to the hard work that makes a marriage beautiful means you will:

- Be willing to lose sleep so an important conversation can be completed.
- Listen and consider when you have communicated a concern.
- Care about your spouse's true needs and gladly work to meet them.
- Work to communicate with your spouse in a way that is patient and kind.
- Look for concrete ways to support and encourage your spouse.
- Do the daily work of forgiveness and reconciliation so that you and your spouse can live in peace.
- Deal with your marital differences in a way that communicates appreciation and respect.
- Make time to enjoy your physical intimacy and friendship.
- Look for ways to help your spouse bear the burden of the responsibilities that he or she carries.
- Partner with your spouse in the daily work of maintaining your physical surroundings.
- Never stop pursuing your spouse romantically.
- Not let the sun go down on a moment of hurt, misunderstanding, or anger.
- Look for ways to encourage and develop your spiritual communion.
- Daily commit to overlooking minor offenses.
- Studiously avoid conflict over things that are unimportant.
- Speak in a way that gives your spouse grace.
- Encourage and support your spouse in areas of interest that you do not share.
- Be willing to make the sacrifices necessary to keep your marriage a priority.
- Daily search for verbal and nonverbal ways to communicate your love.
- Do not leave a conversation until you have reached unity and understanding.
- Never demand of your spouse what you are unwilling to give.
- Continually remind your spouse that he or she is not alone in the marriage.
- Do things you wouldn't normally do simply because they make your spouse happy.
- Fight the busyness that would get in the way of giving your marriage attention.

- Be willing to sacrifice personal activities and leisure for the sake of your marriage.
- Work so your spouse has the downtime, rest, and retreat he or she needs.
- Work to build relationships of love and respect with your family.
- Do not stop working until your marriage is all God intended it to be.

Here is the point: real love for God will always result in a willingness to invest yourself in acts of concrete love for your neighbor. What does this mean for your marriage? It means that a good marriage will be a good marriage because the people in that marriage are committed to the daily labors that make the marriage good. What has this book been about? It has been a detailed description of the daily work of love that must be done with commitment and joy when a flawed person is married to a flawed person and they are living in a fallen world. Your marriage won't just magically become a relationship of unity, understanding, and love. You must work to develop those things. Your marriage won't magically grow to be more loving, understanding, and unified. You will have to work so that those things become deep and strong. And these things won't be maintained magically. You will have to commit to making sure that busyness and selfishness don't drive them away.

There will be moments when you are hurt, angry, exhausted, or discouraged, moments when you will be tempted to abandon the good work that God calls you to do that builds and maintains a beautiful marriage. There will be moments when you won't feel like loving your husband or wife. There will be moments when the issues you face will seem too complicated or too big. There will be moments when it seems that nothing you are doing is making any difference whatsoever. There will be moments when you want to withdraw from your spouse rather than move toward him or her. There will be moments when you will want to strike back and hurt the other in the way that he or she has hurt you. There will be moments when you will want to go your own way. There will be moments when you'd rather scream and yell than listen and encourage. There will be moments when it will seem that you are caring more and working harder. There will be moments when vengeance looks more attractive than forgiveness. There will be moments when you just don't feel like doing the work that every good marriage demands.

It is in these hard moments that husbands and wives choose to do the hard work of love, and weak and immature marriages begin to become mature and good. It is in these moments that you need to get up, get active, and fight for your marriage. It is in these moments that you must determine that you will not allow hurt, anger, exhaustion, laziness, or hopelessness to destroy your marriage. It is in these moments that you must take seriously your calling as a husband or wife and stand together and do the labors of love that God has called you to do.

Driven to Grace

Perhaps, as you have been reading, you have been thinking, "This seems hard. I don't know if I have what it takes to live this way." Or maybe you have wondered how in the world you can do what this book calls you to do as a husband or wife in the middle of the busyness of your schedule and the catalog of responsibilities you carry. Maybe, as you've been reading, you have been thinking, "It seems exhausting just to maintain the status quo let alone working to make my marriage better!" Maybe the street-level call of this book to daily self-sacrificing love has left you a bit hopeless and discouraged. Or maybe you have had to face the fact that you simply do not have inside you the love that a good marriage requires. Perhaps after reading the list of the labors of love in this chapter you feel despondent and discouraged. Maybe this book has given you a lens on your marriage, and, sadly, you have realized that things are worse than you thought. Perhaps you are feeling the standard is too high and the work too hard.

Maybe all this has revealed how selfish your heart really is and left you feeling weak and unable. Well, I am about to say something that will surprise you. If this has been your response, then you are in a very good place. Let me remind you that this is one of the uncomfortable gifts that God is working to give you in your marriage. He has designed marriage to expose the neediness of your heart and, in so doing, to bring you to the end of yourself. Why does God do this? He does it because he knows that it is only when you abandon your own wisdom, strength, and righteousness that you will begin to get excited about his grace.

What is the hope of your marriage? This may seem strange to read at this point in the book, but it must be said: the hope of your marriage is not all the principles, insights, and perspectives found in this book. No, the hope of your marriage can be captured in one glorious, powerful, and transforming word—*grace*. God's grace guarantees that you, in your struggle, will never be alone. God's grace assures you that when you have blown it, there is forgiveness to be found. Grace means that there is strength available when you are weak. Grace assures you that there is wisdom for the moments when you do not know what to do. Grace gives you hope when there seems little to be found. Grace enables you to get up and move forward when inside you want to quit or run away. Grace reminds you again and again that you are not alone.

You see, God knows that this side of heaven there are ways in which we all are weak and unable. There are ways we all fall below his standards. So he has given us the only thing that will rescue, restore, and mobilize us. He has given us himself! In his grace he invades our marriages. He comes with power we don't possess, wisdom unnatural to us, and love beyond anything we have ever known. He is willing to let you see how weak you actually are so that you will begin to seek what you can find only in him. What you should be afraid of in your marriage is not your weakness; being needy is a good place to be. No, what you should be afraid of are your delusions of arrival and strength. When you think you have arrived, and when you are convinced you are strong, you don't reach out for the incredible resources of grace that God freely offers, which will give you what you need to live in a marriage of unity, understanding, and love.

So, in your marriage, God will find ways to drive you to the end of yourself so that you will put your hope and strength in him. Your moments of weakness are not the bad moments of accident or bad luck. No, moments of weakness are there because of divine intention. They are the delivery system of glorious forgiving, empowering, and motivating grace. God is using them to rescue you from you and to make you a person who, in marriage, really is committed to love as you have been loved.

Jack and Shannon were exhausted and discouraged because they had no hope; nothing they did made things better. They felt helpless and alone with no place to turn. Jack knew that he shouldn't be so angry, but he was. Shannon knew she shouldn't be bitter and judgmental, but she didn't know how to deal with her disappointment. There were moments of peace, but those moments were increasingly infrequent and fleeting. The distance and tension between them seemed to grow every day. Their home was no longer a refuge to either one.

One morning Shannon looked out the kitchen window and saw her neighbor working in his yard, and for a brief moment she wondered what it would be like to be married to him. Maybe another man would love her and not demand so much. Jack felt that he was on the edge of throwing in the towel. He just didn't know how long he could go on. He wondered, if they were to work on their marriage, what would they work on? There didn't seem to be much left worth saving. The problems seemed too big, too bad, and too lengthy to ever go away.

Yet they both knew that this was far from the way things were meant to be. Shannon didn't hate Jack; she just felt it was impossible to live with him. Jack didn't hate Shannon; he just didn't like her very much.

As they sat in front of me, I knew they were in a very hard but very good place. Jack and Shannon thought their marriage would be easy. They seemed to have a natural affection for one another, and their courtship had been comfortable and without conflict. They had wondered why other couples talked about how marriage took so much commitment and work. Jack and Shannon really did get married with feelings of arrival. They thought they had something unique and special between them that would make their marriage different. As a result, they developed laziness habits. They allowed themselves to get busy and distracted. They never worked to develop a good-marriage work ethic. In their laziness and busyness, they gave room for misunderstanding and disunity to grow. Sure, at first it was only little moments of disagreement and irritation, but these moments grew in size and frequency. Meanwhile, they both got busier and more discouraged.

Rather than doing the hard work of dealing with their problems, Jack and Shannon developed the skill of working around their problems. But as their problems grew, it became impossible for them to work around them anymore. Their marriage was no longer peaceful and enjoyable. Their home was no longer a place of rest and retreat. So they sat in front of me, exhausted and discouraged. But I knew that it was the exhaustion and discouragement of grace. I knew that God had not turned his back on them but was with them, in them, and for them. And I knew that God had their attention in fresh and new ways.

I didn't start by laying on them all the insights and principles in this book. I knew that that would leave them even more overwhelmed. No, for the first few weeks we met together, I did only one thing: I worked to help them see Jesus. I knew that when they began to see and trust his presence, promises, power, and faithfulness, they would begin to think that maybe they could hope to experience what marriage was designed to be, and they would be willing to do the hard work that would get them there. I knew that they would live with the assurance that God would always give them what they need in order to do what he called them to do.

A long time later I was at a wedding reception with Luella, and to my surprise Shannon and Jack walked up to our table. I hadn't seen them for years. They walked hand-in-hand with smiles on their faces. Shannon greeted me and said, "We were excited when we realized you would be here, because we wanted to share with you what God has done in our marriage. We don't live anymore with the delusion that our marriage will automatically be beautiful somehow. We know that because we are sinners, and we have to work on our marriage every day. But because we love God and one another more than we ever have, we don't mind the work. How did you put it, Paul? 'A good marriage is a good marriage because the people in that marriage work to make it good.' Well, thank you for teaching us to be willing to work and for showing us that God will strengthen us as we do."

It really is true—a marriage of unity, understanding, and love is not rooted in romance. It is rooted in worship. It is when we love God more than we love ourselves and when we quit building our own little kingdom and start seeking his that we will love our spouse. When we really do love our husband or wife, we will be willing to do the hard work that such love requires. When we do the hard work that love requires, we will be humbled by how weak and needy we are when it comes to love, and we will begin to celebrate the love of God that is with us in our moment of greatest need. When we are daily aware that we are being loved, we will be excited about loving our husband or wife in the same way. And when our spouse is being treated with daily love, respect, and appreciation, he or she will be encouraged to love us in return.

Do you want this kind of marriage? If so, worship God above anything else. Do the hard work of love to which he has called you. And trust that he is with you with transforming grace in his hands. You can have a marriage of unity, understanding, and love. By his grace you really can!